Gay Tourism

TOURISM AND CULTURAL CHANGE

Series Editors: Professor Mike Robinson, *University of Birmingham, UK* and Professor Alison Phipps, *University of Glasgow, Scotland, UK*

Understanding tourism's relationships with culture(s), and vice versa, is of ever-increasing significance in a globalising world. TCC is a series of books that critically examine the complex and ever-changing relationship between tourism and culture(s). The series focuses on the ways that places, peoples, pasts and ways of life are increasingly shaped/transformed/created/packaged for touristic purposes. The series examines the ways tourism utilises/makes and re-makes cultural capital in its various guises (visual and performing arts, crafts, festivals, built heritage, cuisine, etc.) and the multifarious political, economic, social and ethical issues that are raised as a consequence. Theoretical explorations, research-informed analyses and detailed historical reviews from a variety of disciplinary perspectives are invited to consider such relationships.

All books in this series are externally peer-reviewed.

Full details of all the books in this series and of all our other publications can be found on http://www.channelviewpublications.com, or by writing to Channel View Publications, St Nicholas House, 31–34 High Street, Bristol BS1 2AW, UK.

TOURISM AND CULTURAL CHANGE: 59

Gay Tourism

New Perspectives

Edited by
Oscar Vorobjovas-Pinta

CHANNEL VIEW PUBLICATIONS
Bristol • Blue Ridge Summit

DOI https://doi.org/10.21832/VOROBJ8427
Library of Congress Cataloging in Publication Data
A catalog record for this book is available from the Library of Congress.
Names: Vorobjovas-Pinta, Oscar - editor.
Title: Gay Tourism: New Perspectives/Edited by Oscar Vorobjovas-Pinta.
Description: Bristol; Blue Ridge Summit: Channel View Publications, 2021. | Series:
    Tourism and Cultural Change: 59 | Includes bibliographical references
    and index. | Summary: "This book examines the emerging and shifting
    issues in the field of gay tourism, how these relate to significant
    societal and technological changes and the implications of these changes
    for theory, policy and practice. It will be a useful resource for
    students, lecturers and researchers in tourism, human geography,
    cultural studies and sociology"—Provided by publisher.
Identifiers: LCCN 2021002783 (print) | LCCN 2021002784 (ebook) | ISBN
    9781845418410 (paperback) | ISBN 9781845418427 (hardback) | ISBN
    9781845418434 (pdf) | ISBN 9781845418441 (epub) | ISBN 9781845418458
    (kindle edition) Subjects: LCSH: Gays—Travel. | Sexual minorities—Travel. |
    Culture and tourism. | Sex tourism. | Tourism—Technological innovations.
Classification: LCC HQ75.25 .G39 2021 (print) | LCC HQ75.25 (ebook) | DDC
    910.86/64—dc23 LC record available at https://lccn.loc.gov/2021002783
LC ebook record available at https://lccn.loc.gov/2021002784

British Library Cataloguing in Publication Data
A catalogue entry for this book is available from the British Library.

ISBN-13: 978-1-84541-842-7 (hbk)
ISBN-13: 978-1-84541-841-0 (pbk)

Channel View Publications
UK: St Nicholas House, 31–34 High Street, Bristol BS1 2AW, UK.
USA: NBN, Blue Ridge Summit, PA, USA.

Website: www.channelviewpublications.com
Twitter: Channel_View
Facebook: https://www.facebook.com/channelviewpublications
Blog: www.channelviewpublications.wordpress.com

The policy of Multilingual Matters/Channel View Publications is to use papers that
are natural, renewable and recyclable products, made from wood grown in
sustainable forests. In the manufacturing process of our books, and to further
support our policy, preference is given to printers that have FSC and PEFC Chain of
Custody certification. The FSC and/or PEFC logos will appear on those books
where full certification has been granted to the printer concerned.

Typeset by Nova Techset Private Limited, Bengaluru and Chennai, India.
Printed and bound in the UK by the CPI Books Group Ltd.
Printed and bound in the US by NBN.

Contents

Acknowledgements

During the past two years there have been so many people who have helped me with this project. First and foremost, I would like to extend my heartfelt appreciation to all the authors who have shared their research. Thank you also to all the reviewers whose contributions have enabled the publication of the book.

I also wish to acknowledge Isaac for his unwavering support and love.

And finally, I would like to thank Anne Hardy, Louise Grimmer and Sarah Hyslop for their editorial assistance and encouragement.

Oscar Vorobjovas-Pinta, Editor
Perth, Australia 2021

Contributors

Helena Andrade holds an MSc in Tourism Management and Planning and a BSc in Tourism from the University of Aveiro (Portugal).

Ana Margarida Barreto is Assistant Professor of Marketing, Consumer Behaviour and Strategic Communication at Universidade Nova de Lisboa (Portugal). She holds a PhD in Strategic Communication and carried out postdoctoral studies in Neuromarketing at the University of Tel Aviv.

Zélia Breda holds a PhD in Tourism, an MA in Chinese Studies (Business and International Relations) and a BSc in Tourism Management and Planning from the University of Aveiro (Portugal), where she is Assistant Professor. She is also Director of the Masters in Tourism Management and Planning, and a member of the Governance, Competitiveness and Public Policies Research Unit.

Wenjie Cai is a Senior Lecturer in the Tourism Research Centre, University of Greenwich (UK). Wenjie joined Greenwich in 2017 after completing his PhD in Tourism at the University of Surrey (UK). Wenjie's research interests include intercultural communication, social inclusion, consumer behaviours, mobilities studies, digital-free tourism, backpacker tourism and qualitative research methods.

Güliz Coşkun is an Assistant Professor in the Department of Recreation Management at Sakarya University of Applied Sciences (Turkey). Güliz holds a PhD in Parks, Recreation and Tourism Management from Clemson University (USA). Her research interests are tourist behaviour, decision making, leisure behaviour and sustainable tourism planning.

Stephan Dahl is an Adjunct Associate Professor at James Cook University and Charles Darwin University (Australia). He is a Fellow of the Royal Society of Arts (London) and the founder of the ecoqueer Quinta Project and Outgrow consultancy, supporting queer, social and sustainable businesses. His research interests include social media, marketing ethics and social marketing, and he has published in national and international journals, including the *Journal of Advertising Research* and the *Journal of Marketing Management*. Stephan is an editorial board member of the

International Journal of Advertising and the *Journal of Consumer Affairs*. He published the books *Social Media Marketing: Theories of Digital Communications*, *Handbook of Marketing Ethics* and *Marketing Ethics & Society* (all with Sage) and is also the co-author of *Social Marketing* (Pearson) and *Integrated Marketing Communications* (Taylor & Francis).

Gorete Dinis holds a PhD in Tourism, an MSc in Innovation, Planning and Development Policies and a BSc in Tourism Management and Planning from the University of Aveiro (Portugal). She is a Deputy Director and Professor of the BSc in Tourism in the School of Education and Social Sciences at the Polytechnic Institute of Portalegre, and a member of the Governance, Competitiveness and Public Policies Research Unit and of the CITUR Algarve.

Xiongbin Gao is a researcher and graduated from the University of Surrey (UK). His research focuses on hitchhiking as a tourist practice in contemporary China, exploring how hitchhiking is articulated and experienced in gendered and sexualised ways through engaging feminist and queer theories.

Louise Grimmer is a Senior Lecturer in Marketing at the University of Tasmania (Australia). Her research focuses on the economic and social impacts of retailing, particularly the role of local shopping precincts in contributing to social well-being. Louise also researches small retail and hospitality firms, retail place marketing and the impact of the visitor economy. She is a mixed-methods researcher with a particular interest in observation, field studies and focus groups. Louise is a Fellow of the Institute of Place Management.

Christiaan Hattingh is a Lecturer in the Department of Tourism and Events Management at the Cape Peninsula University of Technology (South Africa). His primary research interests relate to gay tourism in a developing destination marketing context. His most recent research investigates the 'de-gaying' of Africa's only gay village.

Heather Jeffrey is a Senior Lecturer in the Social Sciences at Middlesex University (Dubai). Heather is a Marie-Curie alumnus, an associate at the charity Equality in Tourism, and was nominated for an emerging scholar profile in the *e-Review of Tourism Research*, where she is now managing editor.

Clifford Lewis is a Senior Lecturer in Marketing at Charles Sturt University (Australia). His research focuses on inclusivity within a rural context, specifically considering the LGBTQI+ community. Before starting his academic career, Clifford was the Head of State (NSW) for a global market research company. In that role, he worked on projects related to regional tourism products, experience and campaign development as well as destination planning. His PhD focused on destination branding and meaning creation.

Carlos Monterrubio received his PhD in Tourism from Manchester Metropolitan University (UK). He is a lecturer and tourism researcher at the Universidad Autónoma del Estado de México (Mexico). Carlos has undertaken research on tourism, gender and sexuality and on the socio-cultural dimensions of tourism in Mexico.

Bình Nghiêm-Phú is an Assistant Professor in the School of Economics and Management at the University of Hyogo (Japan). The majority of his research is directed toward the understanding of consumer perceptions and evaluations of the characteristics or images of products, services, organisations and places. Bình adopts the approaches of applied psychology theories to the implementation of marketing and management activities.

Can-Seng Ooi is a sociologist and Professor of Cultural and Heritage Tourism at the University of Tasmania (Australia). Over two decades he has conducted comparative research between Singapore, Denmark, China and Australia, and on various society-and-tourism issues, including destination branding and social engineering, tourism in cultural development and tourism worker welfare. His personal website is at www.cansengooi.com.

Carol Southall is Course Leader and Senior Lecturer at Staffordshire Business School, Staffordshire University (UK). A former Tour Operations and Training Manager, she entered academia on completion of her MA in Tourism Management in 2008, following a 20-year career in industry. Carol is currently undertaking a PhD focusing on the relationship between cultural awareness and visitor satisfaction in tourism. She has published in the areas of family tourism, culture and LGBT tourism and is also an invited member of the Senior Advisory Board for Harrington Park Press.

Martin Sposato is an Assistant Professor at Zayed University (Dubai). Martin has published on numerous topics, including leadership, postcolonial feminism and qualitative research, in prestigious journals such as *Management and Organization Review* and the *International Journal of Human Resources Management*. Martin is also an academic member of CIPD.

Jillian Rae Suter is an Assistant Professor in the Faculty of Informatics at Shizuoka University (Japan). Her research is directed by social marketing theories. Jillian is implementing research on consumer culture, notably the impact of the rise and fall in popularity of 'Cool Japan' on both the national economy and society, and the global market.

Oscar Vorobjovas-Pinta is a Lecturer in Tourism and Hospitality Management in the School of Business and Law at Edith Cowan University (Australia). He is a leading expert on LGBTQI+ communities in the context of leisure, hospitality and tourism. Oscar's research interests are the sociology of tourism, tourist behaviour and LGBTQI+ tourism. Oscar explores LGBTQI+ travellers as neo-tribes, who come together from disparate walks of life but are united through shared sentiment, rituals and symbols.

Foreword

For those of us who identify under the LGBT umbrella, travel offers opportunities that may not necessarily be so important for heterosexual folk. Some of us are unable to lead the kind of life we would like: free of assumptions, expectations and obligations based on restrictive understandings of sexuality and gender; free of hostility and violence; free of state-sanctioned persecution. Travel to LGBT 'homelands' such as San Francisco, Berlin, New York, Amsterdam, Sydney, or to resort destinations like Provincetown, Palm Springs, Ibiza or Puerto Vallarta, offers a respite – a chance to lead a life more authentically our own. Although such travel offers a temporary escape, it also offers the possibility of creation: building identity, forging new friendships, creating new opportunities for community connection, sexual exploration and romantic experience.

However, opportunities to travel are not easily available to many LGBT people, particularly those with little discretionary income, whether living in advanced or developing economies. My LBGT Papua New Guinean friends, for instance, who wish to travel to Australia, are constrained by lack of financial resources as well as the requirement to be 'sponsored' by an Australian resident in order to obtain a visa. Most will never be able to travel outside PNG. The oft-quoted assumptions about LGBT people being 'natural travellers', because of high incomes and no dependents, wallpaper over the deep inequalities that can be the outcomes of differences in social class, nationality, ethnicity, gender, ability and age, as well as changes to LGBT family structures that have taken place over the past decade or so. In addition, the constraints that operate to oppress and marginalise LGBT citizens may continue to operate if, and when, they travel. While travel can be liberating, at least temporarily, for many people, it is not always so, and can place LGBT tourists in situations characterised by mild intolerance through to violence and/or incarceration.

Nevertheless, LGBT travel continues to be seen as a lucrative market segment for many destinations, propelled by recent growth in same-sex weddings and honeymoons, the sumptuous offering of international and national-scale LGBT events and festivals and a growing LGBT cruise sector. Market research undertaken in 2016 by consulting firm, Out Now, estimated that the global LBGT tourism industry was valued at USD$211 billion and that there had been annual growth over the three years to 2016 of 2%.[1] Data suggest that as a market segment, LGBT travellers show higher levels of resilience to risk and appear to be one of the market segments that recovers quickest after significant disruptions to tourism due to financial crises, terrorist attacks or natural disasters.

Gay Tourism: New Perspectives presents the work of scholars, some established, others emerging, who are critically engaged in understanding the complexities of LGBT travel and tourism. Drawing upon a range of disciplinary and theoretical frameworks, the authors explore the complex, often complicated and contested intersections of travel and tourism with sexualities and genders. New insights emerge from the empirical analyses that compel the reader to consider the political and sociocultural discourses that frame and construct LGBT identities through the spaces of travel and tourism. Importantly, the studies contained in the book are situated well beyond the Western focus of much previous research in this field and come from Argentina, China, Mexico, Portugal and Turkey as well as the African and Southeast Asian regions. There are also chapters on LGBT tourism as it is negotiated within rural regions. The book recognises and examines the social, cultural, gender and sexual diversity of the people who comprise the market for LGBT travel.

This book has been carefully shepherded through the publication process by the energy and enthusiasm of its editor, Oscar Vorobjovas-Pinta, whose PhD dissertation on gay neo-tribes I examined in 2017. Oscar's thesis was original and innovative, being a micro-sociological study of an Australian LGBT resort, which sought to understand critically the intersections of individual and collective gay identity, space and place. Since his PhD work, Oscar has made a sustained contribution to the field. This book, the first edited collection dealing with LGBT tourism in more than two decades, succeeds in being a vehicle to present new perspectives and insights on the topic.

However, when this book was conceived, and as the authors were working on their chapters, the notion that the global tourism industry would be brought to a standstill in 2020 would have been almost inconceivable. However, Covid-19 has proven to be the most disruptive force ever to impact tourism and its repercussions will continue to be felt by the tourism industry – and tourists – for years to come. These changes will affect LGBT tourism as they will the rest of the industry. Events and festivals are major drivers of LGBT tourism across the globe and the pandemic has led to the cancellation of international-scale Pride events in cities such as Los Angeles, London, Tokyo and New York. EuroPride, the largest Pride event in Europe, has been cancelled for 2021. The cruise industry, not surprisingly, has been particularly heavily impacted. Nevertheless, recent market research undertaken in the United States suggests that LGBT travellers are showing the greatest propensity to travel again, particularly the most privileged market segment of white gay men.[2]

As this edited collection shows, LGBT tourism takes place in very different political and sociocultural contexts and spaces today compared to when the nascent industry began to take tentative steps to establish itself in the mid-1970s, following the emergence of the gay rights movement in Europe and North America. Seismic societal and political shifts have occurred which have positively affected LGBT citizens over the past 40 years or so (at least in the West). These shifts have led to the decriminalisation of homosexuality in many countries, the enactment of anti-discrimination legislation and, most recently, marriage equality. Positive representations of LGBT identities and relationships have become mainstream through popular culture and social media. Embedded within this history, however, are the devastating impacts of HIV/AIDS and the political and community responses to its management, which have themselves shaped LGBT travel and tourism patterns and behaviours.

The UN World Tourism Organisation issued its *Second Global Report on LGBT Tourism* in 2017 (the first was issued in 2012). This document examines the various impacts of LGBT travel and tourism, economic and social, and highlights to some extent the inequalities that exist across the globe for LBGT people, including the ability to travel freely. The hope, expressed by John Tanzella, the President/CEO of the International Gay and Lesbian Travel Association, is that by 'reaching out to gay travellers and creating a welcoming infrastructure, tourism businesses are helping to combat homophobia' (UNWTO, 2012: 3). However, it is important that scholars subject such claims to critical scrutiny. The extent to which the LGBT tourism industry can realistically reduce discrimination and homophobia is contested, particularly given that the idealised 'gay traveller' depicted in marketing still seems to be white, male, able-bodied, toned and under the age of 60.

Gay Tourism: New Perspectives will make a valuable contribution to the LGBT travel and tourism literature and it will advance understanding of the intersections between sexuality and tourism. The volume contains new ways of thinking about LGBT tourism that are alert to the possibility of disruption and change and, as such, will help to map out future research directions.

Kevin Markwell
Professor of Tourism
School of Business and Tourism
Southern Cross University
Australia

Notes

(1) LGBT travel market valued at US$211 billion a year. See https://www.cabi.org/leisuretourism/news/25295 (accessed 22 September 2020).

(2) Why the LGBTQ community may be the first to travel again. See https://skift.
     com/2020/05/27/why-the-lgbtq-community-may-be-the-first-to-travel-again/
     (accessed 20 September 2020).

Reference

UNWTO (2012) *Global Report on LGBT Tourism*. AM Reports Vol. 3. Madrid: World
     Tourism Organization. See https://www.e-unwto.org/doi/pdf/10.18111/978928
     4414581.

1 Gay Tourism: New Perspectives

Oscar Vorobjovas-Pinta

Defining Gay Tourism

Gay tourism is a dynamic and vibrant phenomenon. The definition of gay tourism is rather complex; however, it is generally described as a form of niche tourism that refers to the development and marketing of tourism products and services to lesbian, bisexual, transgender, queer/questioning, intersex and other people (LGBTQI+). Although the term 'gay' technically refers to gay men and lesbians, it can also be used in a wider sense to include all other sexual orientations or gender identities under the LGBTQI+ banner. Therefore, the term 'gay tourism' in this book is used loosely and encompasses all forms and combinations of the LGBTQI+ acronym. Indeed, 'gay tourism' has been established as a more recognisable and user-friendly term than 'LGBTQI+ tourism' or any other derivations (Southall & Fallon, 2011).

The origins of gay tourism are commonly dated back to the era of the Grand Tour or perhaps even earlier (Aldrich, 1993). The Grand Tour involved wealthy, well-educated and upper-class gay men from Northern European countries travelling to the Mediterranean in search of exotic cultures, warmer climes and the companionship of like-minded men. Such travel was often associated with an artistic and aesthetic experience (Graham, 2002). Gay tourism flourished in the Victorian period (Aldrich, 1993; Clift & Forrest, 1999; Clift & Wilkins, 1995; Clift et al., 2002; Holcomb & Luongo, 1996). In the late 19th and early 20th centuries, Berlin, Paris and London boasted sizeable gay leisure 'infrastructure', including cafés, cabarets, salons and bathhouses (Hughes, 2006; Peñaloza, 1996; Prickett, 2011). Indeed, Weimar Berlin was considered to be a 'gay mecca' or the 'Eldorado' of the times, offering a safe haven for locals and travellers alike (Clift et al., 2002; Prickett, 2011). One could escape the heteronormative social world and express one's sexuality in a judgement-free space. Due to its tolerance, modernity and inclusive culture, Berlin remained a sanctuary for gay men and women until the Nazi revolution in 1933.

The manifestation of gay culture was not exclusively a European phenomenon. In the later years of the 19th century, New York became known

1

for its numerous bathhouses, brothels and saloons which catered exclusively to gay clientele (Branchik, 2002; Graham, 2002). In 1877, the guidebook *Pictures of New York Life and Character* allegedly contained 'gay' content (Clift *et al.*, 2002). New York's famous bars such as The Slide, Webster Hall and Rockland Palace from the 1890s to the 1930s were part of a flourishing, highly visible LGBTQI+ nightlife and culture which would be integrated into mainstream American life in a way that would be unacceptable just 10–20 years later.

The gay tourism industry has experienced growth since the 1970s. While industry players stand to gain economically from becoming more inclusive, the social implications of such a shift remain critical. Gay tourism is not merely about sexual preference – it plays an integral role in one's self-identification and self-expression. The literature has structured gay tourism into three distinct clusters: identity expression and exploration (Browne & Bakshi, 2011; Hughes, 1997); sense of community and fellowship (Hindle, 1994; Pritchard *et al.*, 2000); and sexual candour (Clift & Forrest, 1999; Hughes, 2006). Therefore, gay tourism is often presented as an idealised escape from the heteronormative strictures of everyday life, and an opportunity to embrace and express one's identity (Vorobjovas-Pinta, 2018). The thirst for escapism has encouraged the establishment of gay spaces, ranging from gay bars and nightclubs in urban environments to the exclusively gay travel resorts and destinations. This phenomenon even extends to gay townships and communities, such as Cherry Grove and Fire Island Pines on New York's Fire Island. Previous studies emphasised the provision of gay space as the primary motivator encouraging the growth of gay travel (Vorobjovas-Pinta, 2018).

Gay tourism and leisure scholars have investigated the interlinked nature of one's sexuality and the space in which it is performed (Binnie & Valentine, 1999; Caluya, 2008; Hughes, 2006; Waitt & Markwell, 2006). Vorobjovas-Pinta (2018) explains:

> Space becomes a vessel for the ideologies, need, practices, and desires of those occupying it, and through this relationship the sexual, racial, and gender categories of its inhabitants become refracted in its imperceptible boundaries. (Vorobjovas-Pinta, 2018: 3)

LGBTQI+ and Societal Change

Historically, a breakthrough in the gay and lesbian movement occurred in the mid-20th century. An assemblage of several historic events and developments led to the liberation and acceptance of LGBTQI+ communities, including: the Stonewell Riots in 1969; a shifting of the demographic composition of the population; changes in cultural ideologies; increased educational levels; and the establishment of LGBTQI+ NGOs and university queer societies (D'Emilio, 1983; Loftus, 2001; Valocchi, 2005; Werum & Winders, 2001). In 1973, the American Psychiatric

Association declassified homosexuality as a mental abnormality vis-à-vis a 'sociopathic personality disturbance' (Morin, 1977; Werum & Winders, 2001). In addition, in 1990 the World Health Organisation removed homosexuality from the list of mental illnesses known as the International Classification of Diseases (King, 2003). These changes paved the way for greater societal acceptance of LGBTQI+ communities, at least in the Global North. The attitudes towards LGBTQI+ individuals considerably differ depending on locality, culture, political climates, history and religion. Countries in the Global North adopted proactive legislative standards to become more inclusive (e.g. marriage equality, the right to adopt for same-sex couples), whereas many African, Asian and Eastern European countries are bounded by social and/or legal norms, which are reflected through the legal discrimination of LGBTQI+ people via prosecution and even the death penalty.

Despite homosexuality being de-pathologised in 1990, LGBTQI+ people are still criminalised in 73 jurisdictions across the world (see Figure 1.1). In 12 jurisdictions the death penalty is imposed or at least is a possible punishment for private, consensual same-sex sexual activity. At least six of these countries actually carry out the death penalty – Iran, Northern Nigeria, Saudi Arabia, Somalia, Sudan and Yemen – and the death penalty is a legal possibility in Afghanistan, Brunei, Mauritania, Pakistan, Qatar and UAE (Human Dignity Trust, 2020). Even in countries with generally tolerant societies, a degree of prejudice still exists within specific areas based on sociodemographic composition and geographic rurality (Ong *et al.*, 2020).

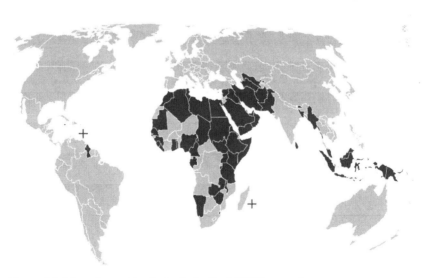

Figure 1.1 Map of countries that criminalise LGBTQI+ people
Source: Human Dignity Trust (2020).

A Demographic Profile of LGBTQI+ Tourists

Gay tourists have often been characterised as high-yield travellers with significantly more disposable income than their heterosexual counterparts (Hughes, 2003). This has been largely attributed to the notion of gays and lesbians being DINKs (i.e. double income, no kids). Indeed, epithets such as a 'dream market' or an 'untapped gold mine' were used to define the gay market (Kahan & Mulryan, 1995; Peñaloza, 1996). This has led to claims that they represent a powerful, profitable and recession-proof market segment (Guaracino, 2007; Melián-González *et al.*, 2011). It is estimated that the annual value of total spending on travel and tourism by LGBTQI+ people exceeds US$218 billion (Out Now, 2018). Gay travellers have also been lauded as trendsetters (Gluckman & Reed, 1997; Guaracino, 2007; Hughes, 2005) and innovators (Vandecasteele & Geuens, 2009), as well as early adopters, hedonists and aesthetes (Hughes, 2005). Gay men and lesbians have been described as industry revivers, as they were the first to support the tourism and hospitality industry after the 9/11 events (Guaracino, 2007). On the other hand, Badgett (1997) and Carpenter (2004) have attempted to debunk the assumptions that gay men and women have more disposable income. Research shows that gay individuals often suffer from salary discrimination and therefore 'using those [higher expenditure] numbers to describe all lesbian and gay people is misleading and, in many cases, deliberately deceptive' (Badgett, 1997: 66). In recent years, an increasing number of married or cohabiting gay and lesbian couples are choosing to have children. An Australian Institute of Family Studies report stated that approximately 11% of gay men and 33% of lesbians in same-sex relationships in Australia have children (Dempsey, 2013).

The collective spending or purchasing power of the LGBTQI+ communities has been branded as the 'pink dollar', 'pink pound' or any other 'pink currency'. In 2016, a study conducted by Roy Morgan (2016) found that 5.2% of Australian men and 3.1% of women agreed with the statement, 'I consider myself homosexual'. While they comprise a relatively low proportion of the total population, gay men and lesbians tend to display distinct purchasing behaviours that reveal their value as a consumer group (Roy Morgan, 2016). The realisation that LGBTQI+ people might possess a distinct purchasing behaviour has resulted in a 'pinkwashing' phenomenon, whereby companies, destination management organisations and even politicians engage in a variety of marketing strategies to promote products, destinations or ideas by publicising gay-friendliness and inclusivity. As such, they are perceived as progressive, modern and tolerant. 'Pinkwashing' is problematic as it appropriates the LGBTQI+ movement to promote a corporate or political agenda; Dahl (2014) explains:

> Companies need to do more than just depict a gay guy, or a lesbian couple, or adorn their products with the rainbow flag – especially when faced with increasingly knowledgeable, and cynical, consumers who hopefully can see through a touch of pink sparkle. (Dahl, 2014)

In tourism, most notably, Israel has come under fire for using 'pink-washing' to embellish 'the positive image of the state by portraying it as a haven for the LGBTQ+ community while deflating issues of the Israeli-Palestinian conflict' (Kama & Ram, 2020: 80). Similarly, in Australia the growing commercialisation and commodification of the Sydney Gay and Lesbian Mardi Gras has led some to believe that the event is being exploited by Australia's business community (De Jong, 2017). Alluding to Mardi Gras' future, Kates (2003) predicted that:

> The darker possibility is that economic factors and meanings involved in Mardi Gras' production may come to dominate and effectively constitute the festival, appropriating and resignificating seemingly progressive and even deviant images to promote capitalist aims. This is done in the context of a global ordering, marketing, and consumption of cultural differences for the benefit of multinational companies. (Kates, 2003: 18)

Gay Tourism in Academic Literature

While the phenomenon of gay tourism has a rich historical background, the academic literature does not reflect this. Achilles (1967), Devall (1979), Harry and Devall (1978) and Weinberg and Williams (1975) were among the first to capture the emergence of gay culture and gay leisure lifestyle (but not 'gay tourism' per se). The early portrayals of gay leisure were grounded in sociological theories attempting to locate the underpinning attributes of gay leisure social worlds. Deval (1979) notes:

> One can participate in homosexual sex without having a gay self-identity or participating in gay leisure social worlds. But having a gay self-identity ('I am a gay') and a gay social identity ('My friends consider me gay') allows a man to participate as an equal in a rapidly emerging leisure social world which is not simply a world of sex or eroticism. (Deval, 1979: 181)

Inadvertently, the debate surrounding gay leisure spaces has led to research into gay tourism. Erik Cohen (1988) was one of the first authors to refer to gay tourists in his article 'Tourism and AIDS in Thailand', published in *Annals of Tourism Research*. As the title and the year of the publication suggest, the paper depicted the realities of a decade that was marked by fear fuelled by the AIDS epidemic. The 1990s saw an increase in scholarly publications pertaining to gay tourism. Early literature focused on gay travellers' demographic characteristics, suggesting that travel allowed gay men to escape the strictures of their heteronormative everyday lives and provided an opportunity to construct their true identity (Hughes, 1997). Nonetheless, the impact of the AIDS epidemic remained palpable as many publications continued to refer to aspects of sexual health and the relationship between sexual health and travel (Clift & Forrest, 1999). It should be noted that these studies were published prior to the major societal changes of the 21st century, where same-sex marriage and family units have been accepted legally and in the broader community.

The 2000s saw the publication of four pioneering books about gay tourism: *Gay Tourism: Culture, Identity and Sex*, edited by Stephen Clift, Michael Luongo and Carry Callister (2002); *Pink Tourism: Holidays of Gay Men and Lesbians* by Howard L. Hughes (2006); *Gay Tourism: Culture and Context* by Gordon Waitt and Kevin Markwell (2006); and *Gay and Lesbian Tourism: The Essential Guide for Marketing* by Jeff Guarancino (2007). These books, each in its own right, attempted to capture the growing interest in gay tourism. They were to a certain degree born out of the necessity to address societal change and the consequential new market imperatives in tourism.

It was not until the second half of the 2010s that there was an exponential increase in academic publications pertaining to gay tourism. These publications were not only rich in the diversity of the topics covered but also more nuanced in portraying research participants (Ong *et al.*, 2020). An emphasis was also placed on gender, and on understanding a variety of identities in diverse contexts such as sport (Elling-Machartzki, 2017), events (Caudwell, 2018), hospitality (Vorobjovas-Pinta, 2018) and tourism (Monterrubio, 2019). Nonetheless, scholarly knowledge addressing the gay travel market continues to lack complexity and fails to represent the heterogeneity embodied within contemporary gay travel (Blichfeldt *et al.*, 2013; Monterrubio, 2009; Ong *et al.*, 2020; Therkelsen *et al.*, 2013; Vorobjovas-Pinta & Hardy, 2016). There is a palpable absence of bisexual, intersex and transgender voices in tourism research. To date, gay travel research has also been dominated by Western perspectives and traditions (Vorobjovas-Pinta & Hardy 2016; Wong & Tolkach, 2017). Voices from non-Western perspectives and cultures remain incidental and minimal. As such, in comparison with other travel sectors, gay tourism remains under-researched, particularly in terms of cultural and social development. It is here that research can play a role by exploring these nuances through a more critical lens.

Structure of the Book

This book addresses the emerging and shifting issues in the field of gay tourism described in this introduction, especially in light of significant societal and technological changes (Monterrubio, 2019; Vorobjovas-Pinta & Dalla-Fontana, 2019; Vorobjovas-Pinta & Hardy, 2016). Arguably, the introduction of marriage equality laws in countries such as Australia, Ireland and the United States, as well as the emergence of gay dating apps such as Grindr, Scruff and Hornet, have disrupted the conventional understanding of gay tourism. While the last decade marked a significant change in LGBTQ+ rights, it also presented new issues and challenges. The dearth of research examining these sociocultural shifts suggests the need for more nuanced and innovative approaches to reimagine gay tourism. Moreover, it is important to discern the implications of these changes for theory, policy and practice. This book brings 19 scholars across 13 chapters to bridge these existing gaps by capturing how societal and technological changes have affected the behaviour and motivations of gay travellers, gay tourism products and the phenomenon of gay tourism itself. The book also incorporates voices from non-Western perspectives and cultures. The emphasis within the small amount of existing literature pertaining to gay travel research in non-Western countries has tended to focus on negative perceptions associated with such travel. This book instead presents a more nuanced and finely grained snapshot of these intriguing cross-cultural dimensions that contribute to a broader understanding of gay tourism on a global scale. The book has been structured into four thematic sections: (1) Gay Tourism: Political and Sociocultural Discourses; (2) Gay Tourism: Profiles and Identities; (3) Gay Tourism: Pleasure and Leisure; and (4) Gay Tourism: Spatial Discourses.

The first section of the book addresses the political and sociocultural discourses evident within the context of gay tourism consumption. In Chapter 2, Can-Seng Ooi situates gay identity politics in tourism practice and research. To do this, Ooi grounds his enquiry in Foucault's (1998) theorisation of identity and poses a question: What has to be renounced when we accept and embrace a certain self-identity and self-imagination? The chapter complements the many streams of gay tourism research by situating gay tourism as part of the perpetual transformation of modern society. Ooi does not focus on queer differences but on understanding how the variety of these differences can be selected, framed and accentuated. For him, some differences are invented and sharpened to define an ever-emerging distinctive queer identity.

In Chapter 3, Carlos Monterrubio argues that travelling away from home is one of the few choices that many gay men have in order to develop their gay identities. The chapter explores the social significance of gay tourism space for local gay men. For them, gay space signifies an opportunity for escape, identity development, socialisation, cruising and learning about gay life. Through interaction with other gay men and gay tourists in gay space, local gay men's self-conceptions, behaviours, attitudes and perceptions of their own sexuality are likely to change. By exploring the importance of gay space for local gay men, Monterrubio not only contributes to the theoretical development of the relations between tourism and socially excluded groups but also promotes the need to manage gay spaces in order to provide shelter from heteronormative constraints and social disapproval.

In Chapter 4, Wenjie Cai and Carol Southall discuss the management of sexuality in heteronormative family holiday spaces. This conceptual chapter examines the literature of inclusive family holiday space and proposes a research agenda. Family holiday spaces continue to be dominated by a heterosexual paradigm (Lucena et al., 2015). The authors call for tourism and hospitality industries to better cater for same-sex parented families by developing and refining products and services. Homosexual families with children continue to experience heightened visibility and often inadvertent disclosure of sexuality on holiday.

In the second section of the book, conceptualisations of gay tourism within the contexts of tourist profiles and identities are explored. In Chapter 5, Christiaan Hattingh challenges the myth that the gay travel market is homogeneous. To do so, Hattingh investigates a sample of African gay leisure travellers' holiday motivations to determine whether there are any critical differences among these travellers' motivations. The chapter contributes towards closing the gap in the literature regarding the heterogeneity of the gay travel market which is much more complex than previously thought.

In Chapter 6, Xiongbin Gao explores Chinese lesbian and gay travel. The chapter demonstrates that Chinese lesbian and gay travel can be very valuable in terms of enabling further understanding and reflection on the homogenisation and homo-normalisation tendencies in current Western-centric gay travel research. Gao also alludes to *xinghun*, a unique queer perspective that allows us to understand lesbian and gay family travel in mainland China.

In Chapter 7, Güliz Coşkun examines gay tourism in a secular Muslim country – Turkey. Coşkun acknowledges the difficulty of researching such a topic, as there is an apparent lack of data about the exact number of LGBT people and same-sex couples residing in Muslim countries. Due to the conservative social, cultural and religious climates, it is difficult to obtain and collect such data. As such, empirical evidence in support of gay tourism in Turkey is rather limited. Coşkun asserts that Turkey is missing a valuable opportunity to position itself as a unique Muslim country that arguably offers a safe space for gay and lesbian travellers.

The third section of the book is centred on the value of tourism that facilitates our engagement with tourism experiences, leisure opportunities and pleasure. In Chapter 8, Oscar Vorobjovas-Pinta explores how employees make sense of working at an exclusively gay and lesbian resort by drawing upon notions of organisational socialisation and sensemaking. Due to the remoteness of the resort, the majority of employees live on-site, blurring the lines between work and leisure. Vorobjovas-Pinta examines the ways in which resort staff negotiate their work and leisure. Employees' relationships with one another, as well as with resort guests, are also considered. It is argued that individuals working at the resort construct their identity in the context of others (i.e. their fellow employees), which in turn affects the way in which they make sense of themselves and their work–leisure environment.

In Chapter 9, Bình Nghiêm-Phú and Jillian Rae Suter identify salient service characteristics for gay patrons at gay saunas, spas and cruise clubs across the Asia Pacific. The data suggest that there are 13 features that are important to massage experiences (e.g. masseurs' skills, facility/location, price/value, friendliness, massage time and masseurs' look/age) and 15 characteristics that are significant to sauna experiences (e.g. co-patrons, cleanliness, staff, cruising areas, steam room, price/value and shower room). Nghiêm-Phú and Suter propose important implications for improving gay client experiences at gay saunas, spas and cruise clubs.

In Chapter 10, Stephan Dahl and Ana Margarida Barreto explore the emerging area of rural LGBT tourism. Drawing upon interviews with participants and netnographic examination (Kozinets, 2019), Dahl and Barreto examine motivations, opportunities and challenges faced by LGBT travellers seeking to 'queer the countryside'. The authors suggest that an eclectic mix of adventure, volunteer and spirituality tourism, brought together in a desire for community seeking and activism, are the contributing factors for the emergence of rural LGBT tourism.

The fourth and final section of the book discusses spatial discourses entrenched within the context of gay tourism. In Chapter 11, Oscar Vorobjovas-Pinta and Louise Grimmer examine the case of Rainbow Tasmania Tourism Accreditation to discuss the development and importance of gay-friendly spaces. Tourism and hospitality businesses use a 'rainbow flag' as a symbol to indicate their support for the LGBTQI+ communities as well as to signal their 'views' and 'leaning'. The chapter explores the marketing and communication effect of 'gay-friendly' spaces and business-related outcomes associated with such marketing.

In Chapter 12, Helena Andrade, Zélia Breda and Gorete Dinis investigate the image of the municipality of Porto (Portugal) as a gay-friendly destination. Andrade, Breda and Dinis carried out a qualitative study to explore whether accommodation service providers in Porto treat potential tourists differently depending on their perceived sexual orientation. To obtain, compare and analyse the data, the authors sent out emails to the accommodation providers posing as couples (homosexual and heterosexual) in order to verify whether responses were similar or if there were signs of preconception based on the sexual orientation of tourists.

In Chapter 13, Heather Jeffrey and Martin Sposato discuss the juxtaposition of authenticity and commodification in tourism research. The chapter utilises interviews with key stakeholders and the examination of publicity materials to discuss the importance of authenticity in the creation of gay destinations alongside the commodification of gay culture in Buenos Aires (Argentina). The chapter contributes to the literature by making salient the concept of participatory planning, which has previously been considered in the development literature but has not been fully explored in studies on gay tourism.

In Chapter 14, Clifford Lewis and Oscar Vorobjovas-Pinta explore considerations in developing rural pride events by reflecting on the town of Hay, New South Wales (Australia), which conducted its inaugural Mardi Gras in 2018. Lewis and Vorobjovas-Pinta highlight relevant considerations that need to be managed and accounted for when developing such events within a rural setting. By drawing upon publicly available reports, the authors suggest that the findings presented in the chapter may be used by regional towns to enhance the process of creating and managing rural pride events.

In summary, this book is designed to present new perspectives in gay tourism. The book will appeal to a range of different readers. It is primarily intended for academic scholars, postgraduate students and educators specialising in tourism, human geography, cultural studies and sociology. The approach taken utilises a broad range of geographical and sociocultural contexts that will appeal to the wider academic community as well as to practitioners and industry. The chapters in the book capture the breadth and depth of gay tourism and bring together a variety of cultural and theoretical approaches to associated topics, contexts and viewpoints. In doing so, the book makes a substantive contribution to the further understanding of the nuances of gay tourism while delivering new insights into contemporary notions of travel and leisure.

References

Achilles, N. (1967) The development of the homosexual bar as an institution. In J. Gagnon and W. Simon (eds) *Sexual Deviance* (pp. 228–294). New York: Harper & Row.

Aldrich, R. (1993) *The Seduction of the Mediterranean: Writing, Art and Homosexual Fantasy*. London: Routledge.

Badgett, L. (1997) Beyond biased samples: Challenging the myths on the economic status of lesbians and gay men. In A.R. Gluckman and B. Reed (eds) *Homo Economics: Capitalism, Community and Lesbian and Gay Life* (pp. 65–71). New York and London: Routledge.

Binnie, J. and Valentine, G. (1999) Geographies of sexuality – a review of progress. *Progress in Human Geography* 23 (2), 175–187.

Blichfeldt, B.S., Chor, J. and Milan, N.B. (2013) Zoos, sanctuaries and turfs: Enactments and uses of gay spaces during the holidays. *International Journal of Tourism Research* 15 (5), 473–483.

Branchik, B.J. (2002) Out in the market: A history of the gay market segment in the United States. *Journal of Macromarketing* 22 (1), 86–97.

Browne, K. and Bakshi, L. (2011) We are here to party? Lesbian, gay, bisexual and trans leisurescapes beyond commercial gay scenes. *Leisure Studies* 30 (2), 179–196.

Caluya, G. (2008) 'The Rice Steamer': Race, desire and affect in Sydney's gay scene. *Australian Geographer* 39 (3), 283–292.

Carpenter, C. (2004) New evidence on gay and lesbian household incomes. *Contemporary Economic Policy* 22 (1), 78–94.

Caudwell, J. (2018) Configuring human rights at EuroPride 2015. *Leisure Studies* 37 (1), 49–63.

Clift, S. and Forrest, S. (1999) Gay men and tourism: Destinations and holiday motivations. *Tourism Management* 20 (5), 615–625.

Clift, S. and Wilkins, J. (1995) Travel, sexual behaviour and gay men. In P. Aggleton, P. Davies and G. Hart (eds) *AIDS: Safety, Sexuality and Risk* (pp. 35–54). London: Taylor & Francis.

Clift, S., Luongo, M. and Callister, C. (2002) *Gay Tourism: Culture, Identity and Sex*. New York: Continuum.

Cohen, E. (1988) Tourism and AIDS in Thailand. *Annals of Tourism Research* 15 (4), 467–486.

Dahl, S. (2014) The rise of pride marketing and the curse of 'pink washing'. *The Conversation*, 27 August. See https://theconversation.com/the-rise-of-pride-marketing-and-the-curse-of-pink-washing-30925.

De Jong, A. (2017) Unpacking Pride's commodification through the encounter. *Annals of Tourism Research* 63, 128–139.

D'Emilio, J. (1983) Capitalism and gay identity. In A. Snitow, C. Stansell and S. Thompson (eds) *Powers of Desire: The Politics of Sexuality* (pp. 100–113). New York: Monthly Review Press.

Dempsey, C. (2013) Same-sex parented families in Australia. CFCA Paper No. 13. Melbourne: Australian Institute of Family Studies. See https://aifs.gov.au/cfca/publications/same-sex-parented-families-australia.

Devall, W. (1979) Leisure and lifestyles among gay men: An exploratory essay. *International Review of Modern Sociology* 9 (2), 179–195.

Elling-Machartzki, A. (2017) Extraordinary body-self narratives: Sport and physical activity in the lives of transgender people. *Leisure Studies* 36 (2), 256–268.

Foucault, M. (1998) *Technologies of the Self: A Seminar with Michel Foucault.* Amherst, MA: University of Massachusetts Press.

Gluckman, A. and Reed, B. (1997) The gay marketing moment. In A.R. Gluckman and B. Reed (eds) *Homo Economics: Capitalism, Community and Lesbian and Gay Life* (pp. 3–9). London: Routledge.

Graham, M. (2002) Challenges from the margins: Gay tourism as cultural critique. In S. Clift, M. Luongo and C. Callister (eds) *Gay Tourism: Culture, Identity and Sex* (pp. 17–41). New York: Continuum.

Guaracino, J. (2007) *Gay and Lesbian Tourism: The Essential Guide for Marketing.* Oxford: Elsevier.

Harry, J. and Devall, W.B. (1978) *The Social Organization of Gay Males.* New York: Praeger.

Hindle, P. (1994) Gay communities and gay space in the city. In S. Whittle (ed.) *The Margins of the City: Gay Men's Urban Lives* (pp. 7–25). Aldershot: Arena Press.

Holcomb, B. and Luongo, M. (1996) Gay tourism in the United States. *Annals of Tourism Research* 23 (3), 711–713.

Hughes, H.L. (1997) Holidays and homosexual identity. *Tourism Management* 18 (1), 3–7.

Hughes, H.L. (2003) Marketing gay tourism in Manchester: New market for urban tourism or destruction of 'gay space'? *Journal of Vacation Marketing* 9 (2), 152–163.

Hughes, H.L. (2005) A gay tourism market. *Journal of Quality Assurance in Hospitality & Tourism* 5 (2–4), 57–74.

Hughes, H.L. (2006) *Pink Tourism: Holidays of Gay Men and Lesbians.* Wallingford: CABI.

Human Dignity Trust (2020) *Map of Countries that Criminalise LGBT People.* See https://www.humandignitytrust.org/lgbt-the-law/map-of-criminalisation/.

Kahan, H. and Mulryan, D. (1995) Out of the closet. *American Demographics* 17 (5), 40–45.

Kama, R. and Ram, Y. (2020) 'Hot guys' in Tel Aviv: Pride tourism in Israel. *Israel Studies Review* 35 (1), 79–99.

Kates, S. (2003) Producing and consuming gendered representations: An interpretation of the Sydney Gay and Lesbian Mardi Gras. *Consumption Markets & Culture* 6 (1), 5–22.

King, M. (2003) Dropping the diagnosis of homosexuality: Did it change the lot of gays and lesbians in Britain? *Australian & New Zealand Journal of Psychiatry* 37 (6), 684–688.

Kozinets, R. (2019) *Netnography: The Essential Guide to Qualitative Social Media Research* (3rd edn). London: Routledge.

Loftus, J. (2001) America's liberalization in attitudes toward homosexuality, 1973 to 1998. *American Sociological Review* 66 (5), 762–782.

Lucena, R., Jarvis, N. and Weeden, C. (2015) A review of gay and lesbian parented families' travel motivations and destination choices: Gaps in research and future directions. *Annals of Leisure Research* 18 (2), 272–289.

Melián-González, A., Moreno-Gil, S. and Araña, J.E. (2011) Gay tourism in a sun and beach destination. *Tourism Management* 32 (5), 1027–1037.

Monterrubio, J.C. (2009) Identity and sex: Concurrent aspects of gay tourism. *Tourismos: An International Multidisciplinary Journal of Tourism* 4 (2), 155–167.

Monterrubio, C. (2019) Tourism and male homosexual identities: Directions for sociocultural research. *Tourism Review* 74 (5), 1058–1069. doi:10.1108/TR-08-2017-0125

Morin, S.F. (1977) Heterosexual bias in psychological research on lesbianism and male homosexuality. *American Psychologist* 32 (8), 629–637.

Ong, F., Vorobjovas-Pinta, O. and Lewis, C. (2020) LGBTIQ+ identities in tourism and leisure research: A systematic qualitative literature review. *Journal of Sustainable Tourism* (online).

Out Now (2018) *LGBT Diversity: Show Me the Business Case.* See http://www.outnow.lgbt/.

Peñaloza, L. (1996) We're here, We're queer, and we're going shopping! *Journal of Homosexuality* 31 (1–2), 9–41.

Prickett, D.J. (2011) 'We will show you Berlin': Space, leisure, flânerie and sexuality. *Leisure Studies* 30 (2), 157–177.

Pritchard, A., Morgan, N.J., Sedgley, D., Khan, E. and Jenkins, A. (2000) Sexuality and holiday choices: Conversations with gay and lesbian tourists. *Leisure Studies* 19 (4), 267–282.

Roy Morgan (2016) Thinking pink: The purchasing power of gay Aussies. Finding No. 6866. See http://www.roymorgan.com.au/findings/6866-power-of-the-pink-dollar-201606271639.

Southall, C. and Fallon, P. (2011) LGBT tourism. In P. Robinson, S. Heitmann and P. Dieke (eds) *Research Themes for Tourism* (pp. 218–232). Wallingford: CABI.

Therkelsen, A., Blichfeldt, B.S., Chor, J. and Ballegaard, N. (2013) 'I am very straight in my gay life': Approaching an understanding of lesbian tourists' identity construction. *Journal of Vacation Marketing* 19 (4), 317–327.

Valocchi, S. (2005) Collective action frames in the gay liberation movement, 1969–1973. In H.N. Johnston and J.A. Noakes (eds) *Frames of Protest: Social Movements and the Framing Perspective* (pp. 53–67). Oxford: Rowman & Littlefield.

Vandecasteele, B. and Geuens, M. (2009) Revising the myth of gay consumer innovativeness. *Journal of Business Research* 62 (1), 134–144.

Vorobjovas-Pinta, O. (2018) Gay neo-tribes: Exploration of travel behaviour and space. *Annals of Tourism Research* 72, 1–10.

Vorobjovas-Pinta, O. and Dalla-Fontana, I.J. (2019) The strange case of dating apps at a gay resort: Hyper-local and virtual-physical leisure. *Tourism Review* 74 (5), 1070–1080.

Vorobjovas-Pinta, O. and Hardy, A. (2016) The evolution of gay travel research. *International Journal of Tourism Research* 18 (4), 409–416.

Vorobjovas-Pinta, O. and Hardy, A. (2021) Resisting marginalisation and reconstituting space through LGBTQI+ events. *Journal of Sustainable Tourism* 29 (2–3), 448–466. doi:10.1080/09669582.2020.1769638

Waitt, G. and Markwell, K. (2006) *Gay Tourism: Culture and Context.* Binghamton, NY: Haworth Hospitality Press.

Weinberg, M.S. and Williams, C.J. (1975) Gay baths and the social organization of impersonal sex. *Social Problems* 23 (1), 124–136.

Werum, R. and Winders, B. (2001) Who's 'in' and who's 'out': State fragmentation and the struggle over gay rights, 1974–1999. *Social Problems* 48 (3), 386–410.

Wong, C.C.L. and Tolkach, D. (2017) Travel preferences of Asian gay men. *Asia Pacific Journal of Tourism Research* 22 (6), 579–591.

Part 1

Gay Tourism: Political and Sociocultural Discourses

2 Gay Tourism: A Celebration and Appropriation of Queer Difference

Can-Seng Ooi

> Queerness is that thing that lets us feel that this world is not enough, that indeed something is missing.
> José Esteban Muñoz, 2009: 1

Members of LGBTQI+ communities travel. Gay tourism in this chapter, however, focuses on only one of many LGBTQI+ communities, namely gay men. Gay tourism can be situated as a challenge to heteronormative practices and values in the tourism industry (Collins, 2009; Coon, 2012; Waitt *et al.*, 2008). It can also be understood as a community coming together to support fellow members in their activities (Auer, 2019; Markwell & Waitt, 2009; Rink, 2008). And from a business perspective, gay tourism emerges because there is a service gap that has to be filled (Guaracino, 2007; Hodes *et al.*, 2007). This chapter complements the many streams of gay tourism research by situating gay tourism as part of the perpetual transformation of modern society. The issue focused on here is not on queer differences but on understanding how these differences are selected, framed and accentuated. Consequently, these processes conflate many shades and layers that characterise LGBTQI+ communities. Instead, some differences are invented, sharpened and accentuated to pursue an ever-emerging distinctive queer identity.

With the growing formal acceptance of LGBTQI+ communities around the world, there seems to be an inherent paradox that the gay identity has become even more pronounced in society. The pursuit of equality and the assertion of gay identity sit together as a paradox. Sexual-identity liberation entails accepting LGBTQI+ communities as part of society and accepting members as regular persons. Queer differences should matter less. But instead, as will be elaborated later, we see queer differences being sharpened, discovered and invented. A 'queer economy' has been founded on how to do gayness and how to travel in a gay way. As we fight for equality for LGBTQI+ communities, asserting that we are like everyone else, we are also selectively asserting queer difference. At the individual level, many gay persons like me may have to grapple with wanting to be recognised as different and yet also wanting to be treated in the same way in the wider heteronormative society. Our asserted difference should not matter to society and yet it matters to us as a community. Where, what, why and how do we assert distinction between the bigger heteronormative society and the queer community? This chapter addresses this dialogical tension in the context of gay tourism, and explores which queer differences are accentuated, promoted and circulated in gay travels. It situates gay tourism in the context of contemporary political economic life.

The fight for equal rights is situated in a set of 'universal' modern values. Modernity and capitalism have brought about prosperity and progress, and have become the primary mode for organising, operating and governing society (Beck *et al.*, 1994; Lash, 1994; Weber & Turner, 1991). Acknowledging the vast differences across the world, all modern societies are organised through a rational and pragmatic logic for achieving administrative efficiency and effectiveness. Despite heterogeneity and diversity, these social systems see all individuals as equal and an individual as a core unit of society, as reflected in democracy (political system), capitalism (economic system) or meritocracy (education and employment). The quest for efficiency and effectiveness in achieving economic prosperity, political stability and social harmony in a society has created the Weberian bureaucratic iron cage (Weber & Turner, 1991: 196–244). Modern society has created and organised a system that has conditioned individuals into thinking about efficiency, rationality and control processes. Emotional and sexual concerns – which are not usually driven by rational thoughts – have also been framed and marginalised so as to fit into a rationally organised society. For instance, a society embracing principles of meritocracy in its education and employment systems, equal participation in its democratic political system and fair economic exchange in capitalism should not discriminate against anyone based on their sexuality.

Fortunately or unfortunately, societies have varying degrees of success in bracing the values of inclusivity and equal opportunity. Minorities are still being discriminated against. Legal and political protests and fights for minority groups, e.g. equal rights for LGBTQI+ persons, equal pay for women and equal treatment for people of colour, still continue around the world. LGBTQI+ communities are diverse, but the inequalities faced by members form common experiences that have brought them together. Besides the fight for equality and justice, there are also emerging sets of norms, behaviours, tastes, symbols and activities that bind these diverse LGBTQI+ communities. In the Durkheimian understanding of religion as a focal point for society (Durkheim, 2014), LGBTQI+ communities have acquired a set of useful totem poles to focus our attention on common interests and concerns. The rainbow flag, pride festivals, celebrities like Lady Gaga and the Village People, movies like *Boys Don't Cry* and *Brokeback Mountain*, coming-out anxiety, marriage equality, decriminalising homosexual acts and supporting gay-friendly establishments have become rallying points for many within the diverse LGBTQI+ communities.

Queer difference is the fundamental basis of queer identity. The constant shaping and maintenance of one's identity is a role that individuals are expected to, and made to, play in modern society. Asserting one's queer identity is now part of living in modernity for members of LGBTQI+ communities. The spirit of modernity requires the constant pursuit of rationalising, formalising and organising society, and economically it is driven by the capitalist pursuit of prosperity and efficiency. The emergence of woke cultures today is underpinned by the spirit of searching for enlightenment as embraced by members of society guided by the principle of self-improvement to bring a higher level of knowledgeability, control and orderliness to one's experience of self (Giddens, 1991). The reflexive person welcomes new information and can act upon new knowledge to achieve new goals and values, such as how gay persons understand and take control of their own situation and condition, and strategically go about achieving equal rights by coming together. A person can consciously adopt values, behaviour and lifestyle options that reflect a desired self-identity. This adoption is also helped and managed by 'experts' and specialists who supposedly know more about values, tastes, fashion, specific topics, etiquette, well-being and all aspects of life (Collier, 2017). These experts and specialists explain and tell us how to dress (e.g. fashion magazine writers), which bars are cool (e.g. entertainment reviewers), how to decorate our homes (e.g. home decoration writers and home renovation show hosts) and what values we should hold (e.g. activists and opinion makers).

In other words, self-reflexivity is both a personal exercise and an institutionalised practice in modern society (Barnard, 2000; Foucault *et al.*, 1988; Lash, 1994). We are expected constantly to 'find' or to 'better' ourselves in terms of who we are, what we stand for and how we should present ourselves. Each of us, as a self-reflexive person, has taken upon ourself as an object to be examined, managed and displayed. We are expected to be 'authentic' and yet be open-minded to change; for instance, we take positions to indicate who we really are, as we consume news, get bombarded by advertisements, support social causes, develop ideological positions and entrench our self-identity. A gay youth leader of a socially conservative student club at the University of Queensland, Wilson Gavin, who opposed same-sex marriage and led protests against various LGBTQI+ activities, took his own life in January 2020 (Taylor, 2020).

The vitriol targeted against him was vicious. Cognitive dissonance can always be squared with self-rationalisation. But there is social pressure and expectations of what a person should value and believe and how they should behave. Even while acknowledging diversity in the LGBTQI+ communities, a gay person is often expected to support certain causes and hold certain values within sub-groups. Increasingly, the struggle for equal rights has led to a gay person being taught and pressured to live a perceived self-righteous life even though the reality is always much more nuanced, layered and complicated. Doing gay tourism is part of that set of activities that woke gay persons are encouraged to if not expected to participate in.

Following Foucault's (1988) technologies of the self, one is expected to be 'consistent' in one's values, beliefs, practices and behaviour, but some disparities have to be ignored and marginalised in order to maintain that consistency. By asserting our difference in everyday activities, we also ignore, marginalise and renounce what we share in common with other members of the wider community. Asserting queer difference is part of the process of overshadowing shared commonalities. Gay tourism does not deny 'general' tourism, but it inadvertently renounces gay-hostile and many gay-neutral businesses by prioritising gay-friendliness as a criterion for defining gay tourism.

With the emergence of modern society, identities are ways to frame and organise people in society, and these identities are also situational and circumstantial (Anderson, 1991; Koning & Ooi, 2013; Ooi, 2019; Stets & Burke, 2000). Gay tourism has become a way for gay men to express their sexuality and identity. Queer difference is used to characterise the LGBTQI+ communities against a heteronormative society. What constitutes that difference? How is that difference constituted? Who constitutes these differences? These are some of the questions that will help us understand the social economic political context that shapes gay tourism today. The following sections will situate gay tourism in this wider context, as I proceed to argue that gay difference is celebrated and appropriated by business.

Constructing Queer Difference and Transnational Gay Knowledge

The acronym LGBTQI+ encompasses many diverse groups of people (Vorobjovas-Pinta & Hardy, 2016). As a classification, it is not a neutral term (Nowak & Mitchell, 2016). The classification is a joint response against the mainstream heterosexual regime and tells of a largely miscellaneous category of humans that encapsulate a range of gender and sexual minorities in relation to heteronormativity (Elizabeth, 2013). It conflates different groups into one category. As alluded to earlier, if there is a sense of community, it is imagined and maintained by a common challenge to heteronormativity.

In the context of gay tourism in this chapter, one might pose a question: How would the propensity of men who have sex with other men translate into social, cultural, economic and political behaviour, practices and activities? Growing up gay, maintaining gay relations and fighting for equality differ across countries, reflecting embedded social institutions and circumstances (see, for example, Kaiser, 1997; Law, 2019; Luther & Ung Loh, 2019; Wotherspoon, 2016). An Australian gay hotel owner in Bali, a visiting German gay couple and the gay Javanese migrant accommodation employee have little in common beyond their commercial transaction and casual social interaction. Coming from different countries, their interaction and comradery is, however, established through common reference points. Many members of the gay community are able to communicate, support each other and come together to fight for equal rights. And in particular for gay tourists, they are able to travel across borders and encounter gay cultures in other countries even if they do not have local knowledge or speak the local vernacular. There is a set of social cultural resources that facilitates interaction among the diverse members of the gay community around the world. Like local knowledge in a community, there seems to be a form of transnational gay knowledge. This transnational gay knowledge is built on at least three interrelated parts.

The first is the shared issues and struggles that are similar around the world. The struggles for equal rights for gay persons manifest differently in different countries but the cause is the same. The call for equal rights in a heteronormative world has brought millions of gay people together. Gay men, for instance, want the right to travel in the same way as straight people. Gay couples get annoyed or embarrassed when, for example, they are asked if they want a room with twin beds instead of a king-size bed at hotels. There are more consequential struggles that galvanise gay communities everywhere, such as the fight to decriminalise sex between men, marriage equality and better sexual healthcare access. Pride is celebrated differently in different countries; for example, the flamboyant and rowdy festivals such as Copenhagen Pride and Sydney Mardi Gras contrast with the subdued and more intellectually framed Pink Dot festival in Singapore. The common cause is that being gay is not wrong and gay persons should be allowed to express their love and intimacy in their own way. The ability for gay men to travel seamlessly and explore their gay desires without discrimination is part of claiming equal treatment.

The fight for equal opportunities, inclusiveness and the right to love are common values that resonate with most members of the gay community. Gay tourism is a sphere of activities that should be accepted, and not just tolerated. International gay tourism supports and exerts these rights and values across borders. It is not just about pleasure and holidaying; it is also about making a statement. In more gay-hostile countries such as Malaysia, Russia and Jamaica, visitors inevitably show solidarity and support to the local gay community through their presence.

The second constituent of transnational gay knowledge is information on what and where common and popular gay-oriented activities are to be found. Pride festivals, gay games and the Eurovision Song Contest attract many gay visitors. People come together in solidarity to assert and champion their rights, as well as to mingle and socialise. Gay dance clubs, pubs and bath houses are also popular with visitors and residents. Gay hook-up apps like Grindr, Blued and Jack'd allow gay men to interact with and meet one another. These places and activities exclude the heterosexual world. Members of the gay community also come together to do non-exclusively gay activities, such as engaging with walking clubs, reading groups and other hobby organizations. While the gay identity is hinged on sexuality, a gay person still does many non-sexual activities; in such groups, members feel comfortable with each other and are able to communicate freely about their deeper social concerns, such as family and relationship matters and discrimination at work. Such places and activities are locations for queer normality, and are safe spaces for gay visitors to meet and interact with residents and fellow tourists. Transnational gay knowledge contains information on types of places to meet, what to do and how to enjoy oneself.

But how would gay visitors from other countries know where to meet? This question is similar to how gay visitors might appreciate the local gay community when they lack local knowledge and are staying only for a short period during which they do not have time to internalise local norms and understanding. It is possible because there are tourism mediators – such as guidebooks (e.g. Spartacus), gay internet sites (e.g. Fridae, Gay Utopia), dating apps (e.g. Grindr, Scruff and Tinder), friends and local guides – that select and present relevant information to visitors (Ooi, 2002). These mediators also help visitors appreciate local gay cultures by explaining and informing them about local norms and practices. Besides knowing where the gay clubs are, for instance, visitors will learn that gay men in China have adopted the term 'comrades' to refer to each other.

The third body of transnational gay knowledge is tied closely to the common causes and knowing what to do and where to meet: it is an assemblage of collective aesthetics and vocabulary. A set of gay norms and aesthetics has been transmitted through the global circuit of cultural production and consumption. Celebrities, cultural icons and entertainment programmes, such as Cher, *Tom of Finland* and *Will and Grace* have popularised certain behaviour as distinctly gay. Gay men learn to flaunt gayness by being camp, taking care of one's skin and concern with one's body shape. By noticing and using clichéd ways of exhibiting gayness, many homosexual men utilise their queer gaze and pick out vibes and cues, often under the name of 'gaydar' (Nicholas, 2004; Wood, 2004). They learn to catch those gazes as well as, sometimes, to strategically avoid being caught displaying queer desires in bars, gyms and other public spaces (Parsi, 1997). In celebration of diversity in gay desires, many gay men across continents picked up the 'hanky codes' or the colour codes in sexual advertising in the United States in the 1970s (Reilly & Saethre, 2013). In the age of Grindr, that set of codes has been translated into stating one's own tribes and preferences in the apps. Many of these gazes have gone global and travelled around the world. These codes, as part of transnational global knowledge, facilitate gay tourism.

Queer difference is constructed and enacted through a myriad set of social dynamics, many of which are found in gay tourism. Queer difference is packaged into a loose set of transnational gay knowledge that provides reference points and shared social cultural resources, including symbols, values, activities, practices and behaviour. Members of gay communities around the world can come together to interact and affirm their queer difference and identity. These cultural resources are also revised and reconstituted over time. And queer difference is increasingly being expressed through commercial means. For instance, fast-moving fashions and tastes are constantly introduced into the gay community, drawing their attention to how members could display their gay identity. Gay tourism is one such commercial channel. The gay tourism industry has adopted the gay cause, including the championing of common agendas and interests, promoting gay-focused activities, doing gay-speak or using gay lingo and maintaining queer difference in relation to 'normal' tourism. This commercial engagement builds a sense of a gay community, generating feelings of togetherness and belongingness based on common values, symbols and practices, while members differentiate themselves from others. Such bonding cuts across borders in gay tourism.

The commercial construction of gay difference has now involved the Othering of heteronormativity. Image maintenance, value-based lifestyle and body shaming are not unique to the gay community. Idealised body forms, lifestyle choices and beauty have shaped the self-reflexive individual in modern society. The gay aesthetic has been appropriated for the straight population. The invention of the metrosexual male is an example of how gay male aesthetics are used to redefine heterosexual commercial masculine aesthetics, through programmes like *Queer Eye for a Straight Guy*, through celebrity icons like David Beckham and Cristiano Ronaldo, and in advertisements like those for Calvin Klein (featuring sexualised male underwear models) and Nespresso (featuring George Clooney). The established gay aesthetic is introduced into the heteronormative straight male population, blurring sexual social representations (Miller, 2005; Sender, 2006). Fashion, taste, etiquette and lifestyle experts and advocates claim that straight guys need to level up and acquire good taste like queer guys. Similarly, Richard Florida has argued that cities that are more diverse and tolerant of diversity will be able to attract more creative workers. Consequently, the measure of tolerance is translated into the so-called gay index. Cities that have a higher proportion of gay persons are found to have more knowledgeable and creative workers, which bodes well for these places as they pursue the creative economy (Florida, 2002; Letellier, 2005; Ooi, 2011).

Living up to imagined queer difference can be difficult for many gay men. For instance, Sydney's Mardi Gras has created great pressure on many gay men, as they are body shamed (Nielsen, 2020). Visitors are not exempted, as many feel compelled to prepare their bodies for display during the festivities (Molz, 2006; Wonders & Michalowski, 2001). Also, the aesthetics of what constitutes a beautiful body change with time (Atkins, 2012; Moore, 1997). This creates challenges for ageing gay men (Jones & Pugh, 2005), men with disabilities (Butler, 1999) and men of colour (Han, 2007; Ibañez et al., 2012). These insecurities arise from their self-reflection on what they ought to be. These insecurities also spur people into action, resulting in the burgeoning industries of instant weight loss, body-beautiful gym programmes, healthy living apps and fashion advice. For instance, in challenging an America-led global dominance in defining gay aesthetics, Balderston and Quiroga (2003) lamented the emergence of a sinister fairyland constituted by sun-kissed, super-toned body image in Latin America, which has been adopted from the fantasies of white gay men in San Francisco. These images unleash a set of gay desires that are unrealistic for most. These issues will be discussed later, and they highlight the irony that the demand for the acceptance of diversity has also led to the homogenisation of gay diversity.

Two Readings of Gay Tourism in Capitalism: Management and Appropriation of Queer Difference

From the discussion above on the construction of queer difference, gay tourism asserts and perpetuates the idea of queer difference. This section will reiterate a couple of points on queer difference and will delve into queer difference as a tourism product. The first reading of gay tourism argues that gay tourism serves a market, and closes a service gap in the industry. The second is a radical reading of the appropriation of queer difference in the tourism industry. By contrasting these two approaches, the paradoxes as addressed in the opening section can be situated and understood.

Serving the market: What is so gay about the gay tourist product?

From the discussion so far, the gay tourism product can be understood at different interrelated levels: providing a gay-friendly environment, offering seamless gay sociality and allowing unfettered self-expression. The gay community has its own needs and gay tourist businesses serve those needs. The gay tourism industry must deliver at least three related services.

The first is that a gay tourism enterprise must provide a safe environment for its customers. Gay tourism encounters the same challenges as tourism in general, that is providing experiences that are seamless, comfortable and enjoyable. Whether gay or not, there are three fundamental tourist conditions: tourists lack local knowledge; their visits are relatively short; and they intend on enjoying themselves. As a result, mediators are at hand to offer short-cuts to enjoying a destination (Ooi, 2002). Mediators allay anxieties that tourists may have because they lack local knowledge and cultural sensitivity (Ma *et al.*, 2018). For example, concerns over food hygiene when eating out in a foreign country can be challenging, especially when visitors want exotic street food experiences in many parts of Asia. To address this problem, Singapore has, for instance, cleaned up its street food culture and provided a secure destination for visitors to experiment and experience the island (Ooi & Tarulevicz, 2019; Tarulevicz & Ooi, 2019). Such health and hygiene concerns apply to both gay and non-gay tourists. In this context, gay tourists are no different from other tourists. Nonetheless, many destinations and venues are not considered gay-tolerant and friendly. Gay tourism businesses and mediators are in the business of providing their customers with a safe and comfortable manner of travelling.

Every destination has its own level of gay-friendliness or hostility. Many countries still criminalise homosexuality, and while anti-discrimination laws have been enacted in many democratic countries, discrimination and hostility against homosexuals remain. Some destinations, such as San Francisco, Tel Aviv and Sydney, offer a general city-wide safe space for gay travellers. Other places such as Singapore, Moscow and Johannesburg are less gay-tolerant, but businesses assure gay travellers that there are still many safe venues for them to visit, such as gay clubs, hotels, cafés, restaurants, resorts and bathhouses. Each destination has its own brand of gay tourism, offering protected spaces for gay interaction. Mediators in gay tourism serve gay visitors by helping them navigate through the different destinations in a safe manner.

The second service that the gay tourism industry offers is the opportunity for gay bonding and interaction. Social behaviour is always situated in context and circumstance. Different interpretations of social expressions can be a source of conflict and anxiety because what might be considered acceptable (or at least tolerable) may be considered highly offensive in some host societies. For instance, an American gay couple posed their bare butts at tourist attractions around the world through their Traveling Butts Instagram account, and were finally caught, fined and jailed in Thailand (BBC, 2017). With disregard to local Thai sensitivities, they 'mooned' at temples in the Buddhist country. Their actions attracted fans and also offended many gay and non-gay persons around the world. If they had taken their selfie while 'mooning' in a Thai gay resort, that would be more widely tolerated, if not accepted. Such a need for sensitivity is not unique to gay tourists. Around the world, people must dress appropriately and not engage in intimate behaviour at places of worship, for instance.

In gay tourism, visitors are informed where they can interact with other members of the gay community without running foul of local social standards. In asserting queer difference in those places, gay tourists can hold hands, use the same lingo and be explicit in displaying their gay desires. Gay travel reviews, travel websites and other mediators facilitate the gay travel experience. At those places, they do not fear barking up the wrong tree if they try to befriend and get intimate with another guy in a dance club, for instance. Gay persons can bond, engage in gay-speak and communicate through their fashion sense, mannerisms and taste. They can be flamboyant and camp, and not be concerned with heteronormative standards.

Besides providing the safe environment and the environment for them to socially interact, the third interrelated service that the gay tourism industry provides is for its gay customers to assert their identity. In gay tourism, gay visitors can be 'themselves', that is, express their same-sex attraction, intimacy and desires without fear and discrimination. One does not have to pretend and 'act straight', and can be comfortable with oneself. Bath houses and dating apps allow one to express one's sexual desires. Gay medical tourism allows persons to go for cosmetic or even sex-transitioning procedures. For many, gay tourism is a break from the routine of everyday life, and also a break from a largely heteronormative social environment they normally live in (Devall, 1979).

Gay tourism is then defined as a form of tourism that provides gay persons with a safe and secure environment where they can travel and interact socially and intimately with each other and that allows them to be free and to be themselves. Gay tourism as an industry fills a jarring service gap for the gay community.

Appropriating gay empowerment: A radical reading of gay tourism

A serving-the-market reading of gay tourism ignores how heteronormative structures have come to define the queer future and utopia that the community is striving for. A more radical reading of gay tourism will show that gay tourism is merely tourism; it is just business-as-usual. Heteronormativity and the current social political and economic system are so closely intertwined that gay difference can only make sense through straight lenses. The gay tourism industry is merely responding to and then adroitly appropriating the gay empowerment cause. As a consequence, the gay community is heteronormalising itself by accepting a market and economic logic of capitalism that embraces heteronormative assumptions.

The Heteronormative Trap: Using a Majoritarian Logic for a Minority

Emotions and affective experiences have become commodities (Anderson & Mullen, 1998; Ooi, 2005; Pine & Gilmore, 1999). In the emotion economy, an effective communication strategy today is to concentrate on selected single issues to champion causes, such as marriage equality, for LGBTQI+ rights. Businesses, activists, politicians and individuals have learned to distil messages into dramatic sound bites. Consequently, armies of woke consumers have been manufactured. The concerns they champion may also create disappointment. This is what Berlant (2011) terms as cruel optimism. The experience of optimism entails an affective structure that drives people towards a fantasy that is obtainable, but the optimism is cruel when the attainment is close to impossible, if not impossible, or when the process creates a situation of profound threat (Berlant, 2011). The normalisation of queer difference is an example.

The pursuit of equality and non-discrimination has led to the absorption of queer difference into mainstream society. The fight for marriage equality, for instance, has inadvertently imposed a heteronormative norm for the gay world, as the narrative shifts to gay couples wanting the same rights as straight ones, and also having to accept the tacit norms of an idealised heteronormative family (i.e. having children, monogamous and everlasting). The rainbow diversity of LGBTQI+ differences to doing social and sexual relationships are measured or contrasted against the heteronormative institutionalised marriage. This leads to criticisms of the normalisation of gay cultures, as the community adopts similar values, behaviour and practices institutionally embedded in the heteronormative society (Harris, 1997). A queer future has consequentially been defined by the present heterosexual culture (Muñoz, 2009). The ideas of sexual avant-gardes, non-uniform family units and other queer social expressions are then subjugated under an institutionalised social practice that is deeply rooted in institutionalised heteronormative practices. Queer differences that are now acceptable and tolerated are those that the heteronormative society sanctions. The wide variety of queer differences have inadvertently been assimilated into a heteronormative set of lenses. The optimism about being accepted in society for gay activists has cruel consequences because the acceptance has resulted in heteronormalising queer difference. Despite being a minority, LGBTQI+ communities have adopted a majoritarian logic.

The current prevalent social economic system is built on a heteronormative majoritarian logic; for instance, heterosexual family units are the basic household consumption units that are used to organise a modern industrialised society. These nuclear family relationships are legally sanctioned and are made stable through formal protection. Parents are obliged to look after and support their children, and the state sees that as the de facto family unit. This has become the unit of analysis for consumption by many businesses, as products and services are sold to households for joint consumption by members (e.g. eating together, sharing a WiFi connection, going on holiday together), and businesses understand the social and emotional dynamics within that unit (i.e. demands on limited resources by members of a family unit). It is this intertwined social, legal and economic dynamics in the proliferation of the nuclear family unit and the pursuit of profit and efficiency that stop other minority social arrangements from getting wider recognition and acceptance. Modern industrialised societies have made the nuclear family the most common unit of consumption. The economy is structured to serve this majority in familial arrangements.

A radical reading of gay tourism must acknowledge the institutionalised economic logic of the tourism industry. It is a logic that attempts to extract the most profit, whether by volume (i.e. serving the majority) or by yield (i.e. focus on people who can pay more). Because the gay community remains a minority, gay tourism takes off because of the 'pink dollar'. All tourist segments have special and unique needs, including those who have more disposable income (Wiltshier & Cardow, 2001). With regard to gay visitors, many are considered higher yield because of their generally bigger spending power arising from gender income inequality and being less likely to support children (Chang, 2013; Kates, 1998). Gay visitors make up for their lack of numbers by being more lucrative. This pink dollar argument – rightly or wrongly conceived – embraces a variation of the majoritarian logic of profit maximisation for tourism businesses.

Products and services are provided for different market segments. The strategy for serving the specific needs of gay tourists is no different from catering to the specific needs of other groups of visitors, such as Chinese tourists (Ooi, 2008). And as part of the strategy, tourism products and services are effectively and efficiently manufactured. Ritzer (1996; Ritzer & Liska, 1997) and his McDonaldisation of society thesis highlights how processes are introduced to manufacture friendly and authentic experiences. He terms it McDisneyisation for the tourism industry. Despite perceived differences, modifications and variation are limited; for instance, on a cruise ship, all passengers are given a basic level of comfort, and those who pay more will have a balcony in their bigger cabins. Running a gay-friendly hotel may just mean changing the decoration and fittings to appear gayer. The cost and the perceived differences are arguably banal, but the economic exchange value is enhanced significantly. Gay tourism is not fundamentally different from general tourism, and the selective expression or assertion of queer difference is cost-efficient and sufficient in pleasing the gay clientele. This clientele is also willing to pay for that difference. So, at one level, catering to gay tourists is merely heteronormative tourism but cloaked through clever marketing and the reframing of standardised products and services.

But the banal differences are further accentuated and elevated by the process of the joint social construction of a safe gay-friendly environment. The experience economy, as defined by Pine and Gilmore (1999), sees the experience product as a 'stage', on which customers relate and react to the props and environment. These stages and props range from public installations where tourists pose playfully for their selfies to bath houses for gay men to meet and live out their sexual fantasies. In gay tourism, gay tourists are given the stage to play out and express their sexuality, with businesses having honed and learned what these customers want and fancy. Not only that and as already pointed out earlier, they use and thus affirm established and emerging gay norms, lingos and tastes. Jointly and through processes of globalisation, many gay persons around the world have acquired some transnational gay knowledge and thus could share ways of expressing gayness, thus adding to their own repertoire of local social behaviour and practices. In the name of co-creation, customers are also responsible for producing their own experiences. It does not, however, mean that local gay cultures are replaced but that global ones are added to the mix. For instance, gay people in Myanmar have established their own secret language, *bansaka*, but many have adopted, adapted and use more global forms of gay expressions (*The Economist*, 2020).

Queer Difference and Global Capitalism: The Complicit Tourism Industry

Businesses in the gay tourism industry, regardless, highlight and market queer difference as their distinctiveness even though many of the products they offer are only different in clichéd ways. They follow the economic logic of a market built on heteronormative models. Gay tourism is part of global capitalism, and if there is such a thing as 'global gay capitalism', it is merely how queer differences are selectively accentuated, appropriated and entrenched into global capitalism.

The use of gay symbols, references to gay icons and hosting of gay-themed activities are parts of the staging of the gay experience product. Such staging communicates versions of gay culture and serves several functions. The symbols become a magnet and rallying point to bring gay customers together. These businesses inevitably promote a particular gayness even though they are just using reference points to attract and cater to gay customers. They normalise certain tastes, behaviour and activities and have become mediators in building up the gay community. American and European travellers have come to dominate the lucrative pink dollar market. Gay references from this group are commonly used throughout the world; consequently, the gay tourist is 'tended to be defined by the industry and in commentaries as wealthy, middle-class, healthy, white, and male' (Crang, 2006: ix). Even local portrayals of local gay persons may carry Orientalist depiction of the locals (Boone, 1995;

Moussawi, 2013). The mass global dissemination of gay symbols has made these symbols popular, and is part of a trove of global gay cultural capital. Following Bourdieu's idea of cultural capital, tastes and cultural knowledge are picked up through everyday behaviour and at home (Bourdieu, 1984; Ooi & Shelley, 2019). Children who come from more affluent and better educated families tend to acquire cultural capital that is more in line with what is taught in school, and consequently these young people will do better academically and, when they grow up, will do better economically. Persons with global gay cultural capital have more knowledge about popular gay issues, struggles, cultures and practices, and will be more comfortable navigating in a gay world. Persons who have just come out, for instance, may feel awkward visiting a gay establishment. Gay tourism is part of the process of building up one's global gay cultural capital, as the gay person is socialised into institutionalised and promoted symbols, icons, mannerism, practices and behaviour. In other words, a person with global gay cultural capital is also one with a large amount of transnational gay knowledge. As alluded to earlier, transnational gay knowledge evolves and is also transmitted in different ways, such as through popular culture, news stories and social interaction. Also as pointed out earlier, information on internationalised gay tastes and aesthetics have been disseminated through programmes like *Next in Fashion* and *Glee*, celebrities like Liza Minnelli and Boy George, popular literature (e.g. Oscar Wilde, Edmund White and Dale Peck), news stories featuring gay symbols (e.g. rainbow flag, pride festivals), commercial gay pornography (body aesthetics, fetishes) and homoerotic advertisements (e.g. Armani Exchange). These are part of the professionalisation of queerness and the commodification of queer difference (Miller, 2005). The queer tastes and fashion elevated often reflect American middle-class values (Miller, 2005; Sender, 2006).

The creation of queer difference also entails its appropriation, sometimes in the guise of pink washing. Many gay tourists embrace the gay cause by supporting gay establishments, visiting gay memorials and joining gay events. The pink dollar is used as 'pink power'. The call for boycotts of gay-hostile places and establishments is often heard. For instance, in 2019 Sultan Hassanal Bolkiah of Brunei passed Islamic criminal laws that allow for the stoning of offenders to death for gay sex and adultery (Holson & Rueb, 2019). Celebrities such as Elton John, Ellen DeGeneres and George Clooney and big global companies rallied behind the boycott of nine luxurious hotels owned by the Sultan, one of the richest men in the world. The United Nations and many governments of democratic countries, such as Australia and Denmark, voiced their disdain. And the effective way of protest seems to be through the wallet. Gay consumption, including how gay persons travel and use their pink dollars, is a response to addressing an injustice and to supporting a good cause. If we are to consume, we might as well bring about some good too.

The economic appropriation of the gay cause highlights a crisis in societies across the world. And this crisis reflects modern society-at-large. The fight for equality and anti-discrimination has mobilised support on both sides of the debate. As with all 'culture wars', people are emotionally consumed by a sense of calamity if things are not changed or are changed. Standing up for a purpose and cause is part of doing self-reflexivity in modernity. This is perpetuated in big and small issues. For instance, Sender (2006) argues that the metrosexualisation of straight guys is part of the neoliberal project to socially engineer and discipline the subject by creating a crisis. In this case, it is the crisis of masculinity, as men have to be better and to rethink their image, appearance and home habits as well as their relationships. The modern person is pliant to advice on their own identity and being more flexible and adaptable to an imagined image of themselves. In neoliberal and transactional economics, the individual is assumed to be and is a resource that can be reallocated to different tasks and jobs (Williamson, 1998). The flexible individual is the best type of employee in that system. The casualisation of the workforce and the metrosexualisation of straight men are manifestations of the neoliberal logic of the efficient, effective and employable pliable individual.

Subsequently, the process of self-reflexivity and how that has been appropriated for consumption has created perverse consequences. In some instances, popularity as an indication of social support has been conflated with the exercise of democracy. For instance, popular reality programmes like *Big Brother* and *The Voice* have given the public the idea that they are able to vote for and shape the consequences of the results. Wide viewership engagement attracts advertisers. Consumption is also seen as an exercise of one's freedom, and freedom is an intricate value of democracy. As a result, China bans such talent shows because viewers can vote for their favourite artists and feel that they are exercising a democratic right; the authorities fear that Chinese citizens may want to exercise their democratic rights after voting in these shows (*The Economist*, 2011). Gay tourism, seen as part of supporting the gay cause, is also an exercise of one's freedom and democratic choice. But those choices are shaped by heteronormative standards and by businesses.

Concluding Remarks

There is a competition of causes – poverty, environmentalism, gender equality, racism – for our attention. Gay tourism has become a cause that serves the gay community. And within that context, the gay cause is also fighting for attention. LGBTQI+ communities have succeeded in many aspects, such as in the decriminalisation of homosexual acts and marriage equality in many countries. Members, regardless of their differences in these communities, come together and rally around selected issues. And as part of the reclamation of equality, members are arguing that they are the same as everyone else. This chapter has not focused on queer differences but on understanding how these differences are selected, framed, accentuated and perpetuated. Those promoted differences often conflate and flatten the shades and layers that celebrate LGBTQI+ communities. Gay tourism is used to illustrate how some differences are invented, sharpened and accentuated to define an ever-emerging distinctive queer identity. In doing so, this chapter points to the importance of the global queer economy, gay cultural capital and transnational gay knowledge. Seamless gay travel is made possible partly by transnational gay knowledge. Gay men with plenty of transnational gay knowledge have more gay cultural capital to interact and enjoy their trips.

While we celebrate queer difference in gay travel and argue that gay tourism closes a service gap, queer difference has also been appropriated by global tourism. There is an apparent paradox that queer difference sets the LGBTQI+ communities apart, but in order to obtain equal rights, members must be seen and be treated the same in modern society. LGBTQI+ communities have navigated the system by asserting that their sexuality is of no consequence to the economic, political and social system of a modern society, but they have asserted those differences regardless, in the spheres of their personal, social and sexual lives. And with such compartmentalisation, gay consumption sits between the personal social life and public economic activities. Gay tourism satisfies the personal and social needs of gay men, and they seem to be in a better position to enjoy their tourism adventures if they acquire and embrace some transnational gay knowledge. The transnational gay knowledge asserts clear distinctions with the heteronormative society but that set of knowledge is constructed through heteronormative structures and logic. Gay tourism celebrates our diversity when many of the flattened differences that are sanctioned are quite banal, and yet that is good enough to exert our queer difference.

References

Anderson, B. (1991) *Imagined Communities: Reflections on the Origin and Spread of Nationalism*. London: Verso.

Anderson, D. and Mullen, P. (eds) (1998) *Faking It: The Sentimentalisation of Modern Society*. London: Penguin.

Atkins, D. (2012) *Looking Queer*. New York: Routledge. doi:10.4324/9780203047477

Auer, J.J. (2019) *Movement and Change: Perspectives on Urban Gay Tourism and Gay Community Building of the Past*. Reno, NV: University of Nevada. See http://hdl.handle.net/11714/6006.

Balderston, D. and Quiroga, J. (2003) A beautiful, sinister fairyland: Gay sunshine press does Latin America. *Balderston* 21 (3), 85–108. See https://www.muse.jhu.edu/article/47174.

Barnard, S. (2000) Construction and corporeality: Theoretical psychology and biomedical technologies of the self. *Theory & Psychology* 10 (5), 669–688. doi:10.1177/0959354300105005

BBC (2017) Bangkok photo: US tourists held for baring buttocks at Thai temple. *BBC News*, 29 November. See https://www.bbc.com/news/world-asia-42164668.

Beck, U., Giddens, A. and Lash, S. (1994) *Reflexive Modernization: Politics, Tradition and Aesthetics in the Modern Social Order*. Cambridge: Polity Press.

Berlant, L. (2011) *Cruel Optimism*. London: Duke University Press.

Boone, J.A. (1995) Vacation cruises; Or, the homoerotics of orientalism. *Publications of Modern Language Association* 110 (1), 89–107. doi:10.2307/463197

Bourdieu, P. (1984) *Distinctions*. London: Routledge.

Butler, R. (1999) Double the trouble or twice the fun? Disabled bodies in the gay community. In R. Butler and H. Parr (eds) *Mind and Body Spaces: Geographies of Illness, Impairment and Disability* (pp. 203–220). London: Routledge.

Chang, A. (2013) The power of LGBT travel. *LGBTQ Policy Journal* 4, 109–114.

Collier, S.J. (2017) Neoliberalism and rule by experts. In V. Higgins and W. Larner (eds) *Assembling Neoliberalism* (pp. 23–43). New York: Palgrave Macmillan US. doi:10.1057/978-1-137-58204-1_2

Collins, D. (2009) 'We're there and queer'. *Gender & Society* 23 (4), 465–493. doi:10.1177/0891243209340570

Coon, D.R. (2012) Sun, sand, and citizenship: The marketing of gay tourism. *Journal of Homosexuality* 59 (4), 511–534. doi:10.1080/00918369.2012.648883

Crang, M. (2006) Foreword. In G. Waitt and K. Markwell (eds) *Gay Tourism: Culture and Context* (pp. ix–xi). London: Routledge. doi:10.1300/5141_a

Devall, W. (1979) Leisure and lifestyles among gay men: An exploratory essay. *International Review of Modern Sociology* 9 (2), 179–195. See https://www.jstor.org/stable/41420700.

Durkheim, E. (2014) *The Elementary Form of Religious Life*. (J.W. Swain, ed.). Scotts Valley, CA: CreateSpace Independent Publishing Platform.

Elizabeth, A. (2013) Challenging the binary: Sexual identity that is not duality. *Journal of Bisexuality* 13 (3), 329–337. doi:10.1080/15299716.2013.813421

Florida, R. (2002) *The Rise of the Creative Class*. New York: Basic Books.

Foucault, M., Martin, L.H., Gutman, H. and Hutton, P.H. (1988) *Technologies of the Self: A Seminar with Michel Foucault*. (L.H. Martin, H. Gutman and P.H. Hutton, eds). London: Tavistock.

Giddens, A. (1991) *Modernity and Self-Identity: Self and Society in the Late Modern Age*. Oxford: Polity Press.

Guaracino, J. (2007) *Gay and Lesbian Tourism: The Essential Guide for Marketing*. Oxford: Butterworth-Heinemann.

Han, C. (2007) They don't want to cruise your type: Gay men of color and the racial politics of exclusion. *Social Identities* 13 (1), 51–67. doi:10.1080/13504630601163379

Harris, D. (1997) *The Rise and Fall of Gay Culture*. New York: Hyperion.

Hodes, S., Vork, J. and Gerritsma, R. (2007) Amsterdam as a gay tourism destination in the twenty-first century. In G. Richards and J. Wilson (eds) *Tourism, Creativity and Development* (pp. 178–188). Abingdon: Routledge.

Holson, L.M. and Rueb, E.S. (2019) Brunei hotel boycott gathers steam as anti-gay law goes into effect. *The New York Times*, 3 April. See https://www.nytimes.com/2019/04/03/world/asia/brunei-hotel-boycotts.html.

Ibañez, G.E., Van Oss Marin, B., Flores, S.A., Millett, G. and Diaz, R.M. (2012) General and gay-related racism experienced by Latino gay men. *Journal of Latina/o Psychology* 1 (S), 66–77. doi:10.1037/2168-1678.1.S.66

Jones, J. and Pugh, S. (2005) Ageing gay men: Lessons from the sociology of embodiment. *Men and Masculinities* 7 (3), 248–260. doi:10.1177/1097184X04265990

Kaiser, C. (1997) *The Gay Metropolis*. London: Phoenix.

Kates, S.M. (1998) *Twenty Million New Customers! Understanding Gay Men's Consumer Behaviour*. New York: Harrington Park Press.

Koning, J. and Ooi, C. (2013) Awkward encounters and ethnography. *Qualitative Research in Organizations and Management: An International Journal* 8 (1), 16–32. doi:10.1108/17465641311327496

Lash, S. (1994) Reflexivity and its doubles: Structure, aesthetics, community. In U. Beck, A. Giddens and S. Lash (eds) *Reflexive Modernization: Politics, Tradition and Aesthetics in the Modern Social Order* (pp. 110–173). Cambridge: Polity Press.

Law, B. (2019) *Growing Up Queer in Australia*. (B. Law, ed.). Carlton, VIC: Black.

Letellier, P. (2005) Success depends on gays. *Advocate* 940, 22.

Luther, J.D. and Ung Loh, J. (eds) (2019) *'Queer' Asia*. London: Zed Books.

Ma, Y., Ooi, C.-S. and Hardy, A. (2018) Chinese travelling overseas and their anxieties. In E. Yang and C. Khoo-Lattimore (eds) *Asian Cultures and Contemporary Tourism: Perspectives on Asian Tourism* (pp. 201–220). Singapore: Springer. doi:10.1007/978-981-10-7980-1_11

Markwell, K. and Waitt, G. (2009) Festivals, space and sexuality: Gay pride in Australia. *Tourism Geographies* 11 (2), 143–168. doi:10.1080/14616680902827092

Miller, T. (2005) A meterosexual eye on queer guy. *GLQ: A Journal of Lesbian and Gay Studies* 11 (1), 112–117. doi:10.1215/10642684-11-1-112

Molz, J.G. (2006) Cosmopolitan bodies: Fit to travel and travelling to fit. *Body & Society* 12 (3), 1–21. doi:10.1177/1357034X06067153

Moore, P.L. (ed.) (1997) *Building Bodies*. London: Rutgers University Press.

Moussawi, G. (2013) Queering Beirut, the 'Paris of the Middle East': Fractal Orientalism and essentialized masculinities in contemporary gay travelogues. *Gender, Place & Culture* 20 (7), 858–875. doi:10.1080/0966369X.2012.753586

Muñoz, J.E. (2009) *Cruising Utopia: The Then and There of Queer Futurity*. New York: New York University Press.

Nicholas, C.L. (2004) Gaydar: Eye-gaze as identity recognition among gay men and lesbians. *Sexuality & Culture* 8 (1), 60–86. doi:10.1007/s12119-004-1006-1

Nielsen, B. (2020) The body image pressures gay men feel around Mardi Gras. *ABC Life*, 28 February. See https://www.abc.net.au/life/the-body-image-pressure-on-gay-men-around-mardi-gras/12009666.

Nowak, K.L. and Mitchell, A. (2016) Classifying identity: Organizing an LGBT library. *Library Philosophy and Practice* (online). See http://digitalcommons.unl.edu/libphilprac/1452?utm_source=digitalcommons.unl.edu%2Flibphilprac%2F1452&utm_medium=PDF&utm_campaign=PDFCoverPages.

Ooi, C.-S. (2002) *Cultural Tourism and Tourism Cultures: The Business of Mediating Experiences in Copenhagen and Singapore*. Copenhagen: Copenhagen Business School Press.

Ooi, C.-S. (2005) A theory of tourism experiences. In T. O'Dell and P. Billing (eds) *Experiencescape: Culture, Tourism and Economy* (pp. 51–68). Copenhagen: Copenhagen Business School Press.

Ooi, C.-S. (2008) The Danish seduction of the China outbound tourism market: New issues for tourism research. In V. Worm (ed.) *China – Business Opportunities in a Globalizing Economy* (pp. 171–191). Copenhagen: Copenhagen Business School Press.

Ooi, C.-S. (2011) Subjugated in the creative industries: The fine arts in Singapore. *Culture Unbound* 3, 119–137. doi:10.3384/cu.2000.1525.113119

Ooi, C.-S. (2019) Asian tourists and cultural complexity: Implications for practice and the Asianisation of tourism scholarship. *Tourism Management Perspectives* 31 (July), 14–23. doi:10.1016/j.tmp.2019.03.007

Ooi, C.-S. and Shelley, B. (2019) The Children's University Tasmania: The transformative power of tourism. In T. Jamal (ed.) *Justice and Ethics in Tourism* (pp. 222–228). London: Routledge.

Ooi, C.-S. and Tarulevicz, N. (2019) From third world to first world: Tourism, food safety and the making of modern Singapore. In E. Park, S. Kim and I. Yeoman (eds) *Food Tourism in Asia* (pp. 73–88). Singapore: Springer. doi:10.1007/978-981-13-3624-9_6

Parsi, N. (1997) Don't worry, Sam, you're not alone. In P.L. Moore (ed.) *Building Bodies* (pp. 103–134). London: Rutgers University Press.

Pine, B.J. and Gilmore, J.H. (1999) *The Experience Economy Work is Theatre and Every Business a Stage*. Boston, MA: Harvard Business School Press.

Reilly, A. and Saethre, E.J. (2013) The hankie code revisited: From function to fashion. *Critical Studies in Men's Fashion* 1 (1), 69–78. doi:10.1386/csmf.1.1.69_1

Rink, B.M. (2008) Community as utopia: Reflections on De Waterkant. *Urban Forum* 19 (2), 205–220. doi:10.1007/s12132-008-9031-z

Ritzer, G. (1996) *The McDonaldization of Society* (revised edn). Thousand Oaks, CA: Pine Forge Press.

Ritzer, G. and Liska, A. (1997) 'McDisneyisation' and 'post-tourism': Complementary perspectives on contemporary tourism. In C. Rojek and J. Urry (eds) *Touring Cultures* (pp. 96–109). London: Routledge.

Sender, K. (2006) Queens for a day: 'Queer Eye for the Straight Guy' and the Neoliberal Project. *Critical Studies in Media Communication* 23 (2), 131–151. doi:10.1080/07393180600714505

Stets, J.E. and Burke, P.J. (2000) Identity theory and social identity theory. *Social Psychology Quarterly* 63 (3), 224. doi:10.2307/2695870

Tarulevicz, N. and Ooi, C.-S. (2019) Food safety and tourism in Singapore: Between microbial Russian roulette and Michelin stars. *Tourism Geographies* (online). doi:10.1080/14616688.2019.1654540

Taylor, J. (2020) Grief over death of Young Liberal Wilson Gavin after drag queen protest. *The Guardian*, 14 January. See https://www.theguardian.com/australia-news/2020/jan/14/grief-over-death-of-young-liberal-wilson-gavin-after-drag-queen-protest.

The Economist (2011) No voting please, we're Chinese. *The Economist*, 24 September. See https://www.economist.com/asia/2011/09/24/no-voting-please-were-chinese.

The Economist (2020) Gay people in Myanmar have adopted a secret language. *The Economist*, 30 May. See https://www.economist.com/asia/2020/05/30/gay-people-in-myanmar-have-adopted-a-secret-language.

Vorobjovas-Pinta, O. and Hardy, A. (2016) The evolution of gay travel research. *International Journal of Tourism Research* 18 (4), 409–416. doi:10.1002/jtr.2059

Waitt, G., Markwell, K. and Gorman-Murray, A. (2008) Challenging heteronormativity in tourism studies: Locating progress. *Progress in Human Geography* 32 (6), 781–800. doi:10.1177/0309132508089827

Weber, M. and Turner, B.S. (1991) *From Max Weber: Essays in Sociology* (H.H. Gerth and C. Wright Mills, trans. and eds). Abingdon: Routledge.

Williamson, O.E. (1998) Transaction cost economics: How it works; where it is headed. *De Economist* 146, 23–58. doi:10.1023/A:1003263908567

Wiltshier, P. and Cardow, A. (2001) The impact of the pink dollar: Wellington as a destination for the gay market. *Pacific Tourism Review* 5 (3), 121–130.

Wonders, N.A. and Michalowski, R. (2001) Bodies, borders, and sex tourism in a globalized world: A tale of two cities – Amsterdam and Havana. *Social Problems* 48 (4), 545–571. doi:10.1525/sp.2001.48.4.545

Wood, M.J. (2004) The gay male gaze. *Journal of Gay & Lesbian Social Services* 17 (2), 43–62. doi:10.1300/J041v17n02_03

Wotherspoon, G. (2016) *Gay Sydney: A History*. Sydney: NewSouth Publishing.

3 The Significance of Gay Tourism Spaces for Local Gay Men: Empirical Evidence from Mexico

Carlos Monterrubio

Introduction

Some researchers have suggested that many gay individuals currently foresee the end of homosexual oppression (Katz, 1992). The liberation movements of lesbians and gay men have politicised and radically altered traditional concepts of homosexuality, as well as the social situations, relationships, ideas and emotions of some homosexuals (Katz, 1992). Gay spaces and public gay events such as parades have also had significant impacts on social, political and cultural meanings, stereotypes and images of gay communities (Markwell, 2002; Marsh & Galbraith, 1995).

While more relaxed attitudes towards homosexuality may exist in some societies, the experience of gay communities in certain cultures – particularly those in which homophobia is still omnipresent – is that of repression. To date, in many countries, discriminatory legislation and religious and social disapproval continue to affect gay populations negatively, making them ready victims of discrimination, stigma, prejudice, violence and abuse (HRW, 2017).

Attitudes towards homosexuality are culturally specific (Weeks, 1989), but they have in general long been repressive. Homosexuality was once thought of as essentially a moral, legal and psychological problem (Katz, 1992), and many people continue to regard this as a deviant sexual preference (Herrera & Scott, 2005) or a mental illness (Herek, 2002). Even though these attitudes are based on irrational fears or mistaken beliefs held by prejudiced individuals (Adam, 1998), being homosexual is subject to discrimination and disapproval in different aspects of life in many societies. Gay expressions of identity such as gay men holding hands, kissing and showing other signs of affection commonly meet with social disapproval in public spaces. This can have serious implications for gay men's lives, as it can cause them to feel isolated and harassed and to become targets of violence (Poria & Taylor, 2001).

In socially, religiously and legally repressive societies, travelling away from home remains for many homosexual men one of the few opportunities to perform their own sexuality and be themselves (Monterrubio, 2019). In tourism destinations, gay spaces – whether physical or symbolic – are important for gay tourists, particularly regarding the construction of their sexual identities (Cox, 2002; Hughes, 1997, 2002b; Pritchard et al., 2002). Being homosexual at home is thus relegated to gay ghettos and privatised spaces in which homosexuals can be themselves (Pritchard et al., 1998).

Since tourism is about both guests and hosts, gay tourism – and gay spaces – may be as significant for local homosexuals as they are for tourists (Monterrubio, 2019). The meanings assigned to space are fluid and negotiated. Tourism spaces are often used by different social actors, including tourists and locals, and therefore perceived in multiple ways (Waitt & Markwell, 2006). Tourism spaces are shared and therefore promote interaction between tourists and locals, although mostly for commercial purposes. While they may be perceived as freedom and pleasure for tourists and work for locals (Krippendorf, 1987), tourism space can become meaningful not only in economic terms but also in many other recreational and identity ways for both groups.

Only limited evidence has thus far been reported confirming that social interactions between homosexual tourists and locals, many of which take place in gay spaces, can have a quite significant impact on local conceptions and practices of homosexuality (Mendoza, 2013; Murray, 2007; Waitt & Markwell, 2014). The significance of gay spaces for local homosexuals, moreover, has not been sufficiently examined since few studies have investigated the relationships between leisure activities, gay spaces and local gay men (Herrera & Scott, 2005). Because the links between gay sexual identity and space are not universally applicable (Visser, 2013), further research is necessary in order to reveal the various dimensions of the diverse relationships between gay spaces and local homosexuals in different contexts.

The aim of this chapter is to explore the significance of gay tourism spaces for local gay men. Exploring their importance is not only useful for the theoretical development of the relations between tourism spaces and socially excluded groups. It may also be useful in order to act on the value of such spaces for the local homosexual population; exploring the importance of tourism spaces for gay local communities can be valuable, for example, for managing such spaces in order to escape heteronormative constraints and avoid discrimination and social disapproval by gay men.

The results are based on data drawn from interviews with local homosexual men in a Mexican destination popular among gay tourists. This study thus focused exclusively on local gay men. Lesbians are considered more difficult to reach as they are less likely to socialise in gay spaces and are more oriented towards private social activities and entertainment (Hughes, 2007). Consequently, lesbians' use of – and the significance they attribute to – gay spaces is likely to differ from that of gay men. Associations between gay spaces and lesbians, particularly in diverse social contexts, remain largely unexamined. Although this chapter recognises the existence of multiple sociocultural constructions and practices of homosexuality, it assumes the existence of 'globalised' expressions of gay identity in which tourism may play an important role. According to Hernández (2013: 72), 'gay identity, as a social category of sexual identification, has undergone a normalization process in which its political connotations has been lost in order to incorporate itself into social life as a "another way" of exercising sexuality'.

Gay Spaces

Gay spaces are understood as physical manifestations of gay communities in discrete concentrations of pubs, clubs, cafés, shops, residences and public areas (Hughes, 1997). These spaces transform particular physical infrastructure and events into symbolic materialisations of safety, acceptance and tolerance (Waitt & Markwell, 2006). They are thus an important component of gay tourism destinations and events. According to Waitt and Markwell (2006):

> Gay tourism destinations are conceptualised as social leisure spaces that afford an opportunity to escape terrains of heteronormativity that are ongoing and constantly becoming through the intersections of sets of heteronormative social relations stretched out over particular spaces and across geographical scales. (Waitt & Markwell, 2006: 18)

Gay events such as the Gay Games are also constructed as meaningful places fostering a sense of pride and belonging through making new acquaintances and friendships. In these events, places, communities and bodies are connected, and heterosexism is interrupted (Waitt, 2003).

For many homosexual men, gay spaces offer the most significant opportunities for confirming their gay identity (Hughes, 2000). Identities are formed in the social domain, so they are socially produced. These need not be understood as being personal and individual. Instead, identities should be understood as produced among people within social interactions, and gay spaces offer an ideal arena for these interactions. All aspects of identity lie inside social relationships, so identities are lived out and negotiated collectively (Lawler, 2008). They therefore involve identification with others (Lawler, 2008), which leads to an affinity with certain social groups.

According to Herrera and Scott (2005), gay spaces allow gay men to express their sexuality freely. These spaces enable not only open displays of behaviour and affection but also, in some cases, access to a variety of gay services and facilities including shops, bars, housing and legal and medical services. They provide homosexuals with a strong sense of safety, and these are arenas in which behaviours do not have to be edited to conform to a heterosexual life. This thus permits gay identity to be validated by relationships with others (Hughes, 1997). Consequently, as Pritchard et al. (1998: 274) state, '[g]ay spaces, in essence, provide community and territory as well as a sense of order and power'. Gay spaces are not merely physical as they can exist in other forms and designs. The emergence of technology-based platforms, in particular, has changed the way gay men interact. Homosexual men are no longer required to be in a physical gay space such as a bar or resort to seek the companionship of other gay men, since gay spaces can be virtual and still important to homosexual individuals (Vorobjovas-Pinta & Hardy, 2016). Whether physical or virtual, these spaces are significant components in the formation, development and consolidation of gay male identities.

While most of the existing literature on this topic has confirmed the importance of gay spaces for gay tourists, these spaces can also become quite significant for local homosexual men in tourism destinations. In tourism destinations, gay spaces are used not only by tourists but also by some sectors of the local gay community (Visser, 2003). Thus, the use of these spaces may be important for local constructions of sexuality. The use and significance of gay spaces by local gay men can be understood as a type of identity travel. Hughes (2000) argues that:

> The fulfilment or achievement of gay identity often involves travel and the search for gay identity is conceptually a form of tourism (though not necessarily in the sense of a holiday). A man may live and work in what is a heterosexual society and visit 'the tourist destination' of gay society in his leisure time. (Hughes, 2000: 25)

Therefore, 'home' is an ambivalent site for many homosexuals, especially if it is not a space of refuge and needs to be escaped (Puar, 2002). Being gay may, therefore, entail seeking out the nearest gay space in which sexuality can be expressed openly. Gay spaces close to or at home become tourist destinations, even if only temporarily, as they enable gay men to express themselves. According to Cox (2002), the distinction between being 'home' and 'away' is largely about emotional experiences. Despite the potential significance that gay spaces can have for local gay men's sexuality and social and emotional life, this topic has not been sufficiently covered in research on tourism and homosexuality.

The significance of gay spaces for local homosexual men may largely lie in their social interaction dimension. In gay tourism spaces, contact provides an exchange of cultural and political information about issues of homosexuality that have an impact on these men's lives (Cantú, 2002). In gay spaces, local gay men may develop friendships with both tourists and other homosexual locals. Although some locals' participation in gay spaces can fulfil commercial or work purposes (e.g. service providers), interactions there may eventually become quite significant for these individuals.

Interactions with other gay males help homosexual men's social lives become more satisfying, and this eventually helps gay men to develop pride in their homosexuality. They acquire interpersonal and observational skills that allow them to make sense of the world around them (Herrera & Scott, 2005). The ability to establish and confirm a gay identity usually necessitates relationships with other gay men (Hughes, 2000). In some destinations, tourism is critical to creating a sense of group identity through social interactions for both tourists and residents, albeit in different ways (Howe, 2001).

The meanings of spaces are constantly being contested and renegotiated (Visser, 2013). In tourism destinations, the significance and meaning of gay spaces and events tend to be subject to homo-heterosexual power relations. Gay spaces that are touristified have the tendency to be de-gayed due to the increasing number of heterosexuals within these spaces and the efforts to meet these individuals' needs. This process takes place at the expense of these places' original significance as sites that provide security, recognition, support and entertainment for sexual minorities (Waitt & Markwell, 2006). Through tourism, gay spaces are thus contested, controlled and negotiated so that the touristification of gay spaces may ultimately de-gay these areas and erase their essentially gay characteristics (Pritchard *et al.*, 1998). In addition, the weakening of the political focus of – and the greater emphasis on carnivalesque elements now associated with – many of the world's pride events have ensured that they are becoming major tourism attractions (Want, 2002).

Study

Setting

Although attitudes towards homosexuality have relaxed in recent years in Mexico (BBC News, 2016), social environments in many parts of the country remain repressive of or even hostile and dangerous to gays (Reding, 2000). These environments are highly influenced by dominant cultural ideals of hypermasculinity (i.e. *machismo*). According to Reding (2000):

> *Machista* ideals of manly appearance and behavior contribute to extreme prejudices against effeminate men, and often to violence against them. The Roman Catholic teaching that homosexuality is a sin further contributes to intolerance, and is seen by many to provide moral sanction for mistreatment. To live an undisturbed gay or lesbian lifestyle in most Mexico, one has to hide it. (Reding, 2000: 1)

As a major gay tourism destination, Mexico has been included on the list of countries with the highest concentration of gay tourism establishments (Ivy, 2001), and it is now considered a highly attractive destination for gay tourism (IGLTA, 2020). There are several destinations with significant concentrations of gay spaces in the country; cities such as Mexico City, Guadalajara, Veracruz, Acapulco, Puerto Vallarta, Cancún and Tijuana are destinations with significant tourism supply for both national and international gay tourists (López López & Van Broeck, 2013). In international tourist guides, Mexico is now advertised as increasingly broad-minded about sexuality and as a destination with rarely open discrimination or violence against gay people (Lonely Planet, 2019).

By 2016, the country received almost 3 million LGBT tourists annually, staying on average four nights during low tourist season and spending around 60% more than mainstream tourists do (Sectur, 2017). Due to the LGBT tourism segment's relevance, the Mexican Tourism Ministry has decided to improve tourism supply, tourism promotion, advertising, commercialisation and tourism providers' training for serving the segment. All this makes several Mexican gay tourism destinations suitable cases in which gay tourism spaces' significance can be examined.

Some tourism destinations in Mexico offer spaces in which individuals can live – albeit temporarily – a gay lifestyle. Even in Mexico's international gay destinations such as Puerto Vallarta, alleged hate crimes against homosexual tourists still take place (MND, 2018). The creation of gay spaces in Mexico has thus been partly the result of demand by foreign gay tourists (Cantú, 2002). For some Mexican gay men, contact with gay tourists occurs more often not through leisure activities but rather through work, as local homosexual men providing services in gay spaces (Cantú, 2002). Therefore, as Cantú (2002) claims, Mexican gay sexualities can be transformed through tourism's transnational processes and links.

Acapulco is a beach destination in southeast Mexico, which is reportedly one of the most popular destinations in Mexico for gay men (Sánchez & López, 2000). Gay space components have been reported as an extremely important resource for gay beach tourism destinations (Melián-González et al., 2011). Most previous studies have highlighted varying degrees of tolerance, acceptance and understanding as key features in homosexuals' choice of destinations, accommodations and types of holiday (Hughes & Deutsch, 2010). Evidence has been found that men who visit resort destinations with an established gay reputation are motivated by opportunities to socialise with gay men and perhaps be sexually active with new partners (Clift & Forest, 1999).

Acapulco is popular with individuals from different socioeconomic backgrounds, and its legendary nightlife is particularly attractive to both domestic and international tourists. This destination offers well-publicised gay and gay-friendly hotels, discos, bars, beach sites and cruising areas for homosexual tourists. Commercial gay sex for tourists is another relevant component of tourism in Acapulco (Vargas & Alcalá, 2013). Despite its popularity as a gay tourism destination, attitudes towards homosexuality in Acapulco are not always positive, and several local gay individuals have been killed there in recent years (Robles, 2018).

Methods

The present study sought to explore the individual and collective significance of tourism spaces for local gay men. Acapulco was adopted as a case study. Researching the relationships between tourism and homosexuality has to deal with specific difficulties because sexuality is often a sensitive topic and individuals may thus be quite reluctant to participate. Therefore, this kind of research must sometimes rely on opportunistic, informal interviews (Hughes, 2000).

To meet its objective, the current study relied on qualitative interviewing. Ten interviews were conducted with local gay men in Acapulco. Theoretical saturation was not necessarily the criterion for determining the sample size; the number of interviews was unfortunately defined based on the time and (the researcher's own) financial resources available for the research. Although this sample size can be noted as a possible limitation of the work, the researcher believes that the topics derived from the interviews were sufficiently described, commented on and illustrated to meet the study's aim.

Although previous qualitative studies with gay tourists have relied on larger samples (see, for example, Casey, 2009; Hughes, 2002a), smaller samples of gay men have also proved useful in related tourism and leisure research. For example, in Herrera and Scott's (2005) examination of the use and significance of leisure travel among gay men living in a small city, the cited researchers set up nine interviews with gay men based on a snowball and purposive sample. This demonstrates that small samples can be quite productive when doing exploratory and grounded tourism research.

The present study's interviews were conducted in 2016. Due to the difficulty in contacting local gay men in the selected destination and their reluctance to participate, snowball sampling was used to recruit participants. In order to incorporate as many experiences as possible, different profiles in terms of age, education, occupation, sexual identity and leisure patterns were sought. The interview guide had three sections. The first was self-definition, which included questions regarding sexual identity and social life. The second focused on the destination to explore participants' awareness and use of local gay spaces and interactions with other gay men including tourists. The last section covered sociodemographics. All interviews were recorded and transcribed verbatim for analysis.

Findings

Participants

Weeks (1989) reports that, in any study of homosexuality, no auto-matic relationship exists between social categorisation and individuals' sense of self or identity. The meaning given to homosexual activities can vary enormously, which was corroborated by the present study. Most of the participants define themselves as gay, but their understanding and practice of sexuality is individually shaped. This concurs with Carrillo's (2003) assertion on the subjective meaning and construction of homo-sexual identities (see Table 3.1), as well as confirming Hughes's (2000) statement that sexuality is an extremely fluid concept and that being homosexual is ultimately a self-defined category. Thus, exploring Participants' self-identity is essential to understanding the significance of gay tourism spaces for locals.

An important issue to report is that, in many cases, local gay men perceive social constraints on being homosexual in the destination. This can partly explain why some only accepted their sexual orientation as adults. Although some are openly gay, they are gay only in private spaces, not in public. Noting how cultural attitudes towards homosexuality are comparatively more tolerant in other countries, David said:

> In their [tourists'] countries, gay couples can walk holding hands in public and nothing happens, but, if you do the same in Acapulco, they yell at you, they get scared [and] they say bad things to you. Here people are not prepared for these things yet.

In addition, while most participants do not deny their sexual orientation and some claim that they are proud to be gay, they are quite careful about revealing their homosexuality to others. Carrillo (2003) observes that many people in Mexico still rely on signs of effeminacy to decide who is a homosexual man and often measure male homosexuality against an essentialist notion of masculinity. Thus, discrimination and physical vio-lence triggered by effeminate homosexual behaviours are also reported by participants. Antonio narrated his experience in this way:

> When I was ten I was sexually abused, and, for a long time, I thought that my being gay was the cause of the abuse, so I pretended not to be gay in order to fit into society [and] to avoid being bullied for being gay, but I failed. I have several times been discriminated against for being both obese and effeminate.

The use of gay tourism spaces is common among the participants. Some attend gay bars, discos and a popular beach for leisure purposes, and most of the time they do so with their friends or partners. Others, however, work at gay bars and discos and, consequently, they are more frequently in contact with gay tourists – both domestic and foreign. This contact is sometimes quite meaningful. As discussed further below,

Table 3.1 Description of participants

Fernando is a 32-year-old cement industry worker. He was born in the destination, and he only finished high school. He defines himself as gay, and he is open about his sexuality although he first accepted his sexual orientation at the age of 30. He is divorced with a four-year-old child, and he is not in a relationship currently. He used to work at a gay bar where he came into contact with gay tourists and locals and met his first male partner.

Alejandro is a 44-year-old hair stylist. He is single, and he has lived in the destination for 30 years. He stopped studying after high school. He has always liked feminine things and used to wear his mom's high heels when he was a child. He was born and raised in a *machista* society although he now feels proud to be gay. When he was younger, he used to go to gay bars and discos where he met tourists and made friends from abroad. He now rarely goes out with his gay friends.

Francisco is a 22-year-old university student born in the destination. He also works as a waiter in a hotel restaurant. He recalls always being aware of his sexual orientation, but he only openly accepted it at the age of 21. He now self-defines as a *macho* gay who does not like effeminate men. He met his current partner through Facebook. He has no children, but he would like to have some in the future. Since meeting his partner, he has visited gay bars and discos where he encounters other gay men.

Rodrigo is 38 and works for the government. He experienced internal conflict when he realised his sexual orientation while in secondary school. He is now open about his sexuality. He lived away from Acapulco for 15 years in large urban cities in Mexico. He worked at a gay hotel and restaurant where he frequently came into contact with gay tourists. Going to gay bars and discos is not important to him any more. He is single, with no children, and he is not currently in a relationship.

Antonio is 27 years old and is studying nursing at university. He works as a receptionist at a gay hotel where he is in contact with gay tourists every day. He had girlfriends but accepted his homosexuality at the age of 15 when he moved to the United States. He lived there for six years and met his first boyfriend there. He was sexually abused as a child, and he has experienced much discrimination for being both gay and obese. He now feels happy and proud of being gay.

David is 39 years old and has his own corporate image design company. He has a university degree, and he has always lived in Acapulco. He feels part of the gay community though he does not identify with the carnivalesque character of what are meant to be gay sociopolitical events. He has had nine relationships with men and one with a woman. He participates in gay pride events and sometimes goes to gay bars and discos with his friends.

Jorge is 28 years old and is studying physical education at university, as well as working for a printing press company. He has lived in Acapulco all his life. He experienced doubt about his sexuality as an adolescent as he felt attracted to both men and women, finally accepting his homosexuality at the age of 18. He likes being masculine and his friends are mostly heterosexual, so he does not identify with the gay community. He has been in a formal relationship with a man for two years. He rarely goes to gay places as he socialises mostly through Facebook.

Pablo is 37 years old and has been working at a gay hotel for seven years, where he is frequently in contact with other gay men. He completed high school. He first visited Acapulco as a tourist and then moved there, where he has been living for eight years. He neither feels part of the gay community nor identifies with gay pride, events and groups. Before accepting his homosexuality, he felt afraid of being rejected and discriminated against, but his first relationship with a man helped him overcome this fear.

Jesús is a 40-year-old department store clerk. He defines himself as gay, but most of his friends are heterosexual. He has lived in Acapulco for 40 years and has worked at restaurants and stores, where he has had contact with gay tourists and locals.

Leonardo is 38 years old. He sees himself as bisexual, but he does not openly publicise his bisexuality. He has a bachelor's degree and no children, and he is not currently in a relationship. He defines himself as antisocial, and he has not had much contact with other local gay men or gay tourists.

Note: Pseudonyms have been used to protect the participants' privacy.

local–tourist interactions play an important role in the life of some local gay men. The following section describes the significance that the use of gay tourism spaces has for some locals.

Significance of Gay Tourism Spaces for Local Gay Men

Escaping

As described previously, although Acapulco is a popular gay tourism destination, local gay men, one way or another, experience social disapproval of their sexuality. They cannot be gay in public spaces dominated by heterosexuality, so they can be who they really are only in private spaces, including gay spaces. Compared with tourists, locals are more vulnerable to being stigmatised because, as Leonardo pointed out, 'tourists are anonymous in Acapulco, [but] local gay men are not'. Francisco added, 'gay bars and discos are necessary in Acapulco if you want to be who you truly are because in other public places such as parks you just cannot be yourself'.

Therefore, gay tourism spaces are significant for local gay men as these spaces allow these individuals to escape the heteronormative world in which many of them live every day. Some local homosexual men need to escape home 'within home'. For some, as Hughes (2006) maintains, being gay may entail seeking out the nearest gay space – often a local bar – in which to be themselves. Hughes (2002b: 178) reports that 'discrimination against gays has encouraged them to find their identity in the leisure sphere'.

In an interview for the present study, Jorge confirmed this when he said, 'gay bars and the gay beach are very important for some gay men. They can be themselves in those spaces, [where] they feel free [and] they can hug or kiss without being criticised or judged'. This confirms Andriotis' (2010) assertion that, in other less commercial gay spaces such as nude beaches, gay men can briefly come out of the closet, meeting like-minded people and expressing their sexuality openly.

Therefore, gay tourist spaces allow not only tourists but also gay locals to escape the repressions of the heteronormative world. For both groups these spaces mean a possibility of being who they really are, an opportunity to get away from the constraints of their everyday world. Gay spaces allow them to enter a world in which being gay is the norm rather than the exception. Thus, for both tourists and locals, gay tourist spaces have practically the same function in terms of an escape from heteronormativity.

Building identities

Identities are socially produced, so they are constructed and negotiated through social interactions. Local–tourist connections take place in gay spaces. Therefore, gay tourism spaces are valuable in terms of the development of local gay identities, and these spaces' significance lies in both individual and collective dimensions. By interacting with other gay men mainly in bars and discos, some individuals have become aware of and accepted their sexual orientation. Due to his interactions with gay tourist customers, Fernando broke off his relationship with a woman when he accepted his sexual orientation. He asserted:

> When I was working at a gay bar, I became aware of the gay lifestyle and accepted my attraction to other men. I realised that I felt comfortable among them. I did not feel judged. I felt accepted. I felt part of the gay community, and that helped me to accept my [sexual] orientation. ... When I was a waiter, I met several men from Mexico and from abroad. I made friends who made me feel I belonged with them. I felt I identified with them. Working at the bar made me aware that I was not the only one.

Jesús added:

> Sometimes I go to the beach and meet gay tourists. Meeting them has influenced my feelings about being part of the gay community. I identify with them. At the beach or in gay bars, I feel more comfortable being who I am, as I do not need to hide.

For gay locals, gay spaces play an important role in their interaction not only with other tourists but also with other locals. Through these interactions, locals can self-define; they manage to distinguish and choose between a heteronormative world and a world to which they can belong more easily. These spaces provide gay men with the opportunity to reflect on their own being and thereby build their own sexual identity.

Socialising

Gay bars, discos and the beach are places where gay men socialise with other homosexual men. In these places, local gay men interact both with other locals and with tourists. For gay men who go to these locations with their friends, gay spaces are significant because they reinforce their gay friendships. With these friends, they can all be who they really are. David said, 'when I was younger, I used to go to bars and discos with my friends. We sang the gay songs we all liked, and, in discos, I could dance with another man, and everything was okay'.

Gay spaces can also be used to expand local gay men's social networks. By frequenting bars, discos and the beach, locals establish new relationships with other people. At gay discos, Alejandro, for example, met many homosexual friends from other urban parts of Mexico, such as Mexico City, Guadalajara and Monterrey, as well as gay men from the United States. David further met two of his best friends through gay social networks on the web. Later, they came to Acapulco to visit him. He took them to the beach where they socialised with David's other local friends.

For locals, unlike tourists, gay spaces have two main roles. On the one hand, they allow locals to expand their social networks by meeting new people, whether tourists or other locals. On the other hand, they offer an opportunity to socialise with local friends. Certainly there are other spaces to socialise with friends, but gay tourist spaces are particularly relevant for locals because they allow socialisation in an environment where they feel free and identified with.

Cruising

The significance of gay tourism spaces is also associated with sexual activity. For some, gay spaces are ideal for meeting new men, although not necessarily for socialising but rather for having casual sexual encounters with other locals and with tourists. This pattern was not reported by all participants, but even those who did not use gay spaces for cruising reported this use of these spaces. For instance, Rodrigo stated:

> At discos, I have made new friends, danced [and] had fun, and, at the beach, I have met gay men with whom I have exchanged telephone numbers, and I have also found someone to have sex with – not a relationship, just casual sex.

In a similar vein, David explained, 'I go to gay discos perhaps twice a month. I go with my gay friends, drink, dance [and] have fun, and, if possible, I meet someone to have sex with'. The cruising-related image of gay tourism places is well established for some participants. Jorge reported, 'gay discos are not for having fun anymore. They are just for cruising. That is why I do not like those places'.

Socialisation at gay spaces may lead to meeting new potential partners, who may form short- or long-term relationships with local gays. For some, these relationships become quite memorable experiences on an affective level. Alejandro described one of his most unforgettable emotional experiences. In a gay 'antro' ('hole'), he met a guy called Alberto, who first came to Acapulco as a tourist. They became friends right away, and Alberto eventually moved to Acapulco to live with Alejandro. After one year of living together, Alberto suddenly disappeared from Acapulco after stealing Alejandro's valuable belongings and savings.

A different story was narrated by Fernando:

> As a waiter, I met a guy two years ago. He was a tourist from Mexico City. I served his table, and he asked me for my telephone number. We could not meet that night, but, when he left Acapulco, we kept in touch. A few months later, he returned to visit me, and we did not meet at the bar. We met at his hotel. Ever since then, he has come to visit me twice a year, or sometimes we meet in other places. So far, we have met seven times outside of Acapulco. He travels quite a lot and invites me to travel with him. When we travel together, we go to ... gay discos where we can

dance, hold hands or kiss. We do not regard each other as a partner, but we meet and call each other quite often. It is a type of relationship. ... He means a lot to me.

Affective relationships between local gay men and male tourists are naturally conditioned by time and distance. They may, however, still be significant, especially when these relationships need to be kept hidden from the eyes of other locals in everyday life. For cases such as the one described by Fernando, gay spaces are seen as meaningful for keeping relationships alive, even if only temporarily and at a distance.

For other locals, tourist spaces are a commercial opportunity. Several gay tourist destinations in Mexico have become an opportunity for sex workers. Although male sex workers do not always hold a gay sexual identity in Mexico (López López & Van Broeck, 2013), they also shape tourist spaces and the type of interactions within tourism spaces. For locals of this type, the tourist areas are ideal for finding customers; they usually establish brief instrumental encounters rather than affective relationships.

Learning

Through interactions with other gay men in gay spaces, local homosexual men learn about gay lifestyles, which can be different from the way the local gays live. This is particularly the case for those who are just starting to develop a gay lifestyle or who have recently accepted their orientation. Fernando, for example, claimed that working at a gay bar allowed him to learn about and discover new things. He discovered the type of music many gay men listen to and the ways other homosexual men dress or behave and observed that some of these patterns vary among gays.

In addition, Antonio learned that, in other countries – especially richer countries – attitudes towards homosexuals are more tolerant than those in Mexico. Pablo, in turn, reported that, through interacting with gay tourists at a gay hotel, he became aware of how, even within the homosexual community, gay men are all different and their cultural backgrounds influence their choices of 'how to be gay'. He thus discovered that gay men are quite diverse in terms of behaviours and consumption patterns.

For the participants, gay spaces allow them to become aware that they are not alone. Francisco said, 'when I started visiting gay discos, I became aware that I was not the only one, and I learnt that not all gays are effeminate [and] that there are other macho gay men like me'. Sharing gay spaces can, therefore, play an important role in building locals' self-esteem and improving their lives. Some participants declared that, before accepting their sexual orientation, they felt afraid, confused, unconfident and frustrated, in addition to experiencing rejection and discrimination. By meeting other gay men – including his partner – Pablo, for instance, gained self-confidence, and he now feels happy and special.

Similarly, some local gay men have felt inspired by gay tourists to improve their life conditions. Antonio's case clearly illustrates this as he asserted:

> I have worked for years at a gay hotel, and I am frequently in contact with gay tourists. I like to listen to them talking about their lives. Some have given me advice on how to become a better person. By talking to them, I have realised what I want and what I do not want for my own life. I have been inspired by tourists' personal and professional achievements. I have met tourists who are professionals, so I said I wanted to be like them [and] I decided to continue my university studies. I am studying nursing now, and, by talking to them [gay tourists], I have also learnt how to take care of my body.

Discussion and Conclusions

In tourism contexts, research on gay spaces has largely centred around tourists. Many studies of the significance of these spaces have analysed their significance for tourists, particularly in relation to their identity development (Cox, 2002; Hughes, 1997; Monterrubio, 2009; Pritchard *et al.*, 2002). This previous research has found that, due to the social constraints experienced by gay men and lesbians in a heteronormative society, many of them need to travel away from home in search of places in which to be gay. Gay spaces in tourism destinations are, for many travellers, one of the few opportunities to perform their true sexuality.

Gay spaces in tourism destinations, however, are far from being significant only to gay travellers. In local people's lives these spaces acquire alternative meanings. While for some individuals, gay spaces offer chances to generate financial gains (e.g. sex workers: Mendoza, 2013; Waitt & Markwell, 2014), for others these are spaces for leisure activities (Herrera & Scott, 2005; Visser, 2003). In terms of events, gay spaces offer a chance for sociopolitical change (Marsh & Galbraith, 1995).

In many cases, gay spaces unite people with different identities and various social, economic, ideological and sexual backgrounds. Prior studies have confirmed that, in non-Western societies, gay spaces are commodified but also culturally and historically significant sites of mobilisation, community building and identity formation (Lewis, 2013). The emergence of alternative subjectivities, identities and practices contributes to the (re)constituting of meanings associated with gay spaces (Nash, 2013). Through interactions with other homosexual local men and tourists, local gay men's self-concepts, behaviours, attitudes and perceptions of their own sexuality are likely to be (re)constructed. Because these constructions can be significant for the everyday lives of many local gay men – both individually and collectively – the significance of gay tourism spaces for local homosexual men needs to be incorporated into further social analyses of tourism. As a general conclusion, gay tourism spaces are important agents of social change. Mainly through interactions with tourists, locals can build new identities and consequently adopt new ways of life and new behaviours. New lifestyles can in turn lead to social and cultural changes in other segments of the population. Greater recognition and acceptance of the homosexual population, for example, can be changes influenced by the existence of gay tourism spaces.

The present study sought to explore the use and meaning of gay tourism spaces for local gay men. On the one hand, this research aimed to incorporate local gay men into the understanding of tourism and leisure spaces as social constructs that are affected by – and have an impact on – gay men as social actors. On the other hand, this study sought to recognise that gay spaces acquire different constructions and meanings depending on the social actors in question. The current research was thus able to reveal that gay spaces play specific roles in local gay men's lives, of which some roles are concurrent with those identified for gay men as travellers while some other roles are not.

Gay tourism spaces provide local gay men with the chance to be gay at home. Even in destinations popular among gay tourists, homosexuality is still disapproved of, so gay men are forced to escape from home. Gay tourism spaces allow them to escape home within home. Thus, these spaces have a special significance for the identity development of certain gay groups. This appears to be especially the case for those who have recently accepted and started to perform their sexuality. Gay tourism spaces also allow these individuals to become more aware of gay lifestyles, particularly those developed in more tolerant countries. For other local homosexual men, these spaces are instead used for socialising and having sexual encounters with other gay men.

Gay tourism spaces are, therefore, socially important for both gay tourists and hosts. However, for local homosexuals, these spaces may represent 'a destination within home' in which they can escape everyday heteronormative constraints. Because not all gay men have the financial resources to travel away from home (Monterrubio & Lopez, 2014), local gay spaces become meaningful, albeit temporarily, as places to (re)construct and perform gay sexualities.

Similar to other research, the present research was subject to limitations. Due to the reduced number of men interviewed, this study's findings should be regarded only as illustrative rather than indicative. Due to the qualitative sampling technique applied, many voices remained unheard, although this limitation offers opportunities for future research.

Analyses are needed of the multiple and varied significance of gay tourism spaces for locals in other more tolerant and/or repressive sociocultural contexts in order to broaden the current understanding of these spaces' roles. Incorporating larger samples including gay men who for any reason have not 'come out' would enrich this understanding further. This, however, will not be an easy task as, according to Hughes and Deutch

(2010), gay men who are less willing to admit openly to their sexual orientation present problems to researchers.

Clearly, quantitative approaches could be a useful way to gain more representative samples and generalised findings. Nonetheless, the relevant literature highly encourages qualitative studies when researchers need to reveal the meaning of gay spaces to those who reside in tourism destinations. Further research also needs to be done on the gender-based significance of gay spaces. Because differences exist in the provision of leisure and holiday spaces for lesbians and gay men (Hughes, 2007), local lesbians' experiences in gay spaces also require exploration.

Pritchard *et al.* (1998) argue that the heterosexual touristification of gay spaces could represent disempowerment, disenfranchisement and a loss of control over crucial gay places. How heterosexually touristified gay spaces are perceived and signified by local homosexual men remains another avenue of research that needs to be explored in order to understand the establishment and negotiation of heterosexual versus homosexual domination in tourism spaces. Finally, the number and use of virtual gay spaces have increased, so the symbolic value and need for physical gay spaces seem to be decreasing (Vorobjovas-Pinta & Hardy, 2016). The significance of virtual gay spaces for local gay men thus could be another interesting future line of research.

References

Adam, B.D. (1998) Theorizing homophobia. *Sexualities* 1 (4), 387–404.

Andriotis, K. (2010) Heterotopic erotic oases: The public nude beach experience. *Annals of Tourism Research* 37 (4), 1076–1096.

BBC News (2016) Mexico leader Pena Nieto proposes legalising same-sex marriage. *BBC News*, 17 May.

Cantú, L. (2002) De ambiente: Queer tourism and the shifting boundaries of Mexican male sexualities. *GLQ* 8 (1–2), 139–166.

Carrillo, H. (2003) Neither machos nor maricones: Masculinity and emerging male homosexual identities in Mexico. In M.C. Gutmann (ed.) *Changing Men and Masculinities in Latin America* (pp. 351–370). Durham, NC: Duke University Press.

Casey, M.E. (2009) Tourist gay(ze) or transnational sex: Australian gay men's holiday desires. *Leisure Studies* 28 (2), 157–172.

Clift, S. and Forrest, S. (1999) Gay men and tourism: Destinations and holiday motivations. *Tourism Management* 20 (5), 615–625. doi:10.1016/S0261-5177 (99)00032-1

Cox, M. (2002) The long-haul out of the closet: The journey from smalltown to boystown. In S. Clift, M. Luongo and C. Callister (eds) *Gay Tourism: Culture, Identity and Sex* (pp. 151–173). London: Continuum.

Herek, G.M. (2002) Gender gaps in public opinion about lesbians and gay men. *Public Opinion Quarterly* 66 (1), 40–66.

Hernández, P.M. (2013) Sexo comercial entre hombres: Una aproximación antropológica en espacios turísticos mexicanos. In A. López López and A.M. Van Broeck (eds) *Turismo y sexo en México: Cuerpos masculinos en venta y experiencias homoeróticas. Una perspectiva multidisciplinaria* (pp. 59–105). México: UNAM.

Herrera, S.L. and Scott, D. (2005) 'We gotta get out of this place!': Leisure travel among gay men living in a small city. *Tourism Review International* 8, 249–262.

Howe, A. (2001) Queer pilgrimage: The San Francisco homeland and identity tourism. *Cultural Anthropology* 16 (1), 35–61.

HRW (2017) 'I have to leave to be me': Discriminatory laws against LGBT peoples in the Eastern Caribbean. *Human Rights Watch*, 21 March. See https://www.hrw.org/report/2018/03/21/i-have-leave-be-me/discriminatory-laws-against-lgbt-people-eastern-caribbean.

Hughes, H. (1997) Holidays and homosexual identity. *Tourism Management* 18 (1), 3–7.

Hughes, H.L. (2000) Gay men's holidays: Profit, sex, and identity. *Téoros. Revue de Recherche en Tourisme* 19 (2), 22–27.

Hughes, H. (2002a) Gay men's holiday destination choice: A case of risk and avoidance. *International Journal of Travel Research* 4 (4), 299–312.

Hughes, H. (2002b) Gay men's holidays: Identity and inhibitors. In S. Clift, M. Luongo and C. Callister (eds) *Gay Tourism: Culture, Identity and Sex* (pp. 174–190). London: Continuum.

Hughes, H. (2006) *Pink Tourism: Holidays of Gay Men and Lesbians*. Wallingford: CABI.

Hughes, H.L. (2007) Lesbians as tourists: Poor relations of a poor relation. *Tourism and Hospitality Research* 7 (1), 17–26.

Hughes, H.L. and Deutsch, R. (2010) Holidays of older gay men: Age or sexual orientation as decisive factors? *Tourism Management* 31 (4), 454–436.

IGLTA (2020) *Mexico*. See https://www.iglta.org/Country/Mexico (accessed 9 February 2021).

Ivy, R.L. (2001) Geographical variation in alternative tourism and recreation establishments. *Tourism Geographies* 3 (3), 338–355.

Katz, J. (1992) *Gay American History: Lesbians and Gay Men in the USA*. New York: Meridian.

Krippendorf, J. (1987) *The Holiday Makers: Understanding the Impact of Leisure and Travelling*. Oxford: Butterworth-Heinemann.

Lawler, S. (2008) *Identity: Sociological Perspectives*. Cambridge: Polity Press.

Lewis, N.M. (2013) Ottawa's le/the village: Creating a gaybourhood amidst the 'death of the village'. *Geoforum* 49, 233–242.

Lonely Planet (2019) Mexico in detail: Gay & lesbian travellers. See https://www.lonelyplanet.com/mexico/gay-and-lesbian-travellers (accessed 14 January 2019).

López López, A. and Van Broeck, A.M. (eds) (2013) *Turismo y sexo en México: Cuerpos masculinos en venta y experiencias homoeróticas. Una perspectiva multidisciplinaria*. México: UNAM.

Markwell, K. (2002) Mardi Gras tourism and the construction of Sydney as an international gay and lesbian city. *GLQ* 8 (1–2), 81–99.

Marsh, I. and Galbraith, L. (1995) The political impact of the Sydney gay and lesbian Mardi Gras. *Australian Journal of Political Science* 30, 300–320.

Melián-González, A., Moreno-Gil, S. and Araña, J.E. (2011) Gay tourism in a sun and beach destination. *Tourism Management* 32 (5), 1027–1037.

Mendoza, C. (2013) Beyond sex tourism: Gay tourists and male sex workers in Puerto Vallarta. *International Journal of Tourism Research* 15 (2), 122–137.

MND (2018) Gay couple attacked in Puerto Vallarta. *Mexico News Daily*, 27 March.

Monterrubio, J.C. (2009) Identity and sex: Concurrent aspects of gay tourism. *Tourismos: An International Multidisciplinary Journal of Tourism* 4 (2), 155–167.

Monterrubio, C. (2019) Tourism and male homosexual identities: Directions for sociocultural research. *Tourism Review* 74 (5), 1058–1069. doi:10.1108/TR-08-2017-0125

Monterrubio, J.C. and López, A. (2014) Recognising homoeroticism in male gay tourism: A Mexican perspective. In T. Thurnell-Read and M. Casey (eds) *Men, Masculinities, Travel and Tourism* (pp. 171–185). London: Palgrave MacMillan.

Murray, D.A.B. (2007) The civilized homosexual: Travel talk and the project of gay identity. *Sexualities* 10 (1), 49–60.

Nash, C.J. (2013) The age of the 'post-mo'? Toronto's gay village and a new generation. *Geoforum* 49, 243–252.

Poria, Y. and Taylor, A. (2001) 'I am not afraid to be gay when I'm on the net': Minimising social risk for lesbian and gay consumers when using the internet. *Journal of Travel & Tourism Marketing* 11 (2–3), 127–142.

Pritchard, A., Morgan, N.J., Sedgely, D. and Jenkins, A. (1998) Reaching out to the gay tourist: Opportunities and threats in an emerging market segment. *Tourism Management* 19 (3), 273–282.

Pritchard, A., Morgan, N. and Sedgley, D. (2002) In search of lesbian space? The experience of Manchester's gay village. *Leisure Studies* 21 (2), 105–123.

Puar, J. (2002) A transnational feminist critique of queer tourism. *Antipode* 34 (5), 935–946.

Reding, A. (2000) Mexico: Update on treatment of homosexuals. Question and Answer series. New York: INS Resource Information Center.

Robles, S. (2018) Pide comunidad gay que no se dé carpetazo al caso del joven degollado. *Quadratín Guerrero*, 20 February.

Sánchez, Á. and López, Á. (2000) Visión geográfica de los lugares gays de la Ciudad de México. *Cuicuilco* 7 (18), 271–286.

Sectur (2017) Fortalece Sectur turismo LGTB para hacer de México un destino vanguardia. See https://www.gob.mx/sectur/prensa/fortalece-sectur-turismo-lgtb-para-hacer-de-mexico-un-destino-vanguardia (accessed 14 January 2019).

Vargas, S. and Alcalá, B. (2013) Aspectos territoriales de la prostitución masculina vinculada al turismo sexual en Acapulco. In A. López and A. Van Broeck (eds) *Turismo y sexo en México: Cuerpos masculinos en venta y experiencias homoeróticas. Una perspectiva multidisciplinaria* (pp. 227–260). México: UNAM.

Visser, G. (2003) Gay men, tourism and urban space: Reflections on Africa's 'gay capital'. *Tourism Geographies* 5 (2), 168–189.

Visser, G. (2013) Challenging the gay ghetto in South Africa: Time to move on? *Geoforum* 49, 268–274.

Vorobjovas-Pinta, O. and Hardy, A. (2016) The evolution of gay travel research. *International Journal of Tourism Research* 18 (4), 409–416.

Waitt, G. (2003) Gay games: Performing 'community' out from the closet of the locker room. *Social & Cultural Geography* 4 (2), 167–183.

Waitt, G. and Markwell, K. (2006) *Gay Tourism: Culture and Context.* New York: THHP.

Waitt, G. and Markwell, K. (2014) 'I don't want to think I am a prostitute': Embodied geographies of men, masculinities and clubbing in Seminyak, Bali, Indonesia. In T. Thurnell-Read and M. Casey (eds) *Men, Masculinities, Travel and Tourism* (pp. 104–119). Basingstoke: Palgrave Macmillan.

Want, P. (2002) Trouble in paradise: Homophobia and resistance to gay tourism. In S. Clift, M. Luongo and C. Callister (eds) *Gay Tourism: Culture, Identity and Sex* (pp. 191–213). London: Continuum.

Weeks, J. (1989) *Sex, Politics and Society.* London: Longman.

4 Managing Sexuality for Gay and Lesbian Parents in Heterosexual Family Holiday Spaces: Setting an Agenda for Research

Wenjie Cai and Carol Southall

Introduction

With societal changes and law reform, the LGBT group has become increasingly accepted. As of May 2017, 47 countries recognise same-sex marriage and/or partnership (ILGA, 2017). The great market potential of LGBT tourism has been identified as the profitable 'pink dollar' and post-disaster revivers (Pritchard *et al.*, 1998; Visser, 2009). There is a growing research interest in the demographic characteristics and motivational factors of the LGBT travel market (Hughes & Southall, 2012; Vorobjovas-Pinta & Hardy, 2016). In the market research, the target profile of gay and lesbian travellers has predominantly concentrated on well-educated, single gay men with high disposable income, whose main travel motivation is to look for sexual encounters and escape from their everyday heterosexual environment (Clift & Forrest, 1999; Gluckman & Reed, 1997; Hughes, 2003). This homogeneity and overrepresentation has been criticised for neglecting the lesbian, transgender and family sectors of the LGBT tourist profile (Badgett, 1997; Lucena *et al.*, 2015). Indeed, Lucena *et al.* (2015) and Hughes and Southall (2012) emphasise the importance of researching the gay and lesbian family, given their distinctive motivations and characteristics. A recent report by the European Travel Commission (ETC, 2018) states that the introduction of gay and lesbian family tourism has broadened the idea of a 'gay vacation' and contributes to a more inclusive concept of LGBT travel.

Holiday spaces are socially constructed spaces in which social interaction, group dynamics and self-identities take place and are negotiated. Heteronormative assumptions (Dinnie & Browne, 2011; Lucena *et al.*,

2015) continue to regulate sexuality in public spaces, often generating tension for gay men and lesbians. Steck and Perry (2017) refer to the marginalising of non-gender-conforming individuals in a heteronormative culture, and the provision of safe spaces to create an inclusive environment. There are 72 countries where the LGBT community is criminalised, limiting the options for holiday choices (ILGA, 2017). For homosexual families with children, there is the added pressure of the potential for heightened visibility and inadvertent disclosure of sexuality on holiday.

This conceptual chapter aims to contribute to the literature on inclusive family holiday spaces and proposes a research agenda. Responding to Lucena *et al.*'s (2015) call for research on how the presence of children affects the ways in which parents navigate their sexuality in public holiday spaces, this chapter focuses on the complexities of performing homosexual family lives, as well as the additional complexities of negotiating space with the fluidity and blurred boundaries between public and private, virtual and physical, and heterosexual and homosexual. Practically, this study will also offer the oft-criticised tourism and hospitality industry implications to better cater to same-sex parented families by developing or refining products and services. In this chapter, the term 'gay' has been used interchangeably to describe gay and lesbian people. The chapter will firstly provide an up-to-date literature review of gay and lesbian tourism and family tourism by addressing key trends and research gaps. The chapter then looks into the multidimensional concept of space, including gay and heterosexual spaces, as well as sexual negotiations in these spaces. The chapter ends by proposing a future research agenda and implications for service providers.

Gay and Lesbian Tourism

Although gay tourism can be traced back to the 18th century (Clift & Wilkins, 1995), gay and lesbian tourism only started to develop and to be recognised following a series of social movements, law reforms and increased social acceptance of the LGBT community after the Stonewall riots in 1969 (Coon, 2012). Commercial market research and academic studies in gay and lesbian tourism have looked into market segments, motivations, destination choice and gay space (Clift & Forrest, 1999; Hughes & Southall, 2012; Southall & Fallon, 2011; Vorobjovas-Pinta & Hardy, 2016). Research shows that by leaving their daily heteronormative environment, gay travellers use tourism as an opportunity to recognise, shape and reinforce their identities. As well as traveller motivations similar to those of heterosexuals, gay travellers, in particular, go on holiday for reasons of escape, finding 'self' and seeking a sense of belonging, which are highly connected to the coming out process (Poria & Taylor, 2002).

In fact, holidays for gay travellers centralise the sense of 'self'. They are more about self-discovery, community-seeking and identity-reinforcement than gazing others. By travelling to cities such as Amsterdam, London and

San Francisco, many gay men and lesbians escape from their everyday heteronormative environment (Waitt & Markwell, 2014), and some have their first sexual experience when on holiday (Hughes, 2006). In addition, engaging in sexual activities has been emphasised as a key distinctive push factor for many gay men (Ryan & Hall, 2005). On the other hand, lesbian tourists may not associate themselves as much with the sexual elements, and emphasise the need for acceptance and escape when choosing destinations (Monterrubio & Barrios, 2016; Pritchard et al., 2000). In general, recognised gay destinations provide a safe and comfortable space where gay travellers can express their identities without anxieties and fears.

Risk avoidance is the primary concern for gay men and lesbians when choosing destinations (Hughes, 2002). Many gay tourists tend to avoid destinations where homosexuality is illegal or not socially accepted. In addition, studies found that gay and lesbian tourists are rather self-conscious in terms of the perceptions of other tourists, especially straight-parented families (Clift & Forrest, 1999; Hughes, 2002). Based on this argument, Lucena et al. (2015) raise the question: If gay travellers rule out family-friendly destinations, what destinations will they choose when they are going on holiday as a family unit?

Vandecasteele and Geuens (2009) and Vorobjovas-Pinta and Hardy (2016) criticise the fact that the current gay travel market literature is outdated in terms of stereotyping the market profile and fails to capture the significant world and societal changes. It is worth noting that, although specific interests and primary motivations have been discussed, most gay travellers have similar motivations to other tourists (Hughes, 1997; Monterrubio, 2019). Vorobjovas-Pinta and Hardy (2016) further argue that the increased visibility and acceptance of the LGBT sector around the world will potentially lead to new motivations, experiences and destination choices, especially for those regions where LGBT lifestyles are legalised and socially accepted. Based on this, we argue that from a new mobilities paradigm, research should go beyond a Eurocentric perspective (Cohen & Cohen, 2015) and examine how gay tourists from Asia, Africa and Muslim countries choose destinations (Wong & Tolkach, 2017), as well as how their experiences are shaped. Furthermore, the stereotypical profile of gay tourists limits the scope of focus on single gay travellers, and overlooks emerging market segments such as senior gay travellers (Hughes & Deutsch, 2010) and gay families (Hughes & Southall, 2012; Lucena et al., 2015), as well as bisexual, transgender and intersex families.

Gay and Lesbian Family Tourism

According to the International Lesbian, Gay, Bisexual, Trans and Intersex Association (ILGA, 2017), there are 26 states that recognise joint adoption and 27 states accepting second-parent adoption (as in

May 2017). With this increased legal protection and social recognition, an increasing number of gay parents are travelling as a family unit to enjoy the benefits of family holidays. According to Hughes and Southall (2012), most gay and lesbian families have similar lifestyles to heterosexual families. Still, they tend to be more egalitarian and exhibit less power imbalance than heterosexual families (Carrington, 1999). Most studies of this issue to date focus on the comparison between heterosexual and homosexual families. Lucena *et al.* (2015) suggest that more research should be conducted to look at the differences between gay and lesbian parents in terms of parenthood and the relationship with children, given the fact that some gay fathers might have less time with their children due to full-time work commitments (Biblarz & Stacey, 2010), while Baetens and Brewaeys (2001) suggest that due to social pressures, lesbians tend to be more likely to have children. Gay and lesbian families' holiday motivations, destination choices and experiences are thus largely impacted by these similarities and differences between homosexual and heterosexual, as well as gay and lesbian families. However, we argue that the differences between gay and lesbian parents are proposed through a patriarchal lens and stereotypes of father and mother roles. An alternative perspective is required to investigate gay and lesbian families.

From a commercial perspective, the huge market potential of gay and lesbian family tourists has been identified (Hughes & Southall, 2012; Puar, 2002), while only a few academic studies explore this issue (see Hughes & Southall, 2012; Lucena *et al.*, 2015).

In the broader tourism context, Carr (2011) argues that with the overfocus on individual tourists, family holiday research, in general, has been overlooked. Research focusing on individual travellers or couples fails to take into account the complexity of families in terms of decision making, dynamics between parents and children, and the voices of children. To add to this complexity, gay parents also face challenges with their sexual identity being exposed with the presence of the child, as well as difficulties in choosing suitable family destinations. Both Hughes and Southall (2012) and Lucena *et al.*'s (2015) studies highlight the significance of the gay-friendliness of the destinations towards the family as a unit when choosing holiday destinations.

Most family research is still dominated by the 'father-mother-children' trinomial. However, in the past decade, tourism scholars have called for a revisiting of the constantly evolving concept of 'family', which should include more diverse family forms reflecting changes in societal values and family structures such as single-parent families and gay and lesbian families (Hughes & Southall, 2012; Schänzel & Yeoman, 2014; Yeoman, 2009). In Lucena *et al.*'s (2015) critical review, they argue that issues of decision making on family holidays such as power relations and assigned

roles in the family are viewed through a heteronormative lens, which overlooks alternative situations of same-sex families.

Acknowledging the differences discussed earlier between single gay
men's and lesbians' travel motivations, we argue that lesbian and gay families share more similarities than differences in their travel motivations. In
addition to common motivations for family holidays such as togetherness,
family bonds and social interactions, same-sex families' travel motivations are impacted by the parents' sexualities (Lucena *et al.*, 2015).

Tourist Space

Tourist spaces are produced and consumed symbolically, socially and
physically (Ponting & McDonald, 2013; Thurnell-Read, 2012). In the
social sciences, the physical features of space refer to material affordances
(Gibson, 1977) or – in performative studies – stages (Edensor, 2000),
which are relational, and do not exist without tourists' practices.
According to Pritchard and Morgan (2000a), spaces are increasingly
regarded as sociocultural constructions rather than physical locations.
Socially, Crouch (2001) argues that relationships and identities are structured through spaces where the embodied engagement and co-performance
of tourists and other stakeholders take place (Crouch, 2016; Mavrič &
Urry, 2009). In his research into gay resort spaces, Vorobjovas-Pinta
(2018b) suggests that collective neo-tribal identity is manifested and performed in the gay space. The representational and symbolic aspects of
space such as destination image and place myth, which are shaped by collective social practices and organisational decisions, have a major power
to influence tourist practices (Larsen, 2006). Crouch (2000) and Wearing
et al. (2009) further suggest that the meanings of tourist spaces, which are
provided by social engagement and the practices of travellers, are dynamic
and constantly changing. Tourist spaces are thus considered fluid and
dynamic not only because of unpredictable social encounters and evolving
meanings but also because tourists negotiate and renegotiate appropriate
behaviours and identities in the public space (Goffman, 1963; Pritchard &
Morgan, 2000b). The performance turn (Haldrup & Larsen, 2009) sheds
light on the understanding of the bidirectional relationship between the
space and the tourist (Vorobjovas-Pinta, 2018b; Weaver, 2011). On the one
hand, the imaginary, social and spatial features of the space largely influence and contextualise tourist performances (Edensor, 2000). On the
other hand, the interactions between tourists and the enactment between
the destination and tourists strongly lead to a reconfiguration of the space.
This argument is further supported by Skeggs (1999), who argues that
space and subjectivities are mutually constituted.

The roles of gender and sexuality have been emphasised in the construction of space (Aitchison & Reeves, 1998; Duncan, 1996; Valentine,
1993). Based on these studies on gender and the sexual identities of space,

the heteronormativity of urban holiday space has been largely addressed by scholars (Blichfeldt *et al.*, 2013; Gorman-Murray *et al.*, 2012; Lucena *et al.*, 2015; Pritchard *et al.*, 1998; Skeggs, 1999). With the heteronormative gaze of the public holiday space, gay and lesbian tourists have been marginalised and pushed to build and find gay havens, where they can express their sexuality and meet like-minded LGBT people with an absence of homophobia (Blichfeldt *et al.*, 2013; Hughes, 2003; Vorobjovas-Pinta & Hardy, 2016). Urban gay space such as Manchester village (Hughes, 2003; Skeggs, 1999), London Soho (Binnie, 1995) and San Francisco (Howe, 2001), as well as exclusive gay resorts (Vorobjovas-Pinta, 2018a, 2018b), have been widely discussed, focusing on issues such as sexualised space, alternative gaze in marketing and the fluidity of sexuality in the tourist space. In Blichfeldt *et al.*'s (2013) qualitative research, three roles of gay space were identified: 'sanctuaries', 'zoos' and 'turfs'. In addition to 'sanctuaries' serving the role of a safe haven addressed earlier, the metaphor of the zoo shows the heterosexual gaze towards gay attractions, while men's turfs are used to demonstrate that the gay spaces are male-oriented. Correspondingly, Skeggs (1999) argues that the predominant masculinity of the gay space leads to the vulnerable feelings of lesbian tourists.

The European Travel Commission (ETC, 2018) predicts that exclusive gay spaces will continue to decline with the trend of urbanisation, gentrification and digitalisation. Vorobjovas-Pinta and Hardy (2016) propose that gay spaces are currently undergoing a 'de-gaying' process with the increasing popularity of virtual gay space and societal change. Online spaces such as online forums, virtual worlds and mobile apps create various gay platforms that facilitate functions similar to physical space such as social movement and socialising (McKenna *et al.*, 2011; Miller, 2015; Vorobjovas-Pinta & Dalla-Fontana, 2019). The de-gaying process not only indicates the potential decline of the traditional physical gay space such as gay bars and saunas (Visser, 2014), but also suggests the blurring of boundaries between heterosexual and homosexual space. With the constant connection to their gay community online, increasing numbers of homosexuals no longer primarily search for physical gay space, as more options have been opened up for holiday choices.

Historically, sex plays a significant role in constructing gay (particularly male) space (Clift & Forrest, 1999; Pritchard *et al.*, 2000). Public gay space with predominantly adult and erotic themes (Binnie, 2001) tends to exclude everyday gay travellers such as gay families and lesbians. In addition, Poria (2006) finds that gay men tend to perceive higher risk in the presence of families with children. There is a dilemma for gay parents on holiday: on the one hand, they are seeking homonormative gay space to express their sexuality and identity freely; on the other, concerns about the lack of family-friendliness of gay spaces potentially pushes them to choose alternative options such as popular family holiday spaces.

Compared with the increasing number of destinations welcoming and transforming for gay men and lesbians without children, popular family destinations still largely adopt the heteronormative model with a marketing focus on and perception of the father-mother-children trinomial (Hughes & Southall, 2012; Lucena *et al.*, 2015). Gay parents, therefore, face challenges to negotiate their sexualities in these family holiday spaces (Valentine & Duncan, 1996).

Lucena *et al.* (2015) summarise various anxieties that gay parents encounter in the heterosexual public space. Whereas it is relatively easy to negotiate or hide their sexualities without the presence of children in the public space, gay parents are 'outed' by their children. On one hand, some gay parents feel anxious that they are forced to disclose their sexuality in the public space by their children; on the other hand, for those decided to hide their sexuality in the heterosexual public space, it adds another level of anxiety of shifting roles between parental identities and sexualities. (Gabb, 2005; Gianino, 2008). We argue that the complicated sexuality negotiation might lead to negative impacts of well-being for both anxious gay parents and confused children in the public holiday space.

Away from their supportive, LGBT-friendly everyday environment, gay parents face challenges to negotiate and manage their sexualities according to various settings in holiday spaces: in the private space, they can retain their everyday sexual-parental identity, while in public they have to negotiate alternative options accordingly, which may involve the participation of the children, depending on their age (Demo & Allen, 1996). The blurred boundaries between public and private holiday spaces have been addressed by Perlesz *et al.* (2006). This fluidity of separation further complicates gay parents' behaviours and possibly leads to negative impacts of their holiday experience. From the children's perspective, Hughes and Southall (2012) argue that when exposed to new audiences, the potential of harassment and stress from fellow holidaymakers' heterosexual gaze might result in children's further disapproval on holiday.

Research Agenda

Synthesising from the existing literature, issues have been identified such as the homogeneity and overrepresentation of gay travellers and gay spaces; under-researched sexuality negotiation and the suppression of gay parents on holidays; and the lack of inclusiveness of family space. Seven research agendas and one marketing implication are proposed to initiate future research directions of gay and lesbian family tourism, particularly in heteronormative holiday space.

Firstly, a queer lens should be introduced to challenge the heteronormative family holiday space conceptually and practically. Denzin (1995) suggests that an alternative gaze, such as a gay gaze, provides a different version of reality and challenges the norms that are produced by white, masculine eyes. Pritchard *et al.* (2000) also call for a more inclusive and insightful approach to replace the heteropatriarchal gaze in order to understand tourism. Although the need has been addressed, there still is a conceptual gap requiring theoretical destabilisation and reconfiguration of the holiday space. A queer paradigm or queer turn with toolkits of worldviews, philosophies and methods is required in understanding inclusive holiday space beyond heteronormativity and homonormativity. Aligned with the theoretical development, more empirical studies should be carried out for inductive contributions to theory or investigations on how inclusive the holiday space is in various contexts.

Secondly, based on existing studies about market segments, motivations and destination choices of gay families (Hughes & Southall, 2012; Lucena *et al.*, 2015), it is worth investigating gay families' contextual and embodied experiences from both the parents' and children's perspectives. The fluidity and instability of sexuality and gender in the tourist space has been addressed in the literature (see Johnston, 2007; Skeggs, 1999), demonstrating that tourists tend to negotiate their sexualities when visiting unfamiliar sexualised spaces. Further studies should depart from the awareness of the complicated mechanism of sexuality negotiation (Lucena *et al.*, 2015), and undertake empirical investigations into the process and outcome of the sexuality negotiation and suppression. As one of the results, the well-being of the children and parents, as well as the dynamics between family members during and after the sexuality negotiation, have the potential for exploration. Schänzel and Yeoman (2014) suggest that children as sophisticated consumers of family tourism require further investigations. More studies should be undertaken to understand how the child perceives the process of negotiation of the sexuality of their same-sex parents during the holiday. Additionally, research should investigate the possibilities that virtual space could provide for supporting gay parents to manage their sexuality in a heterosexual holiday environment.

Thirdly, when challenging the inclusiveness of heterosexual space, it is worth questioning the homogeneity of the gay space. As discussed, contemporary gay space tends to be private, erotic and male-oriented (Blichfeldt *et al.*, 2013; Hughes, 2003), and excludes families and some lesbian holidaymakers. There has been a call for research into a diverse gay consumer profile and the heterogeneity of the gay travel market (Blichfeldt *et al.*, 2013; Hughes & Deutsch, 2010; Vorobjovas-Pinta & Hardy, 2016). The market profile of homosexual travellers is seen as high income, well educated and less family-oriented (Hughes, 2005; Vorobjovas-Pinta & Hardy, 2016); there is a need to address the characteristics and demands of the emerging gay family travellers. Corresponding marketing strategies, tourism products and customer services should also follow. From the supply-led side, more attention should be focused on diversifying the gay space. In fact, these representational images with the presumed relationship between sex and gay space do not appeal to many

LGBT travellers (Blichfeldt *et al.*, 2011). The straight gaze treating these gay space as 'zoos' (Blichfeldt *et al.*, 2013) to some extent intensifies this misconception. Concepts such as non-representational theory (Thrift, 2008) can reduce the misconceptions generated by 'gaze', instead of focusing on embodied practices and material enactments. Future studies should also be based on the de-gaying process (Vorobjovas-Pinta & Hardy, 2016), and explore the blurred boundaries between heterosexual and gay spaces. The inclusiveness of holiday space can only be reached when the boundary disappears.

Fourthly, subjectivities and space are mutually constituted (Skeggs, 1999). This concept is worth expanding on through the theoretical lens of performance studies. It not only emphasises that tourists are co-producers of the space but also shows the research gap of social space co-creation in the sexualised and gendered context. It would be interesting to look at how gay families negotiate and manage their sexual subjectivities when visiting popular straight family destinations, as well as how these practices play a role in the constantly evolving holiday space (Crouch, 2000; Wearing *et al.*, 2009). Concepts such as performance theory could potentially develop a new insight into how tourists' embodied practice together with an affording environment develop the holiday space.

Fifthly, when analysing how gay parents manage their sexuality in a holiday space, it is worth investigating the various stakeholders in this holiday space. Previous studies have addressed how destinations, marketing bodies, fellow travellers and government policies play various roles in gay tourists' (including family tourists') motivations and decision making (Binnie, 2001; Gorman-Murray *et al.*, 2012; Hughes & Southall, 2012; Lucena *et al.*, 2015). A hybrid approach synthesising these influential factors should be proposed and quantitatively tested to indicate relationships between these stakeholders in gay families' holiday experiences.

Sixthly, in order to develop an inclusive holiday space, suitable marketing strategies and product designs are crucial. Schänzel and Yeoman (2014) suggest that innovative and creative marketing campaigns should be developed to target gay and lesbian families. Given the complex nature of gay families on holiday, market research should abandon the outdated single gay male market profile, and undertake a thorough analysis considering both parents' and children's perspectives. The marketing campaign cannot exist without a revolutionary inclusive family holiday product. The holiday product should consider details ranging from operations to human resource management and strategic decision making in order to cater to the requirements of both heterosexual and homosexual families. The gay space undergoing the 'de-gaying' process and the homonormative family holiday destination, which is taking social inclusion into account both have the potential to develop into gay family-friendly holiday destinations.

Seventhly, following the existing research into the de-gaying process of gay space (Vorobjovas-Pinta & Hardy, 2016) and the diversification of the gay market segment, studies should examine the 'mainstreaming' of gay tourism. Discussions on this topic can follow a similar path to 'mainstreaming' in backpacker tourism (O'Reilly, 2006). It is worth noting that discussions about undoing the 'pink tourism' niche, and the movement of merging gay travellers into the mainstream segment, should engage with the critique of heteronormativity of mainstream tourism. A transformative and critical theorisation of mainstream tourism is thus required, with further debates on rethinking the boundaries between mainstream and niche forms of tourism, as well as the power relations between predominated and marginalised groups of travellers.

Conclusion

This book chapter synthesised the contemporary gay and lesbian family holiday literature. Issues such as the overrepresentation and homogeneity of gay holiday space and the heteronormativity of family space were discussed. We emphasised that the fluidity of the holiday space and the bidirectional relationship between space and tourists provide opportunities to reshape and develop an inclusive holiday space. Ranging from conceptual lenses to practical applications, seven research agendas were proposed, focusing on the queer paradigm, the travel experience of individuals in gay and lesbian families, the de-gaying trend of gay space, the fluidity of holiday space, stakeholders in the holiday space, and marketing and product design implications, respectively. By suggesting directions for future research, this book chapter contributes to the value-based knowledge in the tourism knowledge system by raising awareness and proposing practices of an inclusive holiday space.

References

Aitchison, C. and Reeves, C. (1998) Gendered (bed) spaces: The culture and commerce of women-only tourism. In C. Aitchison and F. Jordan (eds) *Gender, Space and Identity: Leisure, Culture and Commerce* (pp. 47–68). Eastbourne: Leisure Studies Association.

Badgett, M.L. (1997) Beyond biased samples: Challenging the myths on the economic status of lesbians and gay men. In A. Gluckman and B. Reed (eds) *Homo Economics: Capitalism, Community, and Lesbian and Gay Life* (pp. 65–72). New York: Routledge.

Baetens, P. and Brewaeys, A. (2001) Lesbian couples requesting donor insemination: An update of the knowledge with regard to lesbian mother families. *Human Reproduction Update* 7, 512–519.

Biblarz, T.J. and Stacey, J. (2010) How does the gender of parents matter? *Journal of Marriage and Family* 72, 3–22.

Binnie, J. (1995) Trading places: Consumption, sexuality and the production of queer space. In D. Bell and G. Valentine (eds) *Mapping Desire: Geographies of Sexualities* (pp. 182–199). New York: Routledge.

Binnie, J. (2001) The erotic possibilities of the city. In D. Bell, J. Binnie, R. Holliday, R. Longhurst and R. Peace (eds) *Pleasure Zones: Bodies, Cities, Spaces* (pp. 103–128). Syracuse, NY: Syracuse University Press.

Blichfeldt, B.S., Chor, J. and Milan, N.B. (2011) 'It really depends on whether you are in a relationship': A study of 'gay destinations' from a tourist perspective. *Tourism Today* 11, 7–26.

Blichfeldt, B.S., Chor, J. and Milan, N.B. (2013) Zoos, sanctuaries and turfs: Enactments and uses of gay spaces during the holidays. *International Journal of Tourism Research* 15, 473–483.

Carr, N. (2011) *Children's and Families' Holiday Experience*. New York: Routledge.

Carrington, C. (1999) *No Place Like Home: Relationships and Family Life among Lesbians and Gay Men*. Chicago, IL: University of Chicago Press.

Clift, S. and Forrest, S. (1999) Gay men and tourism: Destinations and holiday motivations. *Tourism Management* 20 (5), 615–625. doi:10.1016/S0261-5177 (99)00032-1

Clift, S. and Wilkins, J. (1995) Travel, sexual behaviour and gay men. In P. Aggleton, G. Hart and P. Cavies (eds) *AIDS: Safety, Sexuality and Risks* (pp. 35–54). London: Taylor & Francis.

Cohen, E. and Cohen, S.A. (2015) Beyond Eurocentrism in tourism: A paradigm shift to mobilities. *Tourism Recreation Research* 40, 157–168.

Coon, D.R. (2012) Sun, sand, and citizenship: The marketing of gay tourism. *Journal of Homosexuality* 59, 511–534.

Crouch, D. (2000) Places around us: Embodied lay geographies in leisure and tourism. *Leisure Studies* 19, 63–76.

Crouch, D. (2001) Spatialities and the feeling of doing. *Social & Cultural Geography* 2, 61–75.

Crouch, D. (2016) *Flirting with Space: Journeys and Creativity*. Abingdon: Routledge.

Demo, D.H. and Allen, K.R. (1996) Diversity within lesbian and gay families: Challenges and implications for family theory and research. *Journal of Social and Personal Relationships* 13, 415–434.

Denzin, N.K. (1995) *The Cinematic Society: The Voyeur's Gaze*. London: Sage.

Dinnie, E. and Browne, K. (2011) Creating a sexual self in heteronormative space: Integrations and imperatives amongst spiritual seekers at the Findhorn community. *Sociological Research Online* 16, 1–10.

Duncan, N. (1996) *BodySpace: Destabilizing Geographies of Gender and Sexuality*. Hove: Psychology Press.

Edensor, T. (2000) Staging tourism: Tourists as performers. *Annals of Tourism Research* 27, 322–344.

ETC (2018) *Handbook on the Lesbian, Gay, Bisexual, Transgender and Queer (LGBTQ) Travel Segment*. Brussels: European Travel Commission Market Intelligence.

Gabb, J. (2005) Locating lesbian parent families: Everyday negotiations of lesbian motherhood in Britain. *Gender, Place & Culture* 12, 419–432.

Gianino, M. (2008) Adaptation and transformation: The transition to adoptive parenthood for gay male couples. *Journal of GLBT Family Studies* 4, 205–243.

Gibson, J.J. (1977) The theory of affordances. In R.E. Shaw and J. Bransford (eds) *Perceiving, Acting and Knowing* (pp. 67–82). Hillsdale, NJ: Lawrence Erlbaum.

Gluckman, A. and Reed, B. (1997) The gay marketing moment. In A. Gluckman and B. Reed (eds) *Homo Economics: Capitalism, Community, and Lesbian and Gay Life* (pp. 3-10). New York and London: Routledge.

Goffman, E. (1963) *Behavior in Public Places: Notes on the Social Organization of Gatherings*. New York: Free Press.

Gorman-Murray, A., Waitt, G. and Gibson, C. (2012) Chilling out in 'cosmopolitan country': Urban/rural hybridity and the construction of Daylesford as a 'lesbian and gay rural idyll'. *Journal of Rural Studies* 28, 69–79.

Haldrup, M. and Larsen, J. (2009) *Tourism, Performance and the Everyday: Consuming the Orient*. New York: Routledge.

Howe, A.C. (2001) Queer pilgrimage: The San Francisco homeland and identity tourism. *Cultural Anthropology* 16, 35–61.

Hughes, H. (1997) Holidays and homosexual identity. *Tourism Management* 18, 3–7.

Hughes, H. (2002) Gay men's holiday destination choice: A case of risk and avoidance. *International Journal of Tourism Research* 4, 299–312.

Hughes, H. (2003) Marketing gay tourism in Manchester: New market for urban tourism or destruction of 'gay space'? *Journal of Vacation Marketing* 9, 152–163.

Hughes, H. (2005) A gay tourism market. *Journal of Quality Assurance in Hospitality & Tourism* 5, 57–74.

Hughes, H.L. (2006) *Pink Tourism: Holidays of Gay Men and Lesbians*. Wallingford: CABI.

Hughes, H. and Deutsch, R. (2010) Holidays of older gay men: Age or sexual orientation as decisive factors? *Tourism Management* 31, 454–463.

Hughes, H. and Southall, C. (2012) Gay and lesbian families and tourism. *Family Tourism: Multidisciplinary Perspectives* 56, 125–139.

ILGA (International Lesbian, Gay, Bisexual, Trans and Intersex Association) (2017) *Sexual Orientation Laws in the World – Overview*. See https://ilga.org/downloads/2017/ILGA_WorldMap_ENGLISH_Overview_2017.pdf.

Johnston, L. (2007) *Queering Tourism: Paradoxical Performances of Gay Pride Parades*. New York: Routledge.

Larsen, J. (2006) Picturing Bornholm: Producing and consuming a tourist place through picturing practices. *Scandinavian Journal of Hospitality and Tourism* 6, 75–94.

Lucena, R., Jarvis, N. and Weeden, C. (2015) A review of gay and lesbian parented families' travel motivations and destination choices: Gaps in research and future directions. *Annals of Leisure Research* 18, 272–289.

Mavrič, M. and Urry, J. (2009) Tourism studies and the new mobilities paradigm. In T. Jamal and M. Robinson (eds) *The Sage Handbook of Tourism Studies* (pp. 645–657). London: Sage.

McKenna, B., Gardner, L. and Myers, M. (2011) Social movements in World of Warcraft. Paper presented at 17th Americas Conference on Information Systems, Detroit, MI.

Miller, B. (2015) 'They're the modern-day gay bar': Exploring the uses and gratifications of social networks for men who have sex with men. *Computers in Human Behavior* 51, 476–482.

Monterrubio, C. (2019) Tourism and male homosexual identities: Directions for sociocultural research. *Tourism Review*, 74 (5), 1058–1069. doi:10.1108/TR-08-2017-0125

Monterrubio, C. and Barrios, M.D. (2016) Lesbians as tourists: A qualitative study of tourist motivations in Mexico. *Tourismos: An International Multidisciplinary Journal of Tourism* 11 (4), 64–90.

O'Reilly, C.C. (2006) From drifter to gap year tourist: Mainstreaming backpacker travel. *Annals of Tourism Research* 33 (4), 998–1017.

Perlesz, A., Brown, R., Lindsay, J., McNair, R., De Vaus, D. and Pitts, M. (2006) Family in transition: Parents, children and grandparents in lesbian families give meaning to 'doing family'. *Journal of Family Therapy* 28, 175–199.

Ponting, J. and McDonald, M.G. (2013) Performance, agency and change in surfing tourist space. *Annals of Tourism Research* 43, 415–434.

Poria, Y. (2006) Assessing gay men and lesbian women's hotel experiences: An exploratory study of sexual orientation in the travel industry. *Journal of Travel Research* 44, 327–334.

Poria, Y. and Taylor, A. (2002) 'I am not afraid to be gay when I'm on the net': Minimising social risk for lesbian and gay consumers when using the internet. *Journal of Travel & Tourism Marketing* 11, 127–142.

Pritchard, A. and Morgan, N.J. (2000a) Constructing tourism landscapes – gender, sexuality and space. *Tourism Geographies* 2, 115–139.

Pritchard, A. and Morgan, N.J. (2000b) Privileging the male gaze: Gendered tourism landscapes. *Annals of Tourism Research* 27, 884–905.

Pritchard, A., Morgan, N.J., Sedgely, D., Jenkins, A. and Morgan, N. (1998) Reaching out to the gay tourist: Opportunities and threats in an emerging market segment. *Tourism Management* 19, 273–282.

Pritchard, A., Morgan, N.J., Sedgley, D., Khan, E. and Jenkins, A. (2000) Sexuality and holiday choices: Conversations with gay and lesbian tourists. *Leisure Studies* 19, 267–282.

Puar, J. (2002) A transnational feminist critique of queer tourism. *Antipode* 34, 935–946.

Ryan, C. and Hall, C.M. (2005) *Sex Tourism: Marginal People and Liminalities*. New York: Routledge.

Schänzel, H.A. and Yeoman, I. (2014) The future of family tourism. *Tourism Recreation Research* 39, 343–360.

Skeggs, B. (1999) Matter out of place: Visibility and sexualities in leisure spaces. *Leisure Studies* 18, 213–232.

Southall, C. and Fallon, P. (2011) LGBT tourism. In P. Robinson, S. Heitmann and P. Dieke (eds) *Research Themes for Tourism* (pp. 218–232). Wallingford: CABI.

Steck, A. and Perry, D. (2017) Secondary school leader perceptions about the inclusion of queer materials in the school course curricula. *The Curriculum Journal* 28, 327–348.

Thrift, N. (2008) *Non-Representational Theory: Space, Politics, Affect*. New York: Routledge.

Thurnell-Read, T. (2012) Tourism place and space: British stag tourism in Poland. *Annals of Tourism Research* 39, 801–819.

Valentine, G. (1993) (Hetero)sexing space: Lesbian perceptions and experiences of everyday spaces. *Environment and Planning D: Society and Space* 11, 395–413.

Valentine, G. and Duncan, N. (1996) *(Re)negotiating the 'Heterosexual Street': Lesbian Productions of Space*. London: Routledge.

Vandecasteele, B. and Geuens, M. (2009) Revising the myth of gay consumer innovativeness. *Journal of Business Research* 62, 134–144.

Visser, G. (2009) *Gay and Lesbian Tourism: The Essential Guide for Marketing*. Oxford: Butterworth-Heinemann.

Visser, G. (2014) Urban tourism and the de-gaying of Cape Town's De Waterkant. *Urban Forum* 25, 469–482.

Vorobjovas-Pinta, O. (2018a) Gay neo-tribes: Exploration of travel behaviour and space. *Annals of Tourism Research* 72, 1–10.

Vorobjovas-Pinta, O. (2018b) 'It's been nice, but we're going back to our lives': Neo-tribalism and the role of space in a gay resort. In A. Hardy, A. Bennett and B. Robards (eds) *Neo-Tribes: Consumption, Leisure and Tourism* (pp. 71–87). Cham: Palgrave Macmillan.

Vorobjovas-Pinta, O. and Dalla-Fontana, I.J. (2019) The strange case of dating apps at a gay resort: Hyper-local and virtual-physical leisure. *Tourism Review* 74 (2), 1070–1080.

Vorobjovas-Pinta, O. and Hardy, A. (2016) The evolution of gay travel research. *International Journal of Tourism Research* 18, 409–416.

Waitt, G. and Markwell, K. (2014) *Gay Tourism: Culture and Context*. London: Routledge.

Wearing, S., Stevenson, D. and Young, T. (2009) *Tourist Cultures: Identity, Place and the Traveller*. London: Sage.

Weaver, A. (2011) The fragmentation of markets, neo-tribes, nostalgia, and the culture of celebrity: The rise of themed cruises. *Journal of Hospitality and Tourism Management* 18, 54–60.

Wong, C.C.L. and Tolkach, D. (2017) Travel preferences of Asian gay men. *Asia Pacific Journal of Tourism Research* 22, 579–591.

Yeoman, I. (2009) *Tomorrow's Tourist: Scenarios & Trends*. London: Routledge.

Part 2

Gay Tourism: Profiles and Identities

5 Understanding African LGBT Traveller Motivations: A Non-Westernised Perspective

Christiaan Hattingh

Although the Western world (e.g. Northern America and Western Europe) is witnessing several social, cultural and political developments resulting in homosexuality being increasingly visible, tolerated and constitutionally protected, a large majority of countries in the non-Western world, most often those with high levels of religious conviction (Hattingh, 2017), do not outlaw anti-gay discrimination or protect gay[1] rights (Vorobjovas-Pinta & Hardy, 2016). The African continent, in particular, seems to be a competitive arena for violation of gay rights, where 38 of 54 countries strictly outlaw homosexuality (ILGA, 2016). For instance, in 2008 the Gambian President threatened to 'cut off the head' of any homosexual[2] the government 'catches' (Wockner, 2008). In 2014, a British tourist was arrested, tried and found guilty of 'homosexual acts' in Morocco, and sentenced to four months in jail (Strudwick, 2014). That same year, a Kenyan parliamentary committee insisted on applying anti-gay laws more rigorously and warned that homosexuality is 'as serious as terrorism' (Nelson, 2014). In 2016, forced anal examinations, Human Immunodeficiency Virus (HIV) and Hepatitis B tests of men suspected of 'practising' homosexuality were ruled constitutional by a Kenyan Court. In addition, the test results could serve as 'evidence' in criminal prosecutions on homosexuality (HRW, 2016). Although this decision was overturned in 2018, it being argued that these tests 'are both medically worthless and a severe violation of medical ethics', several African countries including Egypt, Cameroon and Tunisia continue to conduct them (HRW, 2018). In 2017, two South African men were arrested in Tanzania for 'promoting homosexuality' (Mzantsi, 2017), while in 2018, 57 Nigerian men were arrested and charged with performing 'homosexual acts'. If convicted, these men could face up to 14 years in prison, considered to be a 'light' sentence compared with the 12 northern Nigerian states with Sharia law, where gays are stoned to death (Jackman, 2018).

The presidents of Uganda and Namibia and the former president of Zimbabwe have been particularly vocal about their anti-homosexual views (Kennedy, 2006), stating that homosexuality is 'un-African' and a Western colonial import (Reddy, 2014). These leaders view homosexuality 'as foreign in all respects to indigenous African culture' (Croucher, 2002: 316) and believe that it threatens the cultural integrity of their countries (Gomes da Costa Santos, 2013). Consequently, with beliefs like these, the gay tourism[3] phenomenon remains largely unexplored in non-Western countries (Hattingh, 2017).

South Africa, however, is the first country in the world to outlaw unfair discrimination against 'sexual orientation' (Gomes da Costa Santos, 2013), and one of the very few non-Western countries and the only country on the African continent that protects the right to 'sexual orientation' in its post-apartheid constitution of 1996 (Gomes da Costa Santos, 2013). But, as with most other non-Western countries (and even some Western countries), the everyday reality for many lesbian, gay, bisexual and transgender (LGBT) South Africans remains grim due to ongoing 'sexual orientation-based' violence and harassment including the heinous practice of 'corrective rape', where the intent of the perpetrators is to enforce conformity and to 'cure' those who 'challenge the dominant heterosexual identity' (Kutsch, 2013). In 2016, a report entitled *Hate Crimes against LGBT People in South Africa* (Out LGBT Well-being, 2016) found that 44% of LGBT South Africans had experienced discrimination in their everyday lives due to their sexual orientation or gender identity (DeBarros, 2016). Therefore, it is crucial to note that the protection of gay rights in South Africa's post-apartheid Constitution is a result of a constitutional order by the progressive new government, the African National Congress, and a commitment to human rights (Jara, 1998), but certainly it is not due to the country's tolerance of homosexuality. The new government and constitution of South Africa are in contrast with the beliefs of many South Africans, who still overwhelmingly oppose gay rights (Ilyayambwa, 2012), often described as 'a deeply conservative, heteronormative country in spite of its progressive politics' (Thoreson, 2008: 682).

The development of a liberal and historic Constitution inevitably resulted in the development of uniquely gay spaces for the gay community (Visser, 2003), which brought about the emergence of a gay leisure market (Visser, 2002). Few South African destinations are, however, taking advantage of gay tourism, with Cape Town being the notable exception (Visser, 2003; Hattingh & Bruwer, 2020; Hattingh & Spencer, 2020). Cape Town – informally known as the 'gay capital of Africa' – is recognised by *The Guardian* as 'one of the 10 most popular gay travel destinations in the world' (UNWTO, 2012: 23). Consequently, it is entirely possible that some LGBT individuals residing in environments where discrimination and marginalisation are still strong are attracted to Cape Town's gay village – the only gay village on the African continent – in search of a safe space in which they can be themselves, even if only temporarily while on holiday. Hattingh and Spencer (2017) found that gay travellers from other provinces in South Africa and non-Western countries who live in conservative environments felt an increasing need to escape from disapproving societies and argued that a safe space is more likely possible in Cape Town than in their heteronormative home environments. Cape Town and its gay village, therefore, seemingly offer a safe escape in a largely conservative country and continent.

To date, apart from a minor number of exceptions, most studies on gay tourism deal with Western gays, resulting in perceptions often being biased towards travellers and destinations within those regions. Indeed, as Vorobjovas-Pinta and Hardy (2016) argue, there remains a 'lack of insight into travel motivations and behaviour of gay travellers going to or, especially, coming from non-Western countries that are hostile towards homosexuals'. As the Western world is considered increasingly 'gay friendly' (Kauhanen, 2015), this could explain why most of the studies conducted to date are unavoidably biased towards the Western world. The hidden nature of the LGBT population makes it nearly impossible to locate informants as it is 'difficult to randomly confront people for an interview because homosexuality is a sensitive sexual identity, which is not visible unless people want to express it themselves' (Månsson & Østrup, 2007: 5). Additionally, the early literature has widely contributed to the belief that gay travel is a highly desirable market to target for tourism, owing to, among other factors, up-scale characteristics such as higher levels of education and incomes as gay couples choose not to have children (so-called DINKs, i.e. double income, no kids). This was believed to allow for flexibility to travel at any desired time, leading to less seasonal behaviour (Pritchard et al., 1998), and led to the myth that gay travellers represent an affluent homogeneous market, resulting in a number of tourism destinations actively targeting these travellers (Hughes, 2005).

Despite individual researchers, some as far back as 20 years ago, arguing that gay travellers are not homogeneous (Blichfeldt et al., 2011; Hattingh & Spencer, 2020; Hughes, 2006; Pritchard et al., 1998), most destinations targeting these travellers continue to regard them as a homogeneous group, which may hinder effective marketing (Hattingh, 2017; Ro et al., 2017) due to their distorted understanding of the needs and desires of gay travellers (Vorobjovas-Pinta & Hardy, 2016). Consequently, Cohen et al. (2014), Herrera and Scott (2005), Hughes (2006) and Ro et al. (2017) called for further consumer research on the diversity among LGBT travellers' behaviour. The current study's aim was therefore twofold: (i) to investigate a sample of non-Western, i.e. African gay leisure travellers' holiday motivations; and (ii) to determine if there were significant differences among these travellers' motivations in order to challenge the myth regarding the homogeneity of this market.

Understanding Tourist Behaviour Through Travel Motivations

Motivation is classically defined as 'a state of tension within the individual which arouses, directs and maintains behaviour toward a goal' (Mullen & Johnson, 1990: 91) or incentive (Luthans *et al.*, 1988) and drives an individual to act in order to reach personal fulfilment (Beerli & Martín, 2004). Goossens (2000) is of the opinion that in order to reach personal fulfilment, an individual must be aware of a service or product, and to perceive that the purchase of that service or product will assist in attaining personal fulfilment and satisfying a need. Tourism services and products can be developed and promoted as a solution to an individual's needs (Fodness, 1994). Therefore, needs are seen as the 'forces which arouse motivated behaviour' (Boekstein, 2012: 85). As Jago (1997) contends, in order to fully comprehend consumer motivation, it is crucial to have in-depth knowledge of the needs that consumers strive to fulfil, and how these needs can be fulfilled.

There is an increasingly important body of research regarding the study of motivation in the travel and tourism industry specifically (Bansal & Eiselt, 2004), with numerous motivation theories having developed over time to help explain the complexity of tourists' behaviour (Isaac, 2008). Undoubtedly, one of the most important contributions to the development of tourism motivational theories is the one proposed by Dann (1977), which suggests that motivations fall into two categories, namely push factors and pull factors. Push factors refer to the 'specific forces that influence a person's decision to take a vacation' and have been theorised as 'motivational factors or needs that arise due to a disequilibrium or tension in the motivational system' (Kim *et al.*, 2003: 170). Push factors include, for example, rest and relaxation, self-actualisation, adventure/nature, status/prestige, novelty, escape, social interaction, nostalgia or romance/sex (Hattingh, 2017). Pull factors can be viewed as relating to the supply dimension and are characterised by the attributes, features or attractions that pull travellers towards a specific destination and include, for example, festivals or special events, recreational activities, cultural resources (Kim & Lee, 2002), sunshine, beaches, sports facilities, inexpensive airfares (Klenosky, 2002), friendliness of local people, population density, urban layout, currency exchange, pricing structures (Prayag, 2003) or any potential activity offered to the traveller (Kassean & Gassita, 2013).

Table 5.1 identifies some of the most common destination attributes (pull factors) and motivational (push) factors from a selection of mainstream tourist motivation studies which all vary in their focus, research design and target groups. Although these studies confirm the preceding common push and pull factors, it has been argued that 'motivations behind travel are constructed out of the social realities of the lives of those who participate in tourism-related activity' (Kinnaird & Hall, 1994: 212), suggesting that the gay traveller may have different travel motivations

Table 5.1 A selection of previous mainstream tourism motivation studies

Researcher(s)	Research approach used	Push factors identified	Pull factors identified
Yuan and McDonald (1990)	Factor analysis of 29 motivational/push items and 53 destination/pull items	Enhancement of kinship relationships, novelty, escape, prestige, hobbies/relaxation	History and culture, budget, wilderness, cosmopolitan environment, hunting, ease of travel, facilities
Uysal and Jurowski (1994)	Factor analysis of 26 motivational/push items and 29 destination/pull items	Escape, sports, cultural experience, re-experiencing family togetherness	Culture/heritage, entertainment, outdoors/nature, rural/inexpensive, resort
Turnbull and Uysal (1995)	Factor analysis of 30 motivation/push items and 53 destination/pull items	Prestige, escape, re-experiencing family, cultural experiences, sports	Comfort/relaxation, city enclave, culture/heritage, outdoor resources, rural/inexpensive, beach resort
Oh et al. (1995)	Canonical correlation analysis of 30 motivational/push items and 52 destination/pull items	Novelty, prestige/entertainment, adventure, knowledge/intellectual, sports, kinship/social interaction, rest/escape	Outdoor/nature, upscale/safety, historical/cultural, budget/inexpensive, sports/activity
Klenosky (2002)	Means-end theory, laddering interviews	New/novel experience, relax/rest, enjoy nature, socialise/meet people, get refreshed/renewed, outdoor recreation, get sun/tan, escape, look good/healthy, know more, date more, fun and enjoyment, be more productive, self-esteem, accomplishment, excitement, learn more, challenge/thrill	Warm climate, beaches, new/unique location, party atmosphere, scenic/natural resources, cultural/historical attractions, skiing
Kim et al. (2003)	Factor analysis of 12 motivation/push items and 12 destination/pull items	Family togetherness and study, appreciating health and natural resources, escaping from everyday routine, adventure and building friendship	Accessibility and transportation, information and convenience of facilities, key tourist resources
Kassean and Gassita (2013)	Factor analysis of 74 motivation/push items and destination/pull items	Social interaction, prestige/recognition, rest and relaxation, self-actualisation, novelty, escape, nostalgia	Unique flora and fauna, authentic Mauritian culture, exotic ambience and atmosphere, special climate and weather, exquisite landscape and scenery, exotic beaches, Mauritian hospitality
Khuong and Ha (2014)	Factor analysis of 17 motivation/push items and destination/pull items	To fulfil my dream of visiting a foreign land/country, to learn something new and interesting, to socialise with local community and meet new people, to visit a place that I have not visited before, to escape from daily routine	Warm and sunny weather, good physical amenities (recreational facilities, transportation, accommodation), cultural, historical, religious and art attractions, special events/festivals and activities, variety of food, safe and easy access destination, beautiful landscape and natural scenery (forests, mountains, beaches)

Source: Researcher construct from secondary data.

from those of the mainstream traveller and even among gay travellers themselves, as there is 'no more reason to believe that gay women's holiday profiles are the same as those of gay men's than there is to believe males and females generally have the same motivations and behaviours' (Hughes, 2006: 58).

Gay travellers' holiday motivations

Clift and Forrest (1999) conducted one of the first empirical investigations into the holiday motivations of gay men and proposed three dimensions of gay travel: 'gay social life and sex', 'culture and sights' and 'comfort and relaxation' (Clift & Forrest, 1999). The authors tentatively conclude that the most important travel motivations for gay travellers are largely similar to those of mainstream travellers, i.e. good food, relaxation and comfort, and sunshine (Clift & Forrest, 1999). Although Pritchard *et al.* (2000) confirmed this notion, they found the need to escape from heterosexism and to interact with like-minded people in an exclusively gay-safe environment were key factors influencing gay travellers' destination choice, particularly for those who hid their sexuality at home.

Hughes (2002: 304) too argued that 'the "types" of holidays that gay men go on are identical to those of the rest of society'. They are attracted (pulled) by destinations that offer scenery, heritage, sea and sun, sport and entertainment, and culture. Push factors such as social interaction, regeneration, evaluation of self, ego-enhancement, escape, freedom and self-realisation apply equally to gay men (Hughes, 2002). Hughes (2002) proposed a typology of gay men's holidays: 'gay-centric', 'gay-related' and 'non-gay'. A 'non-gay' holiday is no different from that taken by mainstream tourists (Hughes, 2006). A 'gay-related' holiday fulfils the desire for a safe and comfortable destination (where gay space or gay friendliness and tolerance are somewhat important but do not outweigh other requirements) (Hughes, 2002). Gay space and experience, on the other hand, are the key attributes looked for in a 'gay-centric' holiday (Hughes, 2006), implying usually, although not always, sun-and-sea holidays in which gay bars, gay clubs, gay saunas, gay beaches, casual sex contact and socialising with other gay men feature predominantly in the tourists' holiday activities (Hughes & Deutsch, 2010).

The influential research of Clift and Forrest (1999), Hughes (2002) and Pritchard *et al.* (2000) led to an important body of research regarding the study of gay travellers' motivations as discussed throughout this chapter. However, as a result of increasing societal tolerance and legislation, the motivations of a modern gay traveller may have substantially changed, especially considering that 'much of the early demographic and motivational research was conducted prior to social and institutional reform in relation to this sector' (Vorobjovas-Pinta & Hardy, 2016: 412). An extensive literature review of this body of research revealed that although some studies suggest gay and mainstream travellers travel for similar reasons to those discussed above, some studies provide evidence suggesting otherwise (Hughes, 2006).

The specific push motivations that distinguish some gay travellers from other groups appear to include (Hattingh & Spencer, 2017):

(i)   Escaping heteronormativity as a result of the need to escape the tension and burdens brought about by the oppressive heteronormative home environment.
(ii) Pursuing sex/romance, especially important to those living in small cities or heteronormative communities that strictly prohibit same-sex sexual activity.
(iii) Constructing and validating gay identity, especially relevant to those more prone to social censure, who could have a need to travel to 'gay-friendly' environments in which they can express their 'true' identities.

The specific pull motivations appear to include (Hattingh & Spencer, 2017):

(i)   Gay friendliness, as their safety and approval and acceptance of their sexuality is more likely in a 'gay-friendly' destination.
(ii) Gay marriage or civil partnerships, which might be illegal in the home environment, which could result in travelling for the purpose of getting married.
(iii) Gay events/festivals, due to the opportunity of being part of a majority gay population, which might not be the case in their home environments.
(iv) Gay space/infrastructure, also referred to as gay-related infrastructure, services and facilities, or the gay scene in which homosexuality is the majority and the norm with no risk of rejection and homophobia.

For a full discussion of these push and pull motivations, see Hattingh and Spencer (2017).

Methodology

This study applied a quantitative research method by means of a self-administered web-based electronic survey to avoid surveying *only* openly LGBT individuals who patronise gay bars/venues at the destination. Respondents could opt to remain anonymous on the web if they wished, which was important considering the heteronormative home environments that some in the study sample have become accustomed to. A judgment sample of eight gay travel agencies and tour operators across South Africa were asked to distribute the survey hyperlink via email to African gay travellers on their databases who had previously travelled to Cape Town.

A list of 13 push factors and 24 pull factors was adapted from a variety of studies including Kassean and Gassita (2013), Kim and Lee (2002) and Zhou (2005). Some specific push and pull motivations for travel among LGBT individuals as found in the literature were also added to the survey. Participants rated the importance level of the push and pull factors on a 5-point Likert scale (1 = not at all important, 2 = unimportant, 3 = neither important nor unimportant (neutrally important), 4 = important, 5 = very important). The survey was available online for eight months (May 2016–January 2017), and was completed by a sample of 250 LGBT travellers from African countries including Botswana, Kenya, Madagascar, Namibia, South Africa, Swaziland, Zambia and Zimbabwe.

Results

African LGBT traveller profile

Most LGBT travellers were married or partnered (61%), and aged between 31 and 40 years (36%). More males (89%) participated in the study than females (11%). Most respondents identified as gay (84%), while lesbians (8%), bisexuals (5%) and transgendered individuals (<1%) made up the balance of the sample. These LGBT travellers were mostly open about their sexuality in their home environments (85%), while 15% were only partially open or concealed their sexuality. Almost two-thirds of respondents (63%) classified their home environments as liberal, while more than a third (37%) originated from conservative environments.

LGBT travel motivations: Push factors

The most important push factors for African LGBT travellers were 'opportunities for rest and relaxation' (4.15), followed by 'escaping from everyday life and daily routine' (4.05) (Table 5.2). These push factors were all relatively close to 4, the value of the 'important' level. Opportunities for rest and relaxation and to escape appeared to be important push factors for mainstream travellers (Kassean & Gassita, 2013) as well as LGBT travellers (Ballegaard & Chor, 2009; Hughes & Deutsch, 2010). These findings tentatively suggest that, despite the deeply conservative and heteronormative attitudes across most South African provinces as well as the unfair discrimination against 'sexual orientation' elsewhere on the African continent, the most important factors that push African LGBT individuals to travel are in line with those of mainstream travellers.

LGBT travel motivations: Pull factors

The most important pull factors attracting LGBT travellers to Cape Town were the 'dramatic/beautiful landscape and scenery' (4.35),

Table 5.2 Push factors' mean scores (*n* = 250)

Rank	Push factor	Mean score	SD
1	Opportunities for rest and relaxation	4.15	1.022
2	Escape from everyday life/daily routine	4.05	1.057
3	Enhancement of kinship relationships (family/friends)	3.72	1.290
4	Novelty (discovering/exploring a new or exciting place)	3.68	1.224
5	Enriching myself intellectually (learn something new)	3.42	1.243
6	Exploration and evaluation of self (gain insight about self)	3.17	1.338
7	Social interaction with other gay people	3.12	1.417
8	Opportunity to develop close friendships/romance	2.97	1.397
9	Nostalgia	2.89	1.334
10	Escape from disapproving society to freely express gay identity	2.61	1.504
11	Opportunity to have a sexual adventure	2.54	1.508
12	Social recognition/ego enhancement	2.52	1.392
13	To get married/go on honeymoon	1.70	1.201

followed by the destination's 'relaxing atmosphere' (4.31) (Table 5.3). The importance attached to these attributes is no surprise – Cape Town is set in some of the most dramatic scenery to be seen anywhere in the world and offers the tourist a world of relaxation (Fisher, 2012). The 'local food and wine' (4.06) was also among the most important attributes that attracted African LGBT travellers, possibly due to Cape Town being named the best food city in the world by the *Condé Nast Traveller World's Best Food Cities Readers' Choice Awards* in 2016 (Voelker, 2016). This accolade, therefore, appears to draw African LGBT travellers. The above findings are supported by Clift and Forrest (1999) and Ersoy *et al.* (2012), who found that comfort/relaxation and good food are strong pull factors for LGBT leisure travel.

The next most important pull factors were the destination's 'safety and security' (3.96) related to LGBT travellers' personal safety, and the 'gay-friendly environment and friendliness of locals towards gays' (3.94). Although the need for safety appears to be a powerful motivational force behind human behaviour and an important consideration in destination selection (Hu & Ritchie, 1993), LGBT travellers do face physical or verbal abuse, discrimination and harassment and even criminalisation initiated by countries that enforce sexuality-based discrimination (Hughes, 2005). Furthermore, some evidence exists that gay friendliness was not an important consideration for LGBT travellers (Blichfeldt *et al.*, 2011; Retnam, 2012). In contrast, most African LGBT travellers regarded the 'gay-friendly' environment and tolerance of the locals in Cape Town to be important, possibly due to its 'gay-friendly' reputation and gay-tolerant society (Hattingh & Spencer, 2017).

Table 5.3 Pull factors' mean scores (*n* = 250)

Rank	Pull factor (destination attribute)	Mean score	SD
1	Dramatic/beautiful landscape and scenery	4.35	0.924
2	Relaxing atmosphere	4.31	0.909
3	Local food and wine	4.06	1.087
4	Safe and secure destination related to LGBT personal safety	3.96	1.190
5	Gay-friendly environment/friendliness of locals towards gays	3.94	1.224
6	Beaches	3.87	1.248
7	General tourist attractions/well known tourist sites	3.82	1.166
8	Ease of access into destination	3.67	1.208
9	Diversity and cosmopolitan reputation	3.66	1.304
10	Climate/weather	3.64	1.209
11	Local gay culture/gay venues (gay village)	3.58	1.313
12	Culture and history (monument, heritage, arts, local customs)	3.38	1.287
13	Nightlife (bars, clubs and other entertainment)	3.34	1.363
14	Shopping facilities	3.26	1.317
15	Cost/value for money	3.25	1.278
16	Unique 'African' city	3.21	1.554
17	Nature, adventure offering (hiking, shark-cage diving, abseiling)	3.17	1.439
18	Same-sex marriage laws	2.99	1.619
19	Unique accommodation	2.93	1.356
20	Gay event	2.74	1.535
21	Gay/nude beach	2.67	1.554
22	Mainstream event	2.66	1.326
23	Wildlife, special animals	2.57	1.322
24	Sport/exercise & wellness facilities	2.48	1.375

The findings in Tables 5.2 and 5.3 have to be carefully considered. Vorobjovas-Pinta and Hardy (2016) are of the opinion that an overemphasis of descriptive data has resulted in the perception of a homogeneous LGBT travel market. In tourism research, sociodemographics such as gender, age, education, relationship status, occupation and income have been widely used for profiling travellers and examining differences among them (e.g. Beerli & Martín, 2004). However, very few empirical studies have examined the sociodemographic differences among LGBT travellers (Ro *et al.*, 2017). Therefore, further statistical analyses were required to test whether there are significant differences in LGBT travellers' motivations. Analysis of variance (ANOVA) was used to analyse the variance within and between means for groups (categories) of data and is represented by the *F*-ratio or *F*-statistic (Saunders *et al.*, 2009). A large *F*-statistic with a probability of less than 0.05 indicates that the variance is statistically significant (Saunders *et al.*, 2009). As the ANOVA only indicates whether there are significant differences between groups (categories), it was supplemented by the post hoc Bonferroni test to determine where the differences lie.

Comparisons of push and pull factors for different age groups

ANOVAs revealed statistically significant differences among the different age groups ($p < 0.05$) (Table 5.4) for some of the push and pull factors. An inspection of the mean scores across age groups indicated that to 'escape from disapproving society to freely express gay identity' (2.81[a]; 2.54[a]), 'social recognition/ego enhancement' (2.84[a]; 2.39[a]) and 'exploration and evaluation of self' (3.60[a]) were more important push factors among younger travellers (between the ages of 18 and 40), while an 'opportunity to have a sexual adventure' (1.59[b]), was less important to senior travellers (61 years and older). Furthermore, the pull factor 'culture and history' (3.37[b]) was less important to 31–40 year olds, while 'nature and adventure offering' (2.70[b]) was less important to senior travellers (61 years and older). The travel behaviours of LGBT travellers of different age groups therefore appear to be varied.

Table 5.4 ANOVA for comparison of push and pull factors by age group ($n = 250$)

Push factor	18–30	31–40	41–50	51–60	61 and older	*F*-ratio	Sig. level
Escape from disapproving society to freely express gay identity	2.81[a]	2.54[a]	2.29[b]	2.10[b]	1.85[b]	4.545	0.001*
Social recognition/ego enhancement	2.84[a]	2.39[a]	2.33[b]	2.51[b]	1.81[b]	4.199	0.002*
Exploration and evaluation of self	3.60[a]	3.20[b,c]	2.72[b]	2.95[b]	2.67[b]	9.658	0.000*
Opportunity to have a sexual adventure	2.78[a]	2.63[a]	2.46[a]	2.58[a]	1.59[b]	3.860	0.004*
Pull factor							
Culture and history	3.71[a]	3.37[b]	3.53[a]	3.49[a]	3.85[a]	2.651	0.033*
Nature, adventure offering (hiking, shark-cage diving, abseiling, etc.)	3.67[a]	3.38[a]	3.22[a]	3.17[a]	2.70[b]	3.442	0.009*

Notes: *Significance at the 5% level.
[a,b,c]Means with different superscripts indicate significant differences. For example, age groups 18–30 and 31–40 (mean values with superscript *a*) differed significantly from age groups 41–50, 51–60 and 61 and older (mean values with superscript *b*) in the push factors 'to escape from disapproving society to freely express gay identity' and 'social recognition and ego enhancement'. Age groups 41–50, 51–60 and 61 and older did not significantly differ from each other in terms of these push factors.

Table 5.5 ANOVA for comparison of pull factors by sexual identities ($n = 250$)

Pull factor	Gay	Lesbian	Bisexual	F-ratio	Sig. level
Gay/nude beach	2.75[a]	1.34[b]	2.57[a]	12.241	0.000*
Nightlife	3.28[a]	2.52[b]	3.03[a,b]	5.029	0.007*
Shopping facilities	3.18[a]	2.55[b]	3.24[a,b]	3.430	0.033*
Gay-friendly environment/friendliness of locals towards gays	3.89[a]	4.14[a]	3.41[b]	3.632	0.027*
Local gay culture/gay venues (gay village)	3.49[a]	2.86[b]	3.16[a,b]	3.880	0.021*
Culture and history (monument, heritage, arts, local customs)	3.63[a]	3.03[b]	3.05[b]	6.922	0.001*

*Significance at the 5% level.
[a,b]Means with different superscripts indicate significant differences. For example, lesbians (mean value with superscript b) differed significantly from gay and bisexual travellers (mean values with superscript a) in the pull factor 'gay/nude beach'. Gay and bisexual travellers did not significantly differ from each other in terms of this pull factor.

Comparisons of pull factors for different sexual identities

The travel motivations of gay, lesbian and bisexual travellers appear to differ according to their sexual identity. ANOVAs revealed statistically significant differences for the three sexual identities ($p < 0.05$) (Table 5.5) for some of the pull factors only. Lesbians attached lower importance to the pull factor 'gay/nude beach' (1.34[b]) when compared with gay and bisexual travellers. Further statistical differences emerged between gay and lesbian travellers in terms of 'nightlife' (3.28[a]; 2.52[b]), 'shopping facilities' (3.18[a]; 2.55[b]) and 'local gay culture/gay venues (gay village)' (3.49[a]; 2.86[b]) in that gay travellers regarded these factors to be more important than lesbians. The pull factor 'gay-friendly environment/friendliness of locals towards gays' (3.41[b]), appears to be a less important motivation for bisexual travellers when compared with the other two sexual identities, while gay men attached a higher importance to the 'culture and history' of a destination (3.63[a]) when compared with lesbians and bisexual men and women.

Comparisons of push and pull factors for different relationship status

The travel motivations of LGBT travellers appear to differ according to their relationship status (Table 5.6) for some of the push and pull factors. An inspection of the mean scores indicated that the push factors 'social interaction with other gay people' (3.38[a]), 'exploration and evaluation of self' (3.39[a]), and the 'opportunity to have a sexual adventure' (2.88[a]) were more important to single travellers, when compared with those who are married/in a civil union or in a relationship. Statistical differences in terms of the push factor 'opportunity to develop close friendships/romance' and the pull factor 'nightlife' emerged between single travellers (3.26[a]; 3.47[a]) and those who were married/in a civil union (2.79[b]; 2.90[b]) in that single travellers regarded these factors to be more important.

Table 5.6 ANOVA for comparison of push and pull factors by relationship status ($n = 250$)

Push factor	Single	In a relationship	Married/ civil union	F-ratio	Sig. level
Social interaction with other gay people	3.38[a]	3.02[b]	2.93[b]	5.201	0.006*
Exploration and evaluation of self (gain insight about self)	3.39[a]	3.01[b]	2.83[b]	7.234	0.001*
Opportunity to have a sexual adventure	2.88[a]	2.45[b]	2.24[b]	8.008	0.000*
Opportunity to develop close friendships/romance	3.26[a]	2.99[a,b]	2.79[b]	4.468	0.012*
Pull factor					
Nightlife	3.47[a]	3.18[a,b]	2.90[b]	7.296	0.001*

*Significance at the 5% level.
[a,b]Means with different superscripts indicate significant differences. For example, single LGBT travellers (mean value with superscript a) differed significantly from those who are married/in a civil union or relationship (mean values with superscript b) in the push factor 'social interaction with other gay people'. LGBT travellers who are married/in a civil union or relationship did not significantly differ from each other in terms of this push factor.

Comparisons of push and pull factors for different classifications of home environments

ANOVAs revealed a statistically significant difference among respondents travelling from a liberal environment and those travelling from a conservative environment ($p > 0.05$) (Table 5.7) for one push factor. To 'escape from disapproving society to freely express gay identity' (2.28[a]) was less important to those travelling from an open-minded city with a

Table 5.7 ANOVA for comparison of push factors by classification of home environment ($n = 250$)

Push factor	Open-minded city with a variety of gay life and venues	Closed-minded city with limited/ no gay life and venues	Village/rural area with limited/no gay life and venues	F-ratio	Sig. level
Escape from disapproving society to freely express gay identity	2.28[a]	2.91[b]	2.52[b]	7.283	0.001*

*Significance at the 5% level.
[a,b]Means with different superscripts indicate significant differences. For example, LGBT travellers travelling from open-minded cities (mean value with superscript a) differed significantly from those who travelled from closed-minded cities and village/rural areas (mean values with superscript b) in the push factor 'escape from disapproving society to freely express gay identity'. LGBT travellers who travelled from closed-minded cities and village/rural areas did not significantly differ from each other in terms of this push factor.

Table 5.8 ANOVA for comparisons of push and pull factors by openness of sexuality ($n = 250$)

Push factor	Conceal sexuality	Open about sexuality	Somewhat (partially) open about sexuality	F-ratio	Sig. level
Escape from disapproving society to freely express gay identity	3.24[a]	2.37[b]	2.53[b]	3.718	0.025*
Opportunity to have a sexual adventure	3.33[a]	2.50[b]	2.72[b]	3.607	0.028*
Pull factor					
Gay/nude beach	3.52[a]	2.63[b]	2.51[b]	3.735	0.025*

*Significance at the 5% level.

[a,b]Means with different superscripts indicate significant differences. For example, LGBT travellers who concealed their sexuality (mean value with superscript a) differed significantly from those who were open or somewhat open about their sexuality (mean values with superscript b) in the push factor 'escape from disapproving society to freely express gay identity'. LGBT travellers who were open or somewhat open did not significantly differ from each other in terms of this push factor.

variety of gay life and venues compared with those who travelled from village/rural areas or closed-minded cities.

Comparisons of push and pull factors for openness of sexuality

ANOVAs revealed statistically significant differences among those who concealed and those who were open about their sexuality ($p < 0.05$) (Table 5.8) for some of the push and pull factors. Those who concealed their sexuality attached more importance to the push factors 'to escape from disapproving society to freely express gay identity' (3.24[a]) and for 'opportunities to have a sexual adventure' (3.33[a]) and the pull factor 'gay/ nude beach' (3.52[a]) when compared with those who were open or somewhat open about their sexuality.

Discussion, Implications and Conclusion

There appears to be a lack of insight into the travel motivations and behaviours of LGBT travellers going to or, especially, coming from non-Western countries. This study marks one of the first attempts to investigate a sample of non-Western LGBT leisure travellers' holiday motivations to Cape Town, an under-researched African destination in the academic literature (Prayag, 2010).

The findings suggest that African LGBT travellers' push motivations, i.e. 'opportunities for rest and relaxation' and 'escaping from everyday life and daily routine', appear not to be influenced by sexual identity and are therefore not specific to these travellers, as the factors pushing LGBT individuals to travel are in line with those of mainstream travellers. The most important destination-specific pull attributes attracting LGBT travellers to Cape Town include the 'dramatic/beautiful landscape and scenery', the 'relaxing atmosphere' and the 'local food and wine'. The importance attached to the gay-related attributes, i.e. 'safety/security' and the 'gay-friendly' environment suggest that African LGBT travellers' sexual identity influences their pull motivations. However, some authors argue that as people are becoming more tolerant towards homosexuality, the need for 'gay-friendliness' appears to be diminishing (Blichfeldt *et al.*, 2011), which is not supported by the current findings and therefore does not seem to fully apply to African LGBT travellers. This could be due to Cape Town's unique 'gay-friendly' environment and tolerant society in comparison with destinations across South Africa and elsewhere on the African continent. These findings should, however, be carefully considered as they can easily create the perception that the LGBT travel market is homogeneous. For instance, would it be accurate to conclude that *most* LGBT travellers are not pushed to experience a sexual adventure, or that *most* are attracted to a gay-friendly environment? Further statistical analyses tested for significant differences in LGBT travellers' holiday motivations and found that there are several variables that suggest that LGBT travellers do not hold the same travel motivations or pursue the same holiday activities, and are therefore not homogeneous.

Firstly, younger LGBT travellers (between the ages of 18 and 40) place a higher importance on escaping from a hostile society. They seem to have a stronger need for ego-enhancement (status) and to discover themselves on holiday. Senior travellers (61 years and older) regard sexual opportunities as less important in comparison with younger travellers. It further appears as if 31–40 year old LGBT travellers are less interested in culture and history when compared with the other age groups, whereas senior travellers (61 years and older) appear to regard the adventure offering of the destination to be less important than the other age groups. These findings contradict Bansal and Eiselt's (2004) argument that it may be a cliché that older travellers are mostly interested in cultural and heritage sites, whereas younger travellers are more interested in the outdoors and adventure activities, as significant differences were found among younger and older age groups for these specific pull factors.

Secondly, the LGBT tourism studies that have included lesbians show that there are substantial differences in the travel motivations of lesbians and gay men (Ballegaard & Chor, 2009; Hughes, 2006; Pritchard *et al.*, 2000). This study therefore supports these previously conducted studies in that lesbians, when compared with gay and bisexual travellers, appear to attach less importance to the gay/nude beach, possibly due to sex and the body not playing a role in lesbians' identity to the same extent as they do in gay men's identity (Hughes, 2006). Gay travellers, when compared with lesbian travellers in particular, attach a higher importance to night-life, shopping facilities and the local gay culture/gay venues (gay village). Hughes and Deutsch (2010) found that the need for frequenting gay space rarely featured among older gay men, while Blichfeldt *et al.* (2013) claimed that the literature may over-emphasise the significance of gay space for gay holidays. It is, however, clear from the findings of this study that the local gay culture and gay venues of Cape Town were more important attributes sought by African gay men when compared with lesbian travellers in particular. African gay men also differ from other sexualities in terms of the higher importance attached to the culture/history of a destination. What is less well known is how bisexual travellers differ from gay and lesbian travellers in terms of holiday motivations. Results of Community Marketing & Insight's 10th Annual LGBT Community Survey (Community Marketing and Insights, 2016) showed no significant differences between gay versus bisexual men or lesbian versus bisexual women (UNWTO, 2017). The findings of this study therefore contradict Community Marketing & Insight's findings in that bisexual travellers indeed have different, although not entirely different, motivations to travel when compared with gay men and lesbians, i.e. a lower importance attached to a 'gay-friendly' environment.

Thirdly, single LGBT travellers place a higher importance on discovering themselves and social interaction with other gay people while holidaying and seem more inclined to travel for sexual adventures when compared with those who are married/in a civil union or in a relationship. Single travellers, when compared with those who are married/in a civil union in particular, also place a higher importance on the opportunity to develop close friendships/romance and the nightlife of Cape Town. According to Storr (2005: 21), the ability to be alone, i.e. single, is 'linked with self-discovery and self-realization; with becoming aware of one's deepest needs, feelings, and impulses' which, based on the current findings, appears to pull through to the holiday. A possible reason why single LGBT travellers, and other travellers, are motivated by a sexual adventure while on holiday, and develop a need to visit a nightclub to form close friendships/romance, might be due to their being 'unattached and because holidays might reduce inhibitions and thus increase the opportunity for sex' (Thomsen, 2008: 61) and/or romance.

Fourthly, those travelling from a liberal home environment attach less importance to escaping from a disapproving society, as this heteronormative environment does not seem to exist. This study therefore supports Clift and Forrest's (1999) and Herrera and Scott's (2005) findings, in that this need for escape applied to LGBT individuals who live in conservative environments that have a limited or no obvious gay community or gay space and who, therefore, have an increased need to escape the oppressive heteronormative home environments. Similarly, travellers who conceal their sexuality attach more importance to escaping from disapproving society, and for sexual adventures, supporting Ballegaard and Chor's

(2009) and Köllen and Lazar's (2012) findings that the need to escape heterosexism depends on whether the individual is open about his/her sexuality or not, as those who live an openly gay lifestyle may not feel a need to escape. Furthermore, the study supports Hughes and Deutsch's (2010) finding that those concealing their sexuality are more likely to travel in pursuit of a sexual adventure. This study also finds that the gay and nude beaches of Cape Town are more important to those who conceal their sexuality, possibly due to the lack of these destination attributes in the home environment, and their being unique to Cape Town when compared with other destinations on the African continent.

These findings provide an important marketing implication. In order to effectively attract LGBT travellers, different marketing strategies and promotional messages will be required for different LGBT travellers. Products and services designed for and promoted to LGBT travellers could be better tailored to their specific needs based on the variables that distinguish their travel motivations, i.e. age, sexual identity, relationship status, classification of home environment and openness of sexuality. Therefore, a single or broad-brush approach will be ineffective to successfully attract *all* LGBT travellers to a destination.

In conclusion, this research provides two significant contributions to the broader LGBT tourism literature: firstly, it contributes to the gap in the literature regarding the travel motivations of non-Western LGBT travellers; secondly, empirical evidence, albeit not universally representative of all African LGBT leisure travellers (given that only eight African nationalities participated in the study and all respondents were internet users), suggests that African LGBT travellers, at least those who visited Cape Town, are not homogeneous and that this market is more complex than previously understood.

The author acknowledges that sample sizes for some of the groups used as part of the ANOVAs are low. Forming statistical conclusions from small sample sizes could violate the normality of distribution required; however, this research should be considered exploratory and does not intend to provide conclusive evidence. The results are nevertheless considered important. Further limitations relating to this research include: (i) respondents self-selected to participate in this study, and findings may therefore be biased towards LGBT individuals that self-identify as such, resulting in those who conceal their sexuality being under-represented. However, respondents could opt to remain anonymous on the web, if they wished, which would not have been the case should personal interviews have been conducted; (ii) the researcher made a judgment about the characteristics (variables or data) to include in the survey. The push and pull factors were borrowed from secondary data sources and did not come from primary data, i.e. open-ended questions in the survey. Therefore, although tourism stakeholders were requested during pilot testing to add push and pull factors that were presumed to be of importance to LGBT travellers but not included in the survey, it may be possible that the final list of motivations was not exhaustive. Future research could implement a qualitative research method such as focus groups to investigate the deeper reasons as to why certain destination attributes and sociopsychological motivations are more important in non-Western LGBT travellers' holiday decision-making processes and travel behaviours. However, the fact that much of the LGBT population in the non-Western world remains hidden will make it difficult to find and interview them, particularly those who conceal their sexualities.

Notes

(1) 'Gay' is sometimes used to describe both male and female homosexuals, i.e. gay men and women, as a 'shorthand' term (Hughes, 2006: 2). In order to keep the writing style fluid, the term 'gay' is used throughout this chapter to cover both male and female homosexuals. To denote a specific gender (where required), gay men, gay women or lesbians are used.
(2) An individual having sexual desire for, or sexual activity with, persons of the same biological sex. In this chapter, the term 'gay' is used interchangeably depending on the context.
(3) A term used to describe the tourism activity of lesbian, gay, bisexual and transgender travellers. Also referred to as LGBT tourism.

References

Ballegaard, N. and Chor, J. (2009) Gay and lesbian tourism: Travel motivations, destination choices and holiday experiences of gays and lesbians. Unpublished Master's thesis, Copenhagen Business School.

Bansal, H. and Eiselt, H.A. (2004) Exploratory research of tourist motivations and planning. *Tourism Management* 25 (3), 387–396.

Beerli, A. and Martín, J.D. (2004) Tourists' characteristics and the perceived image of tourist destinations: A quantitative analysis – a case study of Lanzarote, Spain. *Tourism Management* 25 (5), 623–636.

Blichfeldt, B.S., Chor, J. and Ballegaard-Milan, N. (2011) It really depends on whether you are in a relationship: A study of 'gay destinations' from a tourist perspective. *Tourism Today* 11, 7–26.

Blichfeldt, B.S., Chor, J. and Ballegaard-Milan, N. (2013) Zoos, sanctuaries and turfs: Enactments and uses of gay spaces during the holidays. *International Journal of Tourism Research* 15 (5), 473–483.

Boekstein, M.S. (2012) Revitalising the healing tradition – health tourism potential of thermal springs in the Western Cape. Unpublished Doctor of Technology in Tourism and Hospitality Management thesis, Cape Peninsula University of Technology.

Clift, S. and Forrest, S. (1999) Gay men and tourism: Destinations and holiday motivations. *Tourism Management* 20 (5), 615–625. doi:10.1016/S0261-5177 (99)00032-1

Cohen, S.A., Prayag, G. and Moital, M. (2014) Consumer behavior in tourism: Concepts, influences and opportunities. *Current Issues in Tourism* 17 (10), 872–909.

Community Marketing and Insights (2016) *10th Annual LGBT Community Survey*. San Francisco: Community Marketing Inc. See https://www.communitymarketinginc. com/documents/CMI-10th_LGBT_Community_Survey_US_Profile.pdf (accessed 9 February 2021).

Croucher, S. (2002) South Africa's democratisation and the politics of gay liberation. *Journal of Southern African Studies* 28 (2), 315–330.

Dann, G.M.S. (1977) Anomie, ego-enhancement and tourism. *Annals of Tourism Research* 4 (4), 184–194.

DeBarros, L. (2016) Shocking scale of LGBT discrimination in South Africa revealed. *Mamba Online*, 29 November. See http://www.mambaonline.com/2016/11/29/shocking-scale-lgbt-discrimination-south-africa-revealed/ (accessed 12 September 2018).

Ersoy, G.K., Ozer, S.U. and Tuzunkan, D. (2012) Gay men and tourism: Gay men's tourism perspectives and expectations. *Procedia – Social and Behavioral Sciences* 41, 394–401.

Fisher, S. (2012) Table Mountain one of New7Wonders of nature. *Eyewitness News*, 03 May. See https://ewn.co.za/2012/05/03/Table-Mountain-one-of-New7Wonders-of-Nature (accessed 11 February 2021).

Fodness, D. (1994) Measuring tourist motivation. *Annals of Tourism Research* 21 (3), 555–581.

Gomes da Costa Santos, G. (2013) Decriminalising homosexuality in Africa: Lessons from the South African experience. In C. Lennox and M. Waites (eds) *Human Rights, Sexual Orientation and Gender Identity in the Commonwealth: Struggles for Decriminalisation and Change* (pp. 313–337). London: Human Rights Consortium.

Goossens, C. (2000) Tourism information and pleasure motivation. *Annals of Tourism Research* 27 (2), 301–321.

Hattingh, C. (2017) A typology of gay leisure travellers: An African perspective. Unpublished Doctor of Technology in Tourism and Hospitality Management thesis, Cape Peninsula University of Technology.

Hattingh, C. and Bruwer, J. (2020) Cape Town's gay village: from "gaytrified" tourism mecca to "heterosexualised" urban space. *International Journal of Tourism Cities* 6 (4), 907–928.

Hattingh, C. and Spencer, J.P. (2017) Salient factors influencing gay travellers' holiday motivations: A push-pull approach. *African Journal of Hospitality, Tourism and Leisure* 6 (4), 1–26.

Hattingh, C. and Spencer, J.P. (2020) Homosexual not homogeneous – a motivation-based typology of gay leisure travellers holidaying in Cape Town, South Africa. *Journal of Homosexuality* 67 (6), 768–792.

Herrera, S.L. and Scott, D. (2005) 'We gotta get out of this place!': Leisure travel among gay men living in a small city. *Tourism Review International* 8 (3), 249–262.

HRW (2016) Kenya: Court upholds forced anal exams. *Human Rights Watch*, 16 June. See https://www.hrw.org/news/2016/06/16/kenya-court-upholds-forced-anal-exams (accessed 12 September 2018).

HRW (2018) Kenya: Court finds forced anal exams unconstitutional. *Human Rights Watch*, 22 March. See https://www.hrw.org/news/2018/03/22/kenya-court-finds-forced-anal-exams-unconstitutional (accessed 12 September 2018).

Hu, Y. and Ritchie, J.R.B. (1993) Measuring destination attractiveness: A contextual approach. *Journal of Travel Research* 32 (2), 25–34.

Hughes, H.L. (2002) Gay men's holiday destination choice: A case of risk and avoidance. *International Journal of Travel Research* 4 (4), 299–312.

Hughes, H.L. (2005) The paradox of gay men as tourists: Privileged or penalized? *Tourism, Culture & Communication* 6 (1), 51–62.

Hughes, H.L. (2006) *Pink Tourism: Holidays of Gay Men and Lesbians*. Wallingford: CABI.

Hughes, H.L. and Deutsch, R. (2010) Holidays of older gay men: Age or sexual orientation as decisive factors? *Tourism Management* 31 (4), 454–463.

ILGA (2016) *State-Sponsored Homophobia. A World Survey of Sexual Orientation Laws: Criminalisation, Protection and Recognition*. Geneva: International Lesbian, Gay, Bisexual, Trans and Intersex Association. See http://ilga.org/

downloads/02_ILGA_State_Sponsored_Homophobia_2016_ENG_WEB_150516. pdf (accessed 28 January 2017).

Ilyayambwa, M. (2012) Homosexual rights and the law: A South African constitutional metamorphosis. *International Journal of Humanities and Social Science* 2 (4), 50–58.

Isaac, R. (2008) Understanding the behaviour of cultural tourists: Towards a classification of Dutch cultural tourists. Unpublished Doctor of Philosophy dissertation, NHTV Breda University of Applied Sciences.

Jackman, J. (2018) Police in Nigeria arrest 57 men for having gay sex. *Pink News*, 27 August. See https://www.pinknews.co.uk/2018/08/27/gay-sex-nigeria-police-arrest-57-men/?utm_source=Facebook&utm_medium=Buffer&utm_campaign=PN (accessed 17 August 2018).

Jago, L.K. (1997) Special events and tourism behaviour: A conceptualisation and an empirical analysis from a values perspective. Unpublished DPhil thesis, Victoria University.

Jara, M.K. (1998) Gay and lesbian rights: Forcing change in South Africa. *Southern African Report* 13 (3), 31.

Kassean, H. and Gassita, R. (2013) Exploring tourists' 'push and pull' motivations to visit Mauritius as a tourist destination. *African Journal of Hospitality, Tourism and Leisure* 2 (3), 1–13.

Kauhanen, S. (2015) Think pink in tourism – a study of LGBT+ tourism. Unpublished Bachelor of Tourism thesis, Laurea University of Applied Sciences.

Kennedy, B. (2006) Homosexuals in the periphery: Gay and lesbian rights in developing Africa. *Nebraska Anthropologist* 21, 59–68.

Khuong, M.N. and Ha, H.T.T. (2014) The influences of push and pull factors on the international leisure tourists' return intention to Ho Chi Minh City, Vietnam – a mediation analysis of destination satisfaction. *International Journal of Trade, Economics and Finance* 5 (6), 490–496.

Kim, S.S. and Lee, C. (2002) Push and pull relationships. *Annals of Tourism Research* 29 (1), 257–260.

Kim, S.S., Lee, C. and Klenosky, D.B. (2003) The influence of push and pull factors at Korean national parks. *Tourism Management* 24 (2), 169–180.

Kinnaird, V. and Hall, D. (1994) Conclusion: The way forward. In V. Kinnaird and D. Hall (eds) *Tourism: A Gender Analysis* (pp. 210–216). Chichester: Wiley.

Klenosky, D.B. (2002) The 'pull' of tourism destinations: A means–end investigation. *Journal of Travel Research* 40 (4), 385–395.

Köllen, T. and Lazar, S. (2012) Gay tourism in Budapest: An exploratory study on gay tourists' motivational patterns for travelling to Budapest. *American Journal of Tourism Management* 1 (3), 64–68.

Kutsch, T. (2013) Homosexuality still a crime in 38 African countries. *Aljazeera America*, 14 November. See http://america.aljazeera.com/articles/2013/11/14/senegala-s-criminalizationofhomosexualitypartofaregionaltrend.html (accessed 25 May 2018).

Luthans, F., Hodgetts, R.M. and Rosenkrantz, S.A. (1988) *Real Managers*. Cambridge, MA: Ballinger.

Månsson, M. and Østrup, J.H. (2007) Producing borders of sexuality – the complexity of gay destination marketing. Paper presented at the 16th Nordic Symposium in Tourism and Hospitality Research, Helsingborg, Sweden, 27–30 September.

Mullen, B. and Johnson, C. (1990) *The Psychology of Consumer Behaviour*. Hillsdale, NJ: Lawrence Erlbaum.

Mzantsi, S. (2017) South Africans detained in Tanzania for 'promoting homosexuality'. *Cape Times*, 23 October. See https://www.iol.co.za/capetimes/news/south-africans-detained-in-tanzania-for-promoting-homosexuality-11663994 (accessed 17 August 2018).

Nelson, K.G. (2014) Gay rights ruling in Kenya could reverberate through Africa. *TheWorld*, 17 April. See https://www.pri.org/stories/2018-04-17/gay-rights-ruling-kenya-could-reverberate-through-africa (accessed 13 September 2018).

Oh, H.C., Uysal, M. and Weaver, P.A. (1995) Product bundles and market segments based on travel motivations: A canonical correlation approach. *International Journal of Hospitality Management* 14 (2), 123–137.

Out LGBT Well-being (2016) *Hate Crimes against LGBT People in South Africa*. Pretoria: US Department of State. See https://out.org.za/wp-content/uploads/2020/10/Hate-Crimes-Against-LGBT-People-in-South-Africa-21-November-2016-Web.pdf (accessed 9 February 2021).

Prayag, G. (2003) An investigation into international tourists' perceptions of Cape Town as a holiday destination. Unpublished Master of Business Science thesis, University of Cape Town.

Prayag, G. (2010) Images as pull factors of a tourist destination: A factor-cluster segmentation analysis. *Tourism Analysis* 15 (2), 1–14.

Pritchard, A., Morgan, N.J., Sedgely, D. and Jenkins, A. (1998) Reaching out to the gay tourist: Opportunities and threats in an emerging market segment. *Tourism Management* 19 (3), 273–282.

Pritchard, A., Morgan, N.J., Sedgely, D., Khan, E. and Jenkins, A. (2000) Sexuality and holiday choices: Conversations with gay and lesbian tourists. *Leisure Studies* 19 (4), 267–282.

Reddy, V. (2014) Identity, law, justice: Thinking about sexual rights and citizenship in post-apartheid South Africa. In A.K. Nord and J. Luckscheiter (eds) *Perspectives: Political Analysis and Commentary from Africa: Struggle for Equality – Sexual Orientation, Gender Identity and Human Rights in Africa* (pp. 18–23). Cape Town: Heinrich Böll Foundation Southern Africa.

Retnam, S. (2012) Travel behavior among Malaysian gays: A comparison between Malay, Indian and Chinese ethnicities. Unpublished Master of Business Administration dissertation, University of Malaya.

Ro, H., Olson, E.D. and Choi, Y. (2017) An exploratory study of gay travelers: Sociodemographic analysis. *Tourism Review* 72 (1), 15–27.

Saunders, M., Lewis, P. and Thornhill, A. (2009) *Research Methods for Business Students* (5th edn). Harlow: Pearson.

Storr, A. (2005) *Solitude: A Return to the Self*. New York: Free Press.

Strudwick, P. (2014) Morocco releases British tourist jailed for 'homosexual acts'. *The Guardian*, 7 October. See https://www.theguardian.com/world/2014/oct/07/morocco-releases-british-tourist-jailed-homosexual-acts-ray-cole (accessed 10 September 2018).

Thomsen, A. (2008) Danish homosexual men in a tourism context. Unpublished Master of Tourism dissertation, Aalborg University.

Thoreson, R.R. (2008) Somewhere over the rainbow nation: Gay, lesbian and bisexual activism in South Africa. *Journal of Southern African Studies* 34 (3), 679–697.

Turnbull, D.R. and Uysal, M. (1995) An exploratory study of German visitors to the Caribbean: Push and pull motivations. *Journal of Travel & Tourism Marketing* 4 (2), 85–92.

UNWTO (2012) *Global Report on LGBT Tourism*. Madrid: World Tourism Organization. See https://www.e-unwto.org/doi/pdf/10.18111/9789284414581 (accessed 11 February 2021).

UNWTO (2017) *Second Global Report on LGBT Tourism*. Affiliate Members Global Reports Vol. 15. Madrid: World Tourism Organization. See https://www.e-unwto.org/doi/pdf/10.18111/9789284418619.

Uysal, M. and Jurowski, C. (1994) Testing the push and pull factors. *Annals of Tourism Research* 21 (4), 844–846.

Visser, G. (2002) Gay tourism in South Africa: Issues from the Cape Town experience. *Urban Forum* 13 (1), 85–94.

Visser, G. (2003) Gay men, tourism and urban space: Reflections on Africa's 'gay capital'. *Tourism Geographies* 5 (2), 168–189.

Voelker, J. (2016) The best food cities in the world right now. *CN Traveler*, 7 April. See https://www.cntraveler.com/galleries/2015-04-07/worlds-best-food-cities-readers-choice-awards-2014 (accessed 11 August 2018).

Vorobjovas-Pinta, O. and Hardy, A. (2016) The evolution of gay travel research. *International Journal of Tourism Research* 18 (4), 409–416.

Wockner, R. (2008) Two Spanish men arrested for alleged gay crimes in Gambia. *PrideSource*, 12 June. See https://pridesource.com/article/30767/ (accessed 31 August 2018).

Yuan, S. and McDonald, C. (1990) Motivational determinates of international pleasure travel. *Journal of Tourism Research* 29 (1), 42–44.

Zhou, L. (2005) Destination attributes that attract international tourists to Cape Town. Unpublished Master of Commerce research project, University of the Western Cape.

6 (Re)discovering Chinese Lesbian and Gay Travel

Xiongbin Gao

Introduction

Research into lesbian and gay travel in tourism scholarship has gained increasing interest over the past two decades (e.g. Clift & Forrest, 1999; Guaracino, 2007; Hughes, 2005; Melián-González *et al.*, 2011; Pritchard *et al.*, 1998). The inclusion of the lesbian and gay community in tourism research is crucial to affirming the increasing recognition of lesbian and gay consumers in the fast-growing tourism market. However, most studies of lesbian and gay travel have focused only on middle-class white gay men without children, hence homogenising the gay travel market (Vorobjovas-Pinta & Hardy, 2016). Lesbians and gay men from non-Western countries, therefore, have been significantly absent in the understanding of gay travel (Coon, 2012; Puar, 2002b). Moreover, some critics of the homogenisation of the gay travel market emphasise that lesbian and gay sexualities are seen as an emerging market segment in the supply-and-demand analysis in current research into lesbian and gay travel (Puar, 2002a; Waitt *et al.*, 2008). According to these scholars, reducing lesbian and gay subjects to (or at least overemphasising them as) a market profile sustains acceptable, non-threatening ideas of gayness, that is, homonormativity (Waitt *et al.*, 2008).

Unlike in Western countries where most of the research into lesbian and gay travel is conducted, the recognition of same-sex attraction in contemporary China remains ambiguous. While homosexuality has gained increased acceptance (especially in cyberspace) since the initiation of China's 'reform and opening' in late 1970s, any assumption that being lesbian and gay has ceased to be problematic in China would be inappropriate (Engebretsen & Schroeder, 2015; Jeffreys & Wang, 2018; Kong, 2011). Ho *et al.* (2018: 494) caution that what we have been witnessing in the past four decades is not a progressive '"freeing" of sexuality from "repression"' but a continuous reconstruction of new non-liberating forms of sexual subjectivity. For instance, recent empirical studies (Kam, 2013; Zheng, 2015) have revealed that homosexuality is continually discriminated against and marginalised in China, if not outright repressed. In this case, assuming that homosexuals' travel patterns and experience differ

89

from those of privileged white gay travellers is reasonable. This condition is confirmed by Wong and Tolkach's (2017) study on gay travellers from six Asian cities, including three cities of Chinese origin, Shanghai, Hong Kong and Taipei. Their analysis demonstrates that Asian gay men's travel preferences differ from those of Western gay men.

Critics consider the gay travel market as homogenising and 'homo-normalising' (Vorobjovas-Pinta & Hardy, 2016; Waitt *et al.*, 2008); thus, exploring lesbians' and gay men's travel activities in the non-Western context, such as China, enriches our understanding of lesbian and gay travellers. However, studies on lesbian and gay travel in the Chinese context are limited. Therefore, this chapter aims at building foundations for future exploration of Chinese lesbian and gay travel. Drawing upon the research into homosexuality in China, this chapter clarifies the topic of Chinese lesbian and gay lives that has yet to be introduced to tourism research. The implications of this topic are discussed with reference to existing gay travel literature. The chapter concludes with opportunities and challenges for future research on Chinese lesbian and gay travel. Before discussing the main body of this chapter, it is noteworthy that this chapter focuses primarily on lesbian and gay travellers from mainland China. Due to different sociopolitical environments, lesbian and gay lives in mainland China can vary considerably from those in other Chinese societies, such as Hong Kong and particularly Taiwan, where same-sex marriage was legally recognised in May 2019 (Kong, 2019). Nevertheless, these societies simultaneously share certain traditional Chinese family values that influence their citizens' experience of sexual identity (Jeffreys & Wang, 2018; Kong, 2011). I do not intend to analyse those distinctions and resemblances but aim to clarify that although certain literature referred to in the following discussion is not based on mainland China (e.g. Chou, 2000; Liu & Ding, 2005), they have valuable implications for understanding mainland Chinese lesbians and gay men.

Same-Sex Eroticism in China: From Tolerance to Stigmatisation

Throughout China's history, same-sex eroticism had been largely tolerated as it was not incompatible with heterosexual marriage, that is, marriage based not on 'sexual desire or love but the obligation to continue the family line' (Chou, 2000: 23). To marry and reproduce is central to fulfilling one's familial and social obligations, especially with regard to filial piety in Confucian ethics. However, although such obligations were performed, same-sex relationships outside marriage were not explicitly condemned (Hinsch, 1990). This cultural tolerance reflects male elites' sexual privileges in the patriarchal marital system (Chou, 2000); however, sexual relations between women were also not explicitly prohibited (Sang, 2003). Abundant literature on same-sex relationships and practices between men and between women suggests a vibrant culture of homoeroticism in traditional China (Ruan, 1991).

Cultural tolerance of same-sex eroticism began to fade as the Western concept of 'sex' and 'sexuality', among other modern Western ideas and science, was introduced to China at the turn of the 20th century (Chou, 2000; Hinsch, 1990). In 1912–1949, a 'reconfigured interpretation of homoerotic relationships as immoral, deviant, decadent and, ultimately, the cause of a weak nation' gradually occurred in the Republic of China (ROC). During this period, the term *tongxinglian*, which refers to same-sex love (the translation of homosexuality), emerged in the Chinese language (Zheng, 2015: 39). Homosexuality stigmatisation continued in the Maoist period in China from 1949 to 1976. Although homosexuality was not explicitly outlawed during this period, it became the target of harassment, persecution and administrative and disciplinary sanctions (Li, 2006). In addition, 'marriage was highlighted as a social cause and the fulfilment of a social responsibility to produce children for the communist state'; thus, those who did not marry and did not have children were considered 'socially irresponsible and harmful to the socialist state' (Zheng, 2015: 41). Under such circumstances, the majority of homosexual individuals conceal their sexuality, marry their opposite-sex partner and have children (Li, 2006).

In Post-Mao China, a reconfiguration of sexual culture began to occur due to the unprecedented importation of Western culture enabled by the 'reform and opening' policy initiated by Mao's successor, Deng Xiaoping, in 1978 (Jeffreys & Yu, 2015). Although homosexuality was discussed during this Chinese sexual culture transformation in the 1980s, it continued to be stigmatised. That is, it has been pathologised and (ambiguously) criminalised, respectively, by being 'classified as a sexual disorder in the first version of the Chinese Classification of Mental Disorder' and 'increasingly associated with (and hence penalised as a) type of *liumang zui* ("hooliganism")'[1] (Kong, 2016: 500).

Lesbian and gay communities gradually emerged in the 1990s (Kam, 2013; Zheng, 2015). The deletion of hooliganism and the removal of homosexuality from the list of mental illnesses in 1997 and 2001, respectively, indicates that homosexuality shifted its definition from being deviant and pathological (Ho *et al.*, 2018). In addition, Chinese lesbian and gay space has increased (Engebretsen & Schroeder, 2015; Kong, 2011). However, such space is often monitored; for example: bars and bathhouses inhabited by lesbians and gays are periodically raided and closed down to maintain 'public morality' and 'social order'; homosexual content on the internet, including lesbian and gay websites, are censored; lesbian and gay gatherings are treated as illegal unless approved by the state; and gay-affiliated non-governmental health organisations have to take a 'non-confrontational' approach to gain legitimacy from the government (Cao & Guo, 2016; Kong, 2011; Zheng, 2015).

Various events in the past decade have illuminated positive changes towards lesbian and gay rights in China. These events have ranged from the PRC government's acceptance of the United Nations' (UN) proposal to progress anti-discrimination legislation in 2013 to the landmark case filed by Sun Wenlin in Chinese courts in 2016.[2] However, these positive changes are not without ambivalence. For instance, tighter restriction has been imposed on lesbian and gay content on the internet and social media in recent years (*South China Morning Post*, 2019). Making an assumption, let alone a conclusion, about public opinion on homosexuality in China remains a challenge. For instance, the 2016 United Nations Development Programme's (UNDP) Human Development Report (United Nations Development Programme, 2016) indicates that China's general public have a predominantly positive attitude towards sexual minorities. On the contrary, Xie and Peng's (2018) study suggests that a majority of Chinese citizens considers same-sex sexual behaviour as 'always wrong'. Although the 2016 UNDP Report and Xie and Peng's (2018) analysis are based on data collected at different times and through different sample sizes,[3] their stark contrast still illustrates deeply divided public opinions towards homosexuality in China. Chinese sexual minorities generally tend to 'stay in the closet' as noted in the 2016 UNDP Report. Thus, assuming that Chinese lesbians and gay men continue to face major difficulties in negotiating their sexual identity is reasonable.

Lesbian and Gay Lives in Contemporary China

Chinese lesbian and gay individuals in present-day China identify themselves with the most popular term, *tongzhi*, which is often translated as 'comrades' and literally means 'same spirit or same goal' (Chou, 2000; although lesbians increasingly tend to describe themselves as *lala*, see Kam, 2013). *Tongzhi* is celebrated for its positive connotation and cultural specificity as, respectively, opposed to homosexuality, which was considered as a pathologising medical term, and 'gay', 'lesbian', 'queer', etc., which are Anglo-Saxon terms (Chou, 2000). However, some suggest that the popularity of the term has been overstated (Lau *et al.*, 2017). In Bao's (2012) study of gay spaces in Shanghai, the terms 'gay' and 'homosexuality' are also frequently used by transnational, multilingual same-sex attracted young men and older (often married) men, respectively. In addition, as Bao (2012) observes, the construction of *tongzhi* identity is predominated by the rhetoric of *suzhi* (quality). *Suzhi* is a popular rhetoric in post-Mao China utilised by the government to cultivate citizens and legitimise social inequalities based on location, class and education. This phenomenon should draw our attention to inequality within the lesbian and gay communities. For instance, urban and middle-class *tongzhi* often eagerly distinguish themselves from *tongzhi* from rural areas and 'money boys' (gay male sex workers), who are considered as the 'bad' *tongzhi* (with low *suzhi*) that 'pollute' the *tongzhi* community (Ho *et al.*, 2018; Zheng, 2015).[4] Although this chapter does not intend to discuss the identity preference among Chinese lesbians and gay men or the complicated hierarchy within the *tongzhi* community, the lesbian and gay identity in contemporary China must be acknowledged as a continuously contested and fractured category (Ho, 2010; Wong, 2010).

Regardless of the multiplicity of experiences, lesbian and gay lives in contemporary China are often represented by two interrelated issues: (1) whether or not to tell their parents about their sexuality and (2) how to avoid heterosexual marriage (Jeffreys & Yu, 2015). Although these issues are a partial representation, analysing how they are experienced can provide valuable implications for understanding Chinese lesbian and gay travel as demonstrated in the next section. The issue of 'coming out' to one's parents and marriage seem to be the major concerns for Chinese lesbian and gay individuals, among various difficulties. To marry and to reproduce offspring are the fundamental practices of filial piety that continue to be influential, and marriage is a universal norm. It has been reported that by the age of 34, 93.6% of men and 98.2% of women in mainland China had been married (Ho *et al.*, 2018). Thus, same-sex relationships imply abandoning the duties as a son or daughter and disappointing one's parents (Hu & Wang, 2013). Therefore, lesbian and gay individuals face the predicament between living a homosexual life and entering a heterosexual marriage to meet society's and their family's expectations, particularly those of parents (Chou, 2000; Kam, 2013; Miège, 2009).

Lesbians and gay men avoid social and familial pressure regarding marriage through various strategies. Firstly, they 'go out' (*chuzou*), that is, 'moving away from their place of birth and family home' to metropolitan cities where lesbian and gay culture and community are better developed (Jeffreys & Yu, 2015). Thus, they can pursue a homosexual life for various periods without being constantly pressured by parents and other family members to get married. Nonetheless, it is often a temporary solution as the notion of 'family' is deeply valued in Chinese culture. Therefore, one is unlikely be completely disconnected from one's family. In addition, through 'going out', homosexual life is likely to remain secretive in many aspects, considering that gay and lesbian communities (even in metropolitan cities in China) remain marginal and are often sealed off from society (Zheng, 2015). Moreover, 'going out' should probably be situated within the broader context of mass labour migration from the countryside to urban areas in China since the mid-1980s. That is, migrant distinction is a significant element in the rhetoric of *suzhi*, which is relevant to inequality within Chinese lesbian and gay communities or Chinese society, in general (Zheng, 2015). Hence, migrants who 'go out' to pursue a homosexual life in cities may experience discrimination from their urban counterparts.

Secondly, lesbians and gay men 'come home' (*huijia*), that is, bringing back their same-sex partner to the family home without declaring their same-sex relationship or homosexuality. The intention is to obtain acquiescence from the parents in non-confrontational ways (Jeffreys & Yu, 2015). The significance of 'coming home' lies not so much in the actual practice as in its implications as an indigenous model of queer sexuality that intervenes against the hegemony of the Western-origin 'coming out' model. Chou (2000: 20) argues that, as a confrontational model, coming out is culturally problematic in China as it is founded on the Western value of individualism, whereas in traditional Chinese culture a person exists 'only in the context of family and social relationships' and '[e]veryone is, first, a daughter or a son of her or his parents, which is a role in the social–familial system, before she or he can be anything else'. Coming home is formulated by Chou (2001: 36) as 'a negotiative process of bringing one's sexuality into the family–kin network, not by singling out same-sex eroticism as a site for conceptual discussion but by constructing same-sex relationships in terms of family–kin categories'. However, the model of coming home is construed through silent tolerance of same-sex eroticism in Chinese tradition instead of an open acceptance (Ho et al., 2018). Liu and Ding (2005) criticise that the interface between tolerance and reticence exemplified in coming home can inadvertently contribute to maintaining 'proper' sexual relations. That is, in this model, the subjects of queer must remain in the marginal spaces of the social–familial continuum to maintain its harmony from which they are excluded. The harmonious picture of the Chinese family portrayed by Chou (2000, 2001) is questionable as most Chinese families are unlikely to accept lesbian and gay members and many Chinese lesbian and gay individuals have to enter heterosexual marriages (Jeffreys & Yu, 2015).

Most Chinese lesbians and gay men will probably choose to marry an opposite-sex partner without revealing their sexual orientation while living a 'double life', for example secretly engaging in same-sex practices outside the marriage (Zheng, 2015). However, a unique arrangement of consensual marriage has emerged between lesbians and gay men referred to as *xinghun*, that is, a cooperative/contract/nominal/formality marriage (Choi & Luo, 2016; Huang & Brouwer, 2018b; Liu, 2013). This marriage arrangement allows both parties to 'present themselves to family and work circle as a heterosexual couple' (Jeffreys & Yu, 2015: 91), hence becoming an attractive way to reconcile between preserving space for one's queer sexuality and maintaining familial harmony. However, its success relies chiefly on the 'realness' of heterosexual marriage; that is, for *xinghun* to appear 'real', the gay man and lesbian concerned need to follow gender-specific expressions and play gender-specific roles aligned to the heteronormative understanding of masculinity and femininity (Engebretsen, 2017; Liu, 2013). In addition, concerns such as legal issues regarding finance, pressure of having children (usually from parents on both sides) and the subsequent concerns about child-rearing further complicate such marriages. Thus, it is argued that 'success can only be relative and temporary' (Engebretsen, 2017: 177–178). Nevertheless, Huang and

Brouwer (2018b) acknowledge that *xinghun* may impair the institution of heterosexual marriage. As both 'same-sex partners of some Chinese queers are actively involved in the negotiation and making of such a hetero-marital union', *xinghun* may provide opportunities for practising a queer kinship structure, that is, 'a hetero-marital relationship that includes homosexual intimacy' (Huang & Brouwer, 2018b: 155).

In China, the incessant efforts of developing a culture-specific model of queer sexuality obscure the prominence of the discourse of coming out in a globalising world (Huang & Brouwer, 2018a; Zheng, 2015). However, the discourse of 'coming out' in China does not remain the same as that in Western societies. Bao (2012) notes the nuances between the 'coming out' politics in China (at least among certain queer subjects) and that in the West. For instance, the Chinese aesthetics of 'implicitness' is embedded in the self-identifying phrase 'wo shi gay', which means 'I am gay'. The English word 'gay' is seldom translated into Chinese. The phrase is frequently used by transnational and multilingual gay men in Shanghai in that one does not need to clearly articulate another's (homo)sexuality. It is argued that 'the English term "gay" in this context can be an "out" strategy and a closet' (Bao, 2012: 109). Hence, Bao (2012) highlights 'the complexities of the "closet" and "coming out" politics in the Chinese context', arguing that 'for gays and lesbians in China, one does not need to be completely "in" or "out", and [b]eing "in" and "out" depends on the particular social setting and on the person that they are with' (Bao, 2012: 109).

Implications for Chinese Lesbian and Gay Travel

To my knowledge, research on Chinese lesbian and gay travel is non-existent, except for Liu and Chen's (2010) contribution published in a Chinese journal. Liu and Chen's (2010) research focuses on the travel behaviour of 'post-1980' (born in the 1980s) Chinese lesbians. These lesbians travel to avoid the pressure imposed on them in the heteronormative home environment and to spend quality time with their same-sex partner. Lesbian travel emphasises the going out strategy, as the desire for a temporary escape from the restrictive environment for homosexuality can be identified in both practices. If 'going out' to metropolitan cities within China has been identified as the popular choice for the pursuit of a homosexual life, then it is logical to ask: 'Where do Chinese lesbians and gay men "escape" to in their travel?'

Given the 'escape' and 'romance' motives of the Chinese lesbians in Liu and Chen's (2010) study, a majority of them indicated that the degree of acceptance of homosexuality in a destination affects their choice of travel destination. Furthermore, in their study of Asian gay travellers, including Chinese participants, Wong and Tolkach (2017) observe that those from conservative societies generally prefer to travel to destinations where homosexuality is widely accepted.[5] Therefore, Chinese lesbian and gay travellers who resemble their Western counterparts are assumed to long for a safe and non-judgmental environment where they can express their sexuality in tourism destinations (Hughes, 2002; Waitt & Markwell, 2006).

However, perceiving lesbian and gay travel as an opportunity to negotiate and experience queer sexuality has certain issues. To begin with, regardless of the rapid growth of Chinese outbound tourism, the Chinese passport remains relatively 'weak'; that is, a visa is often required for Chinese citizens when travelling abroad (World Tourism Organization & China Tourism Academy, 2019). Most gay-friendly destinations are located in developed Western countries (see, for instance, Asher & Lyric, 2019) which have restrictive visa policies towards Chinese tourists and are arguably costly to visit. Thus, Chinese lesbians and gay men are likely to have limited access to such destinations.

Although China is one of the least gay-friendly countries according to Asher & Lyric's (2019) index, gay space does exist within China, particularly in urban agglomerations such as Beijing and Shanghai, as indicated by the 'going out' strategy. Through visiting such spaces, Chinese lesbian and gay travellers can arguably practise 'escape'. However, the point is not to congratulate gay-friendly destinations and gayness while condemning those where gay space is often relegated to the 'underground'. Considerable focus on the pursuit of gay-friendliness in destinations can distract us from investigating the underlying racial, class and gender assumptions of liberation.

If lesbian and gay travel is indeed 'an ironic marker of an elitist cosmopolitan mobility', as Puar (2002b: 942) has suggested, then the current hierarchy of mobility must be considered. This hierarchy allows most Westerners and non-Western elites to travel with ease while restricting the movements of the rest (Cohen & Cohen, 2015). Zheng's (2015) research has demonstrated that differentiated accessibility to various gay venues (e.g. bars, bathhouses and public parks) is a characteristic of the economic and social stratification of the Chinese gay community. In the context of tourism, such stratification is likely linked to distinguishing viable consumers of the gay travel market from those who are not. These viable consumers are presumably characterised by their economic, social and cultural ability to afford transnational trips to renowned gay destinations.

Future research on Chinese lesbian and gay travel can learn from extant (mostly Western) research about the awareness of the homogenising and homo-normalising tendency of gay travel marketing (Vorobjovas-Pinta & Hardy, 2016; Waitt et al., 2008). The notion of 'market' may exclude less visible lesbian and gay individuals who engage in travel activities that may not be marketed (and consumed) in terms of 'lesbian-ness/gayness'. Wong and Tolkach (2017) have pointed out that some Asian, including Chinese, gay travellers may prefer to conceal their sexuality and travel to destinations that negatively view homosexuality rather than to avoid them. In the Chinese context, such concealment probably signifies a lack of choice as much as preference. That is, Chinese gay men and lesbians are likely to travel domestically and to less gay-friendly destinations that they can access easily (with their sexuality mostly concealed) rather than not to travel at all. These less visible Chinese lesbian and gay travellers should not be overlooked.

The failure to attend to lesbian and gay travellers who do not identify with the concept of lesbian and gay travel in the extant gay travel research has been noted in Vorobjovas-Pinta and Hardy's (2016) review. One group of such travellers belongs to lesbian and gay families. Although gayness is embedded in a lesbian and gay family structure and same-sex parents tend to avoid homophobic destinations, their holidays are more family-centric than gay-centric (Lucena *et al.*, 2015; Community Marketing and Insights, 2014, in Vorobjovas-Pinta & Hardy, 2016). However, this 'lesbian and gay family' idea arguably relies on the legal recognition and public acceptance of same-sex marriage, which has to yet be found in contemporary China. Thus, Chinese lesbians' and gay men's family travel may provide valuable cases for exploring travel activities alternative to those of the 'homonormative' lesbian and gay families emerging in the West.

Family tourism in China has been growing rapidly (Wu & Wall, 2016). Confucian ethics on child-rearing, eldercare for family members and the importance of extended families have important implications for understanding Chinese family tourism (Wu & Wall, 2016). These attributes affect Chinese lesbian and gay travellers as indicated by the impact of Confucian ethics of filial piety on their (family) lives. In this case, Chinese lesbian and gay individuals will likely engage in various travel activities with their parents, relatives and children.

Wong and Tolkach (2017) note that, in Asian contexts, when travelling in a large group of families (or friends) that includes gay and straight members, gay venues are generally perceived by gay members as not suitable. However, their research does not explicate whether the sexuality of the gay members is known to other group members, though avoiding gay venues may be reasonably understood as an effort of concealing one's homosexuality. Nevertheless, I propose that this finding can be interpreted if translated into the Chinese context. Firstly, Bao's (2012) remark on the ambiguity of being 'in' or 'out' states that family travel can be considered as a setting where a lesbian or gay man must stay in the closet, whereas travelling singly or as a homosexual couple can be a setting where one can be 'out' (as indicated in Wong & Tolkach, 2017). In this case, the concept of 'travel companions' may be more relevant than that of 'lesbian and gay destinations' in understanding Chinese lesbian and gay travel. This phenomenon is implied in Wong and Tolkach's (2017) remark. That is, the preference for gay space, rather than being a primary concern as often is the case in Western lesbian and gay travel (Vorobjovas-Pinta & Hardy, 2016), is significantly influenced by the sexual orientation of the travel companions.

Secondly, avoidance of gay venues when travelling in a large group of families or friends can be interpreted through Liu and Ding's (2005) critique of the reticence in 'coming home', especially if the sexuality of the gay members is known by other group members. Thus, the gay members must maintain harmony within the heteronormative group by eliminating signs of gayness. In this case, they give up visiting gay venues. From this perspective, travel activities labelled as 'lesbian and gay', whether featuring lesbian and gay destinations, spaces, products or travel companions, reflect lesbian and gay individuals' heterosexual hegemony (a point also remarked in Waitt *et al.*, 2008). Thus, the marketability of lesbian and gay travel may neglect the mechanism by which lesbian and gay individuals are marginalised in the heteronormative tourism world. That is, homosexual travellers differ from heterosexual travellers premised on that marginalisation. Hence, investigation into lesbian and gay travel in a heteronormative setting, such as family travel by Chinese lesbians and gay men, is as important as that in lesbian- and gay-specific settings.

Xinghun families, especially those who have children, can be an interesting case for exploring the complex interplay of homosexual and heterosexual norms in various travel settings for Chinese lesbian and gay individuals. In general, investigation into the daily organisation of *xinghun* families is limited, especially with regard to child-rearing. A child's knowledge about the *xinghun* nature of his/her family would be a primary concern. Thus, the following questions about tourism are worth considering in the study of *xinghun* families. How is a family holiday arranged? Considering that the same-sex partners of the parents are often closely involved in such a hetero-marital union (Huang & Brouwer, 2018b), does the family holiday involve the child and parents only or the child and both the same-sex couples? Do the same-sex couples respectively travel with the child, or does each same-sex couple travel as a couple, leaving the child to the other same-sex couple? How do these different arrangements affect travel motivations, behaviour and experience? The travel of *xinghun* families is crucial not only to Chinese lesbian and gay travel but also to gaining valuable insights into the phenomenon of *xinghun* per se.

Conclusion

This chapter has outlined the understanding of Chinese lesbian and gay lives through a literature review on sexuality in China and discussed the implications of such an understanding for future research into Chinese lesbian and gay travel. Thus, the chapter provides foundations for future exploration of lesbian and gay travel in the Chinese context, hence contributing to a new research area. The chapter also responds to Vorobjovas-Pinta and Hardy's (2016) call for the diversification of gay travel research. The exploration of Chinese lesbian and gay travel not only challenges the homogenisation of the global Western-centric gay travel market but also urges us to rethink the concept of a gay travel market. The acceptance of homosexuality in China remains ambiguous and lags behind many Western countries. Thus, in the Chinese context, if most lesbian and gay travellers cannot, or prefer not to, travel openly as lesbian and gay, then should they not be included in the gay travel market? Is it possible to reinvent the gay travel market to accommodate the less visible and feasible demand for tourism characterised by gayness (and lesbian-ness)? Such rethinking may enable the gay travel market to expose its elitism (Puar, 2002b) and open up possibilities for a more inclusive understanding of the various forms of travel performed by lesbians and gay men. Particularly, family travel is given as a valuable case for exploring the multifaceted travel performed by Chinese lesbians and gay men. Unlike the nuclear lesbian and gay family in Western countries, research on Chinese lesbian and gay family travel must consider the Confucian ethics of filial piety and value of family harmony in addition to the importance of child-rearing. Chinese lesbian and gay members' engagement in the primarily heteronormative setting of family travel calls into question the straightforward distinction between 'staying in the closet when in the home environment' ('in') and 'being out of the closet when travelling out of the home environment to gay destinations' ('out'), which is often assumed in the tourism-as-escape formulation. Questions about the family travel of lesbians and gay men involved in *xinghun* can also bring a unique queer perspective to understanding lesbian and gay family travel, which has only begun to receive research interest and remains Western-centric. In the broadest sense, the chapter has demonstrated that Chinese lesbian and gay travel can be a valuable case on which we can further reflect upon the homogenising and homo-normalising tendency in the currently Western-centric gay travel research (Vorobjovas-Pinta & Hardy, 2016; Waitt *et al.*, 2008).

However, research on Chinese lesbian and gay travel faces immense challenges given the difficulty in conducting sexuality research in China. The country's sociopolitical context has considered sexuality as a source of social instability (Ho *et al.*, 2018). Therefore, researchers are inclined to 'avoid[ing] being too critical, especially when dealing with potentially politically sensitive issues' (Ho *et al.*, 2018: 492). On the one hand, Chinese sexuality studies remain dominated by biomedical models that frame homosexuality under the notion of 'public health' to be openly discussed and researched (Kong, 2016). Consequently, the radical politicisation of sex, desire and identity is eliminated in these studies (Kong, 2016). Ho *et al.* (2018) also observe that although radical voices on the matter of sexuality appeared in China in the early 2000s, they are rapidly minimised due to the intensification of authoritarianism. On the other hand, most of the analytical and critical accounts of lesbian and gay lives in China (including those referenced in this chapter) are produced by Taiwanese and Hong Kong researchers and overseas Chinese scholars (Ho *et al.*, 2018). Although they seemingly face less limitation than domestic

Chinese scholars, they often encounter challenges such as onerous negotiations to gain access to certain research settings (Engebretsen & Schroeder, 2015). Additionally, China's tourism research tends to privilege topics closely related to the state's orientation and industry trends, such as tourism development and planning (Bao *et al.*, 2014; Huang & Chen, 2016), where lesbian and gay travel is often excluded. Although this chapter has discussed Chinese lesbian and gay travel under such circumstances as an important research area, additional efforts from other researchers are urgently needed to further develop this research area.

Notes

(1) Hooliganism was a general term that referred to myriad forms of social misbehaviour. Although homosexuality was not specified on the list of hooliganism, same-sex attracted people (especially men) were often arrested or harassed under this catch-all crime (see Kong, 2016). Hence, one may argue that although homosexuality has never been officially considered as a crime in China, it was criminalized ambiguously through hooliganism.

(2) Sun Wenlin sued the Civil Affairs Bureau in the city of Changsha which refused Sun and his same-sex partner Hu Mingliang's request to be registered as a married couple in June 2015. This case was accepted by a court in Changsha in January 2016. On 13 April, this case was dismissed shortly after the hearing began. However, it was regarded as a landmark case in China's lesbian and gay community as it was the first of its kind.

(3) Xie and Peng's analysis is based on data from the 2013 Chinese General Social Surveys whereas the UNDP survey was conducted in 2015. The analytical sample is 28,454 and 11,058 for the UNDP report and Xie and Peng's (2018) study, respectively.

(4) Considering the complication embedded in the term *tongzhi*, I do not intend to use it in this chapter.

(5) The extensive reference to Wong and Tolkach's (2017) study about Asian gay travellers throughout this chapter does not imply that Chinese gay (and lesbian) travellers are simply the same as other Asian gay travellers. However, certain insights into Chinese lesbian and gay travel can be obtained from their study which includes participants from mainland China (Shanghai) and other Chinese cities (Hong Kong and Taipei). Given the lack of research focusing on Chinese lesbian and gay travellers, such insights should be valued.

References

Asher & Lyric (2019) The worst (& safest) countries for LGBTQ+ travel in 2019. *Asher & Lyric*, 12 November. See https://www.asherfergusson.com/lgbtq-travel-safety/.

Bao, H. (2012) Queering/querying cosmopolitanism: Queer spaces in Shanghai. *Culture Unbound: Journal of Current Cultural Research* 4, 97–120.

Bao, J., Chen, G. and Ma, L. (2014) Tourism research in China: Insights from inside. *Annals of Tourism Research* 45, 167–181.

Cao, J. and Guo, L. (2016) Chinese 'Tongzhi' community, civil society, and online activism. *Communication and the Public* 1 (4), 504–508.

Choi, S.Y.P. and Luo, M. (2016) Performative family: Homosexuality, marriage and intergenerational dynamics in China. *British Journal of Sociology* 67 (2), 260–280.

Chou, W. (2000) *Tongzhi: Politics of Same-Sex Eroticism in Chinese Societies*. Binghamton, NY: Haworth Press.

Chou, W. (2001) Homosexuality and the cultural politics of Tongzhi in China. *Journal of Homosexuality* 40 (3–4), 27–46.

Clift, S. and Forrest, S. (1999) Gay men and tourism: Destinations and holiday motivations. *Tourism Management* 20 (5), 615–625. doi:10.1016/S0261-5177 (99)00032-1

Cohen, E. and Cohen, S.A. (2015) A mobilities approach to tourism from emerging world regions. *Current Issues in Tourism* 18 (1), 11–43.

Coon, D.R. (2012) Sun, sand, and citizenship: The marketing of gay tourism. *Journal of Homosexuality* 59 (4), 511–534.

Engebretsen, E.L. (2017) Under pressure: Lesbian-gay contract marriages and their patriarchal bargains. In G. Santos and S. Harrell (eds) *Transforming Patriarchy: Chinese Families in the Twenty-First Century* (pp. 163–181). Seattle, WA: University of Washington Press.

Engebretsen, E.L. and Schroeder, W.F. (eds) (2015) *Queer/Tongzhi China: New Perspectives on Research, Activism and Media Cultures*. Copenhagen: NIAS Press.

Guaracino, J. (2007) *Gay and Lesbian Tourism: The Essential Guide for Marketing*. Oxford: Elsevier.

Hinsch, B. (1990) *Passions of the Cut Sleeve: The Male Homosexual Tradition in China*. London: University of California Press.

Ho, L.W.W. (2010) *Gay and Lesbian Subculture in Urban China*. Abingdon: Routledge.

Ho, P.S.Y., Jackson, S., Cao, S. and Kwok, C. (2018) Sex with Chinese characteristics: Sexuality research in/on 21st-century China. *Journal of Sex Research* 55 (4–5), 486–521.

Hu, X. and Wang, Y. (2013) LGB identity among young Chinese: The influence of traditional culture. *Journal of Homosexuality* 60 (5), 667–684.

Huang, S. and Brouwer, D.C. (2018a) Coming out, coming home, coming with: Models of queer sexuality in contemporary China. *Journal of International and Intercultural Communication* 11 (2), 97–116.

Huang, S. and Brouwer, D.C. (2018b) Negotiating performances of 'real' marriage in Chinese queer *Xinghun*. *Women's Studies in Communication* 41 (2), 140–158.

Huang, S. and Chen, G. (2016) Current state of tourism research in China. *Tourism Management Perspective* 20, 10–18.

Hughes, H.L. (2002) Gay men's holiday destination choice: A case of risk and avoidance. *International Journal of Tourism Research* 4, 299–312.

Hughes, H.L. (2005) A gay tourism market. *Journal of Quality Assurance in Hospitality & Tourism* 5 (2–4), 57–74.

Jeffreys, E. and Wang, P (2018) Pathways to legalizing same-sex marriage in China and Taiwan: Globalization and 'Chinese values'. In B. Winter, M. Forest and R. Sénac (eds) *Global Perspectives on Same-Sex Marriage: A Neo-Institutional Approach* (pp. 197–219). Cham: Palgrave Macmillan.

Jeffreys, E. and Yu, H. (2015) *Sex in China*. Cambridge: Polity.

Kam, L.Y.L. (2013) *Shanghai Lalas: Female Tongzhi Communities and Politics in Urban China*. Hong Kong: Hong Kong University Press.

Kong, T.S.K. (2011) *Chinese Male Homosexualities: Memba, Tongzhi and Golden Boy*. Abingdon: Routledge.

Kong, T.S.K. (2016) The sexual in Chinese sociology: Homosexuality studies in contemporary China. *The Sociological Review* 64, 495–514.

Kong, T.S.K. (2019) Transnational queer sociological analysis of sexual identity and civic-political activism in Hong Kong, Taiwan and Mainland China. *British Journal of Sociology* 70 (5), 1904–1925.

Lau, H., Yeung, G., Stotzer, R.L., Lau, C.Q. and Loper, K. (2017) Assessing the *Tongzhi* label: Self-identification and public opinion. *Journal of Homosexuality* 64 (4), 509–522.

Li, Y. (2006) Regulating male same-sex relationships in the People's Republic of China. In E. Jeffreys (ed.) *Sex and Sexuality in China* (pp. 82–101). Abingdon: Routledge.

Liu, H. and Chen, R. (2010) '80后' 女同性恋旅游行为特征研究 [Research on the travel behaviour of the post-80 lesbians]. *Modern Business* 29, 130–131.

Liu, J. and Ding, N. (2005) Reticent poetics, queer politics. *Inter-Asia Cultural Studies* 6 (1), 30–55.

Liu, M. (2013) Two gay men seeking two lesbians: An analysis of *Xinghun* (formality marriage) ads on China's Tianya.cn. *Sexuality & Culture* 17, 494–511.

Lucena, R., Jarvis, N. and Weeden, C. (2015) A review of gay and lesbian parented families' travel motivations and destination choices: Gaps in research and future directions. *Annals of Leisure Research* 18 (2), 272–289.

Melián-González, A., Moreno-Gil, S. and Araña, J.E. (2011) Gay tourism in a sun and beach destination. *Tourism Management* 32, 1027–1037.

Miège, P. (2009) 'In my opinion, most Tongzhi are dutiful sons!': Community, social norms, and constructive of identity among young homosexuals in Hefei, Anhui Province. *China Perspectives* 1, 40–53.

Pritchard, A., Morgan, N., Sedgley, D. and Jenkins, A. (1998) Reaching out to the gay tourists: Opportunities and threats in an emerging market segment. *Tourism Management* 19 (3), 273–281.

Puar, J. (2002a) Circuits of queer mobility: Tourism, travel, and globalization. *GLQ: A Journal of Lesbian and Gay Studies* 8 (1–2), 101–137.

Puar, J. (2002b) A transnational feminist critique of queer tourism. *Antipode* 34 (5), 935–946.

Ruan, F.F. (1991) *Sex in China: Studies in Sexology in Chinese Culture.* New York: Plenum Press.

Sang, T.D. (2003) *The Emerging Lesbian: Female Same-Sex Desire in Modern China.* London: University of Chicago Press.

South China Morning Post (2019) Fewer rainbows, less social media for China's LGBT community. *South China Morning Post*, 16 May. See https://www.scmp.com/news/china/politics/article/3010475/fewer-rainbows-less-social-media-chinas-lgbt-community.

United Nations Development Programme (2016) *Human Development Report 2016: Human Development for Everyone.* New York: United Nations. See http://hdr.undp.org/sites/default/files/2016_human_development_report.pdf (accessed 9 February 2021).

Vorobjovas-Pinta, O. and Hardy, A. (2016) The evolution of gay travel research. *International Journal of Tourism Research* 18, 409–416.

Waitt, G. and Markwell, K. (2006) *Gay Tourism: Culture and Context.* Binghamton, NY: Haworth Hospitality Press.

Waitt, G., Markwell, K. and Gorman-Murray, A. (2008) Challenging heteronormativity in tourism studies: Locating progress. *Progress in Human Geography* 32 (6), 781–800.

Wong, C.C.L. and Tolkach, D. (2017) Travel preferences of Asian gay men. *Asia Pacific Journal of Tourism Research* 22 (6), 579–591.

Wong, D. (2010) Hybridization and the emergence of 'gay' identities in Hong Kong and in China. *Visual Anthropology* 24 (1–2), 162–170.

World Tourism Organization & China Tourism Academy (2019) *Guidelines for Success in the Chinese Outbound Tourism Market.* Madrid: UNTWO. See https://www.e-unwto.org/doi/book/10.18111/9789284421138.

Wu, M. and Wall, G. (2016) Chinese research on family tourism: Review and research implications. *Journal of China Tourism Research* 12 (3–4), 274–290.

Xie, Y. and Peng, M. (2018) Attitudes toward homosexuality in China: Exploring the effects of religion, modernizing factors, and traditional culture. *Journal of Homosexuality* 65 (13), 1758–1787.

Zheng, T. (2015) *Tongzhi Living: Men Attracted to Men in Postsocialist China.* Minneapolis, MN: University of Minnesota Press.

7 The Search for Gay Space, Relationship Dynamics and Travel Decisions among Same-Sex Couples in a Secular Muslim Country

Güliz Coşkun

Introduction

In recent years there has been a significant increase in the number of people publicly identifying themselves as LGBT in Western countries. For instance, in 2017, 5.1% of men and 3.9% of women in the United States identified as LGBT (Statista, 2019b). This pattern also holds among EU countries: in 2016, 7.4%, 6.9% and 6.5% of the population in Germany, Spain and the UK, respectively, identified as LGBT (Statista, 2019a). Among the reasons for this recent trend may be growing media coverage of celebrities' coming-out, the growing number of countries legislating gay marriage and child adoption and recognition of same-sex civil unions, as well as more positive general attitudes about gay people (Vorobjovas-Pinta & Hardy, 2016).

However, there is no relevant statistical information about the LGBT population residing in non-Western and Muslim countries. The reasons underlying this lack of information include the oppression and discrimination of gay people living in Muslim countries, which result in many LGBT people feeling unsafe in their environment (Banning-Lover, 2017). In fact, homosexuality is still a crime in 72 countries, with ISIS attacks on gay individuals in Iraq, executions in Iran and the arrests of LGBT people in Egypt. Most recently, Brunei has introduced the death penalty for gay sex and adultery (Beswick, 2019). In this context, acquiring statistical information and conducting research on LGBT individuals in Muslim countries is challenging. Accordingly, relevant research in this area is very scarce.

Turkey is a compelling case in this regard. Although Turkey is a secular Muslim country where homosexuality is not criminalised, the oppression of homosexuals in Turkey has considerably intensified in recent years (Faulkner, 2018). However, it remains unknown how this adverse trend has impacted inbound and outbound gay tourism.

In the tourism literature, travel has been widely viewed as a way to escape from routine life and as a measure towards helping an individual on his/her search for self-identity (Cohen, 2010; Wang, 1999). Accordingly, people identifying themselves as LGBT may see travel as a way to fill their need to escape from an oppressive society and find their true selves. However, considering the lack of data about the exact number of LGBT people and same-sex couples residing in Muslim countries, empirical evidence in support of this assumption is rather limited. In this context, there is a clear need for empirical research on travel preferences and corresponding decision-making processes among gay and lesbian couples residing in non-Western and Muslim countries. This study seeks to bridge the aforementioned gap in the literature by presenting a case study of Turkey. As mentioned above, Turkey is an interesting location for such research: one the one hand, it is a secular country; on the other hand, under the current conservative government, Turkey has been positioned as a country with a strong Muslim identity.

Overall, the process of consumer decision making has been conceptualised to consist of the following four stages: (1) need recognition; (2) information search; (3) evaluation of alternatives; (4) final decision; (4) consumption; and (5) post-purchase evaluation (Mayo & Jarvis, 1981). Travel decision making is a well-researched area in tourism literature. Since travel is not commonly an individual activity, decisions regarding travel are not usually made by one individual. Previous research has identified several factors that can influence travel decisions, including the role of companions (Gardiner et al., 2013; Hernández-Méndez et al., 2013) and family members (Chen et al., 2013; Jenkins, 1978; Mottiar & Quinn, 2004; Zalatan, 1998). However, the decision-making process regarding travel in gay couples and families has rarely been investigated. Despite recent growth of the interest in gay and lesbian tourists' travel preferences, very few relevant studies have focused on same-sex couples (Hughes, 2002; Poria, 2006; Vorobjovas-Pinta, 2018; Wong & Tolkach, 2017), and none of these studies has been conducted in a Muslim country. Therefore, in this chapter we will examine the situation in Turkey by reviewing relevant academic literature and media reporting.

Homosexuality in Muslim Countries and Turkey

While gender diversity is increasingly accepted in Western cultures (Vorobjovas-Pinta, 2018), the situation is very different in Muslim countries. In most countries where Islam is the main religion, an individual's engagement in a homosexual relationship is a crime. Furthermore, at present, there are eight Muslim countries where homosexuality is punishable by death (Duncan, 2017). However, the (death) penalty for homosexuality is a relatively recent phenomenon which was introduced with the creation of the Westernised 'homosexual' label (Massad, 2002). In fact, homosexuality has had a long history in Muslim countries. In the past, homosexual acts and relationships used to be common and explicit and were accepted as normal. For example, in the Ottoman Empire, homosexual relationships were not perceived as unnatural until the 19th century, when the influence of European culture was stronger than ever before (Hür, 2013). Pederasty was also very common among the members of the Janissary (Ottoman Army), who were not allowed to get married or to have a family (Murray, 2007). The Janissary used to have troops consisting of boys to meet the sexual needs of the soldiers (Hür, 2013). In Muslim countries, men who were having sex with other men were not identified as gay, as having sex with both genders was accepted as normal (Massad, 2002). Therefore, it can be argued that, in the past, Muslim countries used to offer some form of gay spaces, although at that time such practices were prohibited among Christian nations.

Due to its secular regime, Turkey has been perceived as a modern Muslim state. Until very recently, the country has been very liberal in its policies concerning LGBT individuals. For example, Gay Pride had been held every year since 2003, without incident. Furthermore, at the start of the 2000s, Turkey was increasingly considered an attractive destination for gay people, as it was perceived as a safe destination compared with other Muslim countries. At that time, according to Ivy (2001), Turkey had the potential to become a critical gay destination in Eastern Europe and the Islamic world.

However, in the 2010s, the country's stance towards LGBT individuals shifted. In 2014, Gay Pride was banned (Middle East Eye, 2016) and in 2015 the Municipality of Ankara (the capital of Turkey) banned all LGBT events, including movies, shows, panels, exhibitions and plays, supposedly for security reasons. In a press release, the Ankara Police Department explained the reason for the ban as follows: '[S]uch events may trigger hatred among citizens with different social status, ethnicity, and religion' (Cumhuriyet, 2018). The media also reported that people engaged in such events had been exposed to violence by the police and local residents (Faulkner, 2018). Similarly, in 2014 Turkey withdrew its participation from Eurovision because it broadcast a drag artist (Duffy, 2018).

Due to the change in approach outlined above, and even though no statistical information on the number of incoming and outgoing gay tourists in Turkey is available, it can be assumed that there has been a decline in the number of gay tourists visiting the country. In 2010, 26 Turkish tourism companies were members of the International Gay and Lesbian Travel Association (IGLTA) (Posta, 2010), and at present this number is eight. As demonstrated by the results of a single case study conducted in Turkey on LGBT people, gay men do not feel safe, confident and comfortable in Turkish society (Saraç & McCullick, 2017). The study's authors note 'the strong and detrimental influence of religion on prejudice towards and rejection of same-sex acts in the Turkish context' (Saraç & McCullick, 2017: 351). Indeed, even though Turkey is a secular country, 99% of the population is Muslim. Therefore, most gay men in Turkey experience many difficulties, such as living closeted lives or marrying a woman (Bereket & Adam, 2006).

Finally, given that there is currently no legislation protecting the rights of sexual minorities in Turkey, gay men, bisexuals and lesbians fear discrimination at work and even job loss if they come out (Ozturk, 2011). This restrictive environment may lead gay people in Turkey to travel to gay-friendly destinations in search of their true identity. Even though travel offers only a temporary escape from daily life (Cohen, 2010), as same-sex couples do not have the freedom to explicitly manifest their relationships in their home country, they may feel the need to be in a place where they can freely show their love for their partners without being judged.

Travel Decision-Making Stages

As discussed above, previous research on travel decision-making processes has been conceptualised to consist of the following five stages: (1) problem or need recognition; (2) information search; (3) final decision; (4) consumption; and (5) post-purchase feeling (Mayo & Jarvis, 1981). Since the main focus of this chapter is on the relationship between the search for gay spaces and the travel decision-making processes of gay couples residing in Muslim countries, we will focus only on the three pre-trip stages, (1)–(3) above. In the remainder of this section, these three steps will be discussed in further detail.

Problem or need recognition

The first stage in the travel decision-making process is problem or need recognition, which emerges from internal and external factors (Mayo & Jarvis, 1981; Um & Crompton, 1990). For instance, in a qualitative study, Desforges (2000) found that the timing of travel is congruent with the time when tourists' self-identity is open to question and when they seek to re-imagine themselves. While gay people may have motivations similar to those of other population cohorts, such as to explore other cultures, relax and enjoy their time with friends (Pritchard et al., 2000; Weeden et al., 2016), for many, their primary motivation to travel is to be themselves and to escape from heterosexual society (Lucena et al., 2015). Indeed, for LGBT individuals in Turkey, daily life neither offers a platform for their self-making (Wang, 1999) nor fulfils their need to escape from the repressive society (Dann, 1977). Therefore, their intention to travel is frequently underpinned by the desire to express themselves in a non-judgmental environment, as well as to connect with like-minded people (Vorobjovas-Pinta, 2018: 8). Consequently, homosexual individuals will be looking for gay spaces on vacation in order to experience their true selves, even if only for a short period of time.

The search for gay space during a holiday is usually associated with looking for sexual experience. However, even though most gay men have their first sexual experience away from home (Annes & Redlin, 2012), the main reasons for searching for gay spaces during travel is not for sex, but for self-expression and freedom. LGBT individuals therefore look for a place where they can escape from social norms (Blichfeldt *et al.*, 2013; Haslop *et al.*, 1998), experience shared sentiments and perform rituals of belonging (Vorobjovas-Pinta, 2018). For many gay men, therefore, sex is not an important motive for travel (Vorobjovas-Pinta & Hardy, 2016). According to a recent estimate, 79% of gay men and lesbians do not seek sexual experience during their travel (Weeden *et al.*, 2016). Rather, gay spaces provide collective experiences (Gorman-Murray & Nash, 2014), which offer gay people a chance to feel unique, rather than peripheral as they do in their daily lives where heterosexuality is accepted as the norm (Vorobjovas-Pinta, 2018).

In previous research, gay spaces have also been discussed in the context of mobility. According to Knopp (2004: 124), many people seek pleasure in 'movement, displacement, and placelessness'. Mobility is a must in travel; therefore, travel itself offers a safe space for people, regardless of their motivation. In this context, mobility will be even more valuable to gay people who live in a restricted society. Seeking to escape from a society that restricts their behaviour, gay people living in Muslim countries will be in search of gay spaces during their travel – spaces where they can learn to accept themselves, build their gay identity and experience an array of positive emotions (Noy, 2004).

The emotional component of travelling is particularly important for LGBT people, especially those who are also Muslim. Homosexuality is perceived as a sin in Islam (Bilancetti, 2011); however, through travelling, Muslim gays can gain a new perspective, interpret religion universally and come to terms with their daily lives. In sum, travelling to gay-friendly places and interacting with other gay people may reduce the inner conflicts of Muslim gays.

Information search and evaluation of alternatives

After the process of need recognition outlined above, the second stage of the travel decision-making process is the information search that travellers perform to evaluate available alternatives before making a final decision about their trip. According to previous studies, important factors that influence the travel intentions of heterosexual couples are their family and friends (Gardiner *et al.*, 2013). Likewise, the results of several studies on the destination choices of gay travellers have revealed that LGBT people's decisions are to a great extent influenced by their companions (Hughes, 2002; Wong & Tolkach, 2017). For instance, Wong and Tolkach (2017) found that gay men in relationships make their travel destination choices based on their partners' opinions. Furthermore, single gay people were found to be more inclined to look for gay spaces during their travel, as they want to meet other gay people (Hughes, 2002). In contrast, lesbian travellers were found to avoid choosing gay-friendly destinations because of a fear of being recognised (Poria, 2006) or due to the perception that gay spaces are dominated by men (Blichfeldt et al., 2013).

According to Ivy (2001: 352), 'gay people are like everyone else' in their destination choices. However, gay men still prefer gay-friendly destinations over others, and they avoid typical family destinations and Muslim countries (Hughes, 2002; Hughes & Deutsch, 2010). While several studies have emphasised the importance of sexuality and gay spaces in choosing holiday destinations (Lucena et al., 2015; Melián-González et al., 2011; Vorobjovas-Pinta, 2018; Weeden et al., 2016), others have revealed that gay men and lesbians are not necessarily searching for gay spaces during their holidays (Blichfeldt et al., 2013; Hughes, 2002). Yet some destinations in Western countries have created pull factors for gay and lesbian travellers. For instance, many US cities such as San Francisco, Miami and Boston are marketed as gay-friendly to increase market share (Boyd, 2008). In Florida, a pink dot is used on business premises to show that gay tourists are welcome. Furthermore, gay games and 'Gay day at Disney' are examples of events designed to promote gay tourism (Holcomb & Luongo, 1996). Therefore, it can be argued that Western countries offer safe gay spaces for LGBT people and that this market segment makes up an essential share of the tourism market.

Just like heterosexual individuals, gay people desire to experience diversity both in their daily lives and during travel. Anecdotally, some gay neighbourhoods, such as those in Sydney (Australia) and Amsterdam (The Netherlands), have been gentrified by white, well-educated, high-income people, and not all gay people are content about this change (El-Tayeb, 2012; Gorman-Murray & Nash, 2014). Similarly, some gay people avoid attending gay spaces on holidays. For instance, in a study on holiday decisions among older gay men, Hughes and Deutsch (2010) found that gay people do not want to participate in activities targeting only the gay population; rather, they prefer activities that are open to everyone. Some gay men and lesbians stated that, in gay spaces, they feel like animals in the zoo (Blichfeldt et al., 2013). Accordingly, as argued by Wong and Tolkach (2017), while those gay men who are comfortable with their gay identity prefer gay-friendly destinations, others still want to visit non-gay friendly destinations at the cost of hiding their gay identity. In Muslim countries, gay men and lesbians prefer to use the latter strategy (that of non-disclosure of their identity) for fear of being unable to book double rooms, experiencing a hostile environment and even getting a fine for engaging in public displays of affection with their partner (Hughes, 2002).

Overall, there is some variance in the travel preferences of gay people in Western and Eastern countries. Compared with Western gay men, Asians are generally unwilling to explicitly demonstrate their sexual orientation, particularly in non-gay friendly locations (Wong & Tolkach, 2017). Similarly, Israeli lesbians tend to avoid gay spaces, since they are neither looking to meet other lesbians nor want to be seen in gay spaces (Poria, 2006). Similar to LGBT people living in other Asian countries, gay men and lesbians in Turkey are not explicit about their sexuality and, accordingly, they could be expected to prefer to hide their sexuality during vacations. Available evidence supports this notion: the results of Ersoy *et al.*'s (2012) survey of 71 gay people in Turkey revealed that 54.5% of the respondents were in a relationship and preferred travelling with their partner. The most popular vacation destinations among Turkish gay men were, in descending order of preference, Amsterdam, the Greek Islands and Paris. The finding that Amsterdam was the most popular destination suggests that, in their choice of travel destination, Turkish gay men sought for gay-friendliness, gay accommodation and availability of gay spaces. In terms of choosing the way to obtain these, Turkish gay men relied on personal recommendations, networks, repeat visits and the gay and lesbian travel guides available on the internet (Hughes, 2002).

Final decision and relationship dynamics

The third stage of the travel decision-making process to be reviewed in this chapter is the final decision. A central factor that influences final travel decisions is couple dynamics. The results reported in previous research on family travel decision making demonstrate that the roles of husband, wife and children have evolved over the years. In an earlier study that involved interviewing women, Jenkins (1978) found that most decisions, except for those related to children, were made by husbands. However, in a more recent study, Litvin *et al.* (2004) established that decisions can be either joint or divided among members of the family depending on the type of decision to be made. Interestingly, there is also evidence that the main aspects of the travel decision-making process influenced by women include collecting pre-trip information through various channels, such as the internet, travel agencies and friends, while men retain more control over major budget decisions (Chen *et al.*, 2013; Mottiar & Quinn, 2004; Thornton *et al.*, 1997; Zalatan, 1998). The reason underlying this distribution of tasks within heterosexual couples is that, compared with men, women have higher relaxation needs (Mottiar & Quinn, 2004; Schänzel *et al.*, 2005 and experience a more comprehensive range of emotions (Brebner, 2003; Brody & Hall, 1993). There is also evidence showing that, compared with men, women are more likely to make purchase decisions based on emotions (Coley & Burgess, 2003; Dittmar *et al.*, 1995). Since travel is an experiential product, the involvement of emotion during both planning and consumption may lead to a conflict among heterosexual couples. However, other studies failed to find distinct roles of men and women regarding specific travel decisions so that, even if information was collected individually by different family members, final decisions were made jointly (Rojas-de-Gracia *et al.*, 2018).

Based on the above, it appears that, in heterosexual couples, gender may play an important role in determining the primary decision maker at each stage of the travel planning process. In case of same-sex couples, similar differences were also observed between gay and lesbian couples in their daily life, based on the distribution of gender roles in each couple. While there is limited empirical evidence on travel decision making among gay and lesbian couples, reasonable predictions can be based on their daily life decision-making strategies, since the roles of husbands and wives on travel decisions were found to be similar to their role in the decisions taken in daily life (Mottiar & Quinn, 2004). Of note, compared with gay couples, lesbian couples are more egalitarian in their decision making, since members of the couple share work outside and inside the home (Biblarz & Savcı, 2010; Kurdek, 2006; Vanfraussen *et al.*, 2003). Therefore, it can be argued that, similar to that which occurs in their everyday life, lesbian couples may follow a more egalitarian approach in their travel decision-making process. However, factors influencing family/couple decision-making processes are not limited to gender roles. In this respect, several previous studies have also highlighted the important impact of the education level and working status of women on the decision-making process (Rojas-de-Gracia *et al.*, 2018; Zalatan, 1998). For instance, in a comparative study on the division of labour in heterosexual and lesbian couples, Patterson *et al.* (2004) showed that, compared to heterosexuals, lesbian couples more evenly share work both at home and outside, and there is less difference in partners' income levels. The similar level of income of the members of a lesbian couple may increase the likelihood of a joint travel decision-making process.

Furthermore, due to the similar needs of both parties in same-sex unions, the relationship dynamics of such couples could be expected to be less influenced by gender, and even be less prone to conflict. Indeed, there is evidence showing that, compared with heterosexual partnerships, same-sex couples are more successful in resolving conflicts, as 'they perceive their worlds through similar lenses' (Kurdek, 2005: 252). In addition, due to societal pressure and stigmatisation, same-sex couples engaged in long-term relationships develop some specific coping strategies, experiencing humour, optimism and resilience together (Rostosky *et al.*, 2016). It is well known that shared experience, especially a negative one, makes people closer to each other. Since same-sex couples feel as if they are involved in a constant battle with the external world, they become more resilient to smaller problems within the relationship, and they tend to understand each other better. In this connection, Solomon *et al.* (2005) found that, while women are more expressive and emotional in heterosexual couples, in same-sex couples both parties are equally expressive. The coping strategies developed by same-sex couples lead them to become more expressive to each other in solving relationship problems. Given the severe opposition that couples living in Muslim countries have to face, it would be interesting to consider the influence of their relationship dynamics on the decision-making process among couples living in these countries.

At present, there is no research on the travel preferences and motivations of lesbians or same-sex couples in Turkey and other Muslim countries. Likewise, there is a lack of information on the travel habits of lesbians residing not only in Muslim countries, but also in the Western states (Vorobjovas-Pinta & Hardy, 2016). This area of research is particularly challenging to study, as the lesbian identity is hidden in Muslim countries (Bilancetti, 2011). On the other hand, some arguments may be developed based on the available literature about gay populations in Turkey. In terms of couple dynamics, Turkish gay men have stronger roles such as 'active-passive', and some of them perceive themselves as 'girls' in their relationships (Bereket & Adam, 2006). Overall, in defining couple roles and understanding the tourist experience, culture is an essential factor to consider (Poria, 2006). Given the evidence that, during the period of the Ottoman Empire, men would engage in sexual relationships with young boys who were dressed like females (Murray, 2007), it can be argued that male-female roles in same-sex relationships are grounded in the Turkish culture. Furthermore, gender and 'active-passive' roles among Turkish couples may influence their travel decision-making process. Given the lack of previous research on lesbian couples in Turkey, it is difficult to make reasonable predictions about the impact of relationship dynamics on their travel decisions. Overall, the research for same-sex couples in Turkey and other Muslim countries is still in its initial stage.

Conclusion

Previous research on gay and lesbian tourists, particularly with regard to the travel decision-making process, has mainly focused on Western societies where these population cohorts can freely demonstrate their sexuality and legally get married. However, the status quo is very different in Eastern and Muslim countries, where gay men and lesbians experience discrimination, suppression and stigmatisation. Accordingly, most LGBT individuals in these countries choose to hide their sexuality in their daily life and live a closeted life with their partners. Driven by this lack of freedom in expressing their true selves, gay and lesbian tourists may engage in searching for gay spaces. Gay-friendly destinations can be expected to be particularly attractive to same-sex couples residing in Muslim

countries, as these people are under constant fear of facing the conse-
quences of their actions. Albeit for a short period of time, a vacation may
be an escape from the repressive daily environment for LGBT people in
Turkey. Under the current conservative government, Turkey has been publicising its hostility towards LGBTQ members in the international media.
The country is missing a valuable opportunity to position itself as a unique
Muslim country that offers a safe space to gay and lesbian travellers.
Therefore, future studies should focus on both incoming and outgoing gay
tourism in Turkey. An understanding of gay and lesbian couples' travel
preferences, motivations and decision-making processes will be useful for
the development of both inbound and outbound gay tourism in Turkey.
Hopefully, the development of research in this area will promote mutual
understanding and respect among people living in the same society.

References

Annes, A. and Redlin, M. (2012) Coming out and coming back: Rural gay migration and
the city. *Journal of Rural Studies* 28 (1), 56–68.

Banning-Lover, R. (2017) Where are the most difficult places in the world to be gay or
transgender? *The Guardian*, 1 March. See https://www.theguardian.com/global-
development-professionals-network/2017/mar/01/
where-are-the-most-difficult-places-in-the-world-to-be-gay-or-transgender-lgbt.

Bereket, T. and Adam, B.D. (2006) The emergence of gay identities in contemporary
Turkey. *Sexualities* 9 (2), 131–151.

Beswick E. (2019) Brunei anti-LGBT laws: Gay community, activists, and public figures
speak out. *Euronews*, 3 April. See https://www.euronews.com/2019/04/03/brunei-an
ti-lgbt-laws-gay-community-activists-and-public-figures-speak-out-thecube.

Biblarz, T.J. and Savci, E. (2010) Lesbian, gay, bisexual, and transgender families. *Journal
of Marriage and Family* 72 (3), 480–497.

Bilancetti, I. (2011) The hidden existence of female homosexuality in Islam. *Jura Gentium*
64. See https://www.juragentium.org/topics/islam/mw/en/bilancet.htm.

Blichfeldt, B.S., Chor, J. and Milan, N.B. (2013) Zoos, sanctuaries and turfs: Enactments
and uses of gay spaces during the holidays. *International Journal of Tourism
Research* 15 (5), 473–483.

Boyd, N.A. (2008) Sex and tourism: The economic implications of the gay marriage movement. *Radical History Review* 100, 223–235.

Brebner, J. (2003) Gender and emotions. *Personality and Individual Differences* 34 (3),
387–394.

Brody, L.R. and Hall, J.A. (1993) Gender and emotion. In M. Lewis and J. Haviland (eds)
Handbook of Emotions (pp. 447–460). New York: Guilford Press.

Chen, Y.S., Lehto, X., Behnke, C. and Tang, C.H. (2013) Investigating children's role in
family dining-out choices: A study of casual dining restaurants in Taiwan. Paper
presented at the 18th Annual Graduate Education and Graduate Student Research
Conference in Hospitality and Tourism, Washington, DC.

Cohen, E. (2010) Searching for escape, authenticity and identity: Experiences of 'lifestyle
travellers'. In M. Morgan, P. Lugosi and J.R.B. Ritchie (eds) *The Tourism and Leisure
Experience: Consumer and Managerial Perspectives* (pp. 27–42). Bristol: Channel
View Publications.

Coley, A. and Burgess, B. (2003) Gender differences in cognitive and affective impulse
buying. *Journal of Fashion Marketing and Management* 7 (3), 282–295.

Cumhuriyet (2018) Ankara Valiliği'nden LGBTİ Yasağı. *Cumhuriyet*, 9 October. See http://www.cumhuriyet.com.tr/haber/turkiye/1107074/Ankara_Valiligi_nden_LGB Ti_yasagi.html.

Dann, G.M. (1977) Anomie, ego-enhancement and tourism. *Annals of Tourism Research* 4 (4), 184–194.

Desforges, L. (2000) Traveling the world: Identity and travel biography. *Annals of Tourism Research* 27 (4), 926–945.

Dittmar, H., Beattie, J. and Friese, S. (1995) Gender identity and material symbols: Objects and decision considerations in impulse purchases. *Journal of Economic Psychology* 16 (3), 491–511.

Duffy, N. (2018) Turkey won't return to Eurovision because of LGBT contestants. *Pink News*, 6 August. See https://www.pinknews.co.uk/2018/08/06/turkey-eurovision -lgbt-contestants/.

Duncan, P. (2017) Gay relationships are still criminalized in 72 countries, report finds. *The Guardian*, 27 July. See https://www.theguardian.com/world/2017/jul/27/ gay-relationships-still-criminalised-countries-report.

El-Tayeb, F. (2012) 'Gays who cannot properly be gay': Queer Muslims in the neoliberal European city. *European Journal of Women's Studies* 19 (1), 79–95.

Ersoy, G.K., Ozer, S.U. and Tuzunkan, D. (2012) Gay men and tourism: Gay men's tourism perspectives and expectations. *Procedia – Social and Behavioral Sciences* 41, 394–401.

Faulkner, C. (2018) Turkey's LGBT community vows to march for Pride despite crackdown fears. *Middle East Eye*, 21 June. See https://www.middleeasteye.net/news/ turkey-s-lgbti-community-vows-march-pride-despite-crackdown-fears-493921046.

Gardiner, S., King, C. and Grace, D. (2013) Travel decision making an empirical examination of generational values, attitudes, and intentions. *Journal of Travel Research* 52 (3), 310–324.

Gorman-Murray, A. and Nash, C.J. (2014) Mobile places, relational spaces: Conceptualizing change in Sydney's LGBTQ neighborhoods. *Environment and Planning D: Society and Space* 32 (4), 622–641.

Haslop, C., Hill, H. and Schmidt, R.A. (1998) The gay lifestyle – spaces for a subculture of consumption. *Marketing Intelligence & Planning* 16 (5), 318–326.

Hernández-Méndez, J., Muñoz-Leiva, F. and Sánchez-Fernández, J. (2013) The influence of e-word-of-mouth on travel decision-making: Consumer profiles. *Current Issues in Tourism* 18 (11), 1001–1021.

Holcomb, B. and Luongo, M. (1996) Gay tourism in the United States. *Annals of Tourism Research* 23 (3), 711–713.

Hughes, H. (2002) Gay men's holiday destination choice: A case of risk and avoidance. *International Journal of Tourism Research* 4 (4), 299–312.

Hughes, H.L. and Deutsch, R. (2010) Holidays of older gay men: Age or sexual orientation as decisive factors? *Tourism Management* 31 (4), 454–463.

Hür, A. (2013) Elinde tesbih, evinde oğlan, dudağında dua. *Radikal*, 10 November. See http://www.radikal.com.tr/yazarlar/ayse-hur/ elinde-tesbih-evinde-oglan-dudaginda-dua-1159964/.

Ivy, R.L. (2001) Geographical variation in alternative tourism and recreation establishments. *Tourism Geographies* 3 (3), 338–355.

Jenkins, R.L. (1978) Family vacation decision-making. *Journal of Travel Research* 16 (4), 2–7.

Knopp, L. (2004) Ontologies of place, placelessness, and movement: Queer quests for identity and their impacts on contemporary geographic thought. *Gender, Place & Culture* 11 (1), 121–134.

Kurdek, L.A. (2005) What do we know about gay and lesbian couples? *Current Directions in Psychological Science* 14 (5), 251–254.

Kurdek, L.A. (2006) Differences between partners from heterosexual, gay, and lesbian cohabiting couples. *Journal of Marriage and Family* 68 (2), 509–528.

Litvin, S.W., Xu, G. and Kang, S.K. (2004) Spousal vacation-buying decision making revisited across time and place. *Journal of Travel Research* 43 (2), 193–198.

Lucena, R., Jarvis, N. and Weeden, C. (2015) A review of gay and lesbian parented families' travel motivations and destination choices: Gaps in research and future directions. *Annals of Leisure Research* 18 (2), 272–289.

Massad, J.A. (2002) Re-orienting desire: The gay international and the Arab world. *Public Culture* 14 (2), 361–385.

Mayo, E.J. and Jarvis, L.P. (1981) *The Psychology of Leisure Travel: Effective Marketing and Selling of Travel Services*. Boston, MA: CBI Publishing.

Melián-González, A., Moreno-Gil, S. and Araña, J.E. (2011) Gay tourism in a sun and beach destination. *Tourism Management* 32 (5), 1027–1037.

Middle East Eye (2016) Istanbul police break up LGBT rally held in spite of ban. *Middle East Eye*, 17 June. See https://www.middleeasteye.net/news/istanbul-pride-cancelled-due-to-security-concerns-384742710.

Mottiar, Z. and Quinn, D. (2004) Couple dynamics in household tourism decision making: Women as the gatekeepers? *Journal of Vacation Marketing* 10 (2), 149–160.

Murray, S.O. (2007) Homosexuality in the Ottoman Empire. *Historical Reflections/Réflexions Historiques* 33 (1), 101–116.

Noy, C. (2004) This trip really changed me: Backpackers' narratives of self-change. *Annals of Tourism Research* 31 (1), 78–102.

Ozturk, B.M. (2011) Sexual orientation discrimination: Exploring the experiences of lesbian, gay and bisexual employees in Turkey. *Human Relations* 64 (8), 1099–1118.

Patterson, C.J., Sutfin, E.L. and Fulcher, M. (2004) Division of labor among lesbian and heterosexual parenting couples: Correlates of specialized versus shared patterns. *Journal of Adult Development* 11 (3), 179–189.

Poria, Y. (2006) Tourism and spaces of anonymity: An Israeli lesbian woman's travel experience. *Turizam: medunarodni znanstveno-stručni časopis* 54 (1), 33–42.

Posta (2010) Gay turizminde Türkiye patlaması. *Posta*, 24 September. See https://www.posta.com.tr/gay-turizminde-turkiye-patlamasi-44351.

Pritchard, A., Morgan, N.J., Sedgley, D., Khan, E. and Jenkins, A. (2000) Sexuality and holiday choices: Conversations with gay and lesbian tourists. *Leisure Studies* 19 (4), 267–282.

Rojas-de-Gracia, M.M., Alarcón-Urbistondo, P. and González Robles, E.M. (2018) Couple dynamics in family holidays decision-making process. *International Journal of Contemporary Hospitality Management* 30 (1), 601–617.

Rostosky, S.S., Riggle, E.D., Rothblum, E.D. and Balsam, K.F. (2016) Same-sex couples' decisions and experiences of marriage in the context of minority stress: Interviews from a population-based longitudinal study. *Journal of Homosexuality* 63 (8), 1019–1040.

Saraç, L. and McCullick, B. (2017) The life of a gay student in a university physical education and sports department: A case study in Turkey. *Sport, Education and Society* 22 (3), 338–354.

Schänzel, H.A., Smith, K.A. and Weaver, A. (2005) Family holidays: A research review and application to New Zealand. *Annals of Leisure Research* 8 (2–3), 105–123.

Solomon, S.E., Rothblum, E.D. and Balsam, K.F. (2005) Money, housework, sex, and conflict: Same-sex couples in civil unions, those not in civil unions, and heterosexual married siblings. *Sex Roles* 52 (9–10), 561–575.

Statista (2019a) *Europe's LGBT Population Mapped*. See https://www.statista.com/chart/6466/europes-lgbt-population-mapped/ (accessed February 2019).

Statista (2019b) *Share of Americans who Identify as LGBT from 2012 to 2017, by Gender*. See https://www.statista.com/statistics/719697/american-adults-who-identify-as-homosexual-bisexual-or-transgender-by-gender (accessed February 2019).

Thornton, P.R., Shaw, G. and Williams, A.M. (1997) Tourist group holiday decision-making and behavior: The influence of children. *Tourism Management* 18 (5), 287–297.

Um, S. and Crompton, J.L. (1990) Attitude determinants in tourism destination choice. *Annals of Tourism Research* 17 (3), 432–448.

Vanfraussen, K., Ponjaert-Kristoffersen, I. and Brewaeys, A. (2003) Family functioning in lesbian families created by donor insemination. *American Journal of Orthopsychiatry* 73 (1), 78–90.

Vorobjovas-Pinta, O. (2018) Gay neo-tribes: Exploration of travel behaviour and space. *Annals of Tourism Research* 72, 1–10

Vorobjovas-Pinta, O. and Hardy, A. (2016) The evolution of gay travel research. *International Journal of Tourism Research* 18 (4), 409–416.

Wang, N. (1999) Rethinking authenticity in tourism experience. *Annals of Tourism Research* 26 (2), 349–370.

Weeden, C., Lester, J.A. and Jarvis, N. (2016) Lesbians and gay men's vacation motivations, perceptions, and constraints: A study of cruise vacation choice. *Journal of Homosexuality* 63 (8), 1068–1085.

Wong, C.C.L. and Tolkach, D. (2017) Travel preferences of Asian gay men. *Asia Pacific Journal of Tourism Research* 22 (6), 579–591.

Zalatan, A. (1998) Wives' involvement in tourism decision processes. *Annals of Tourism Research* 25 (4), 890–903.

Part 3

Gay Tourism: Pleasure and Leisure

8 LGBTQI+ Resort Workers: Blurring the Lines of Work and Leisure

Oscar Vorobjovas-Pinta

Introduction

Research pertaining to LGBTQI+ tourism has predominantly focused on the demand-led aspects, such as the demographic characteristics of LGBTQI+ travellers and their motivations to travel, as well as on the supply-led facets such as consumer behaviour and the use of gay space (Vorobjovas-Pinta & Hardy, 2016). A small body of research has examined the impacts of gay tourism on local communities (Hughes *et al.*, 2010; Monterrubio, 2008; Vorobjovas-Pinta & Hardy, 2021), and gay hospitality workers in the context of sex tourism (Collins, 2012; Mendoza, 2013). However, there is limited knowledge about people working in the LGBTQI+ tourism and hospitality industries, such as LGBTQI+ resorts. For the purpose of this research, LGBTQI+ resorts are defined as self-contained commercial establishments catering to predominantly LGBTQI+ clientele. Such resorts usually offer a variety of amenities including entertainment, health and recreational activities. Historically, many such resorts were also known to have spots for outdoor cruising and 'recreational sex' opportunities (Hughes, 2006; Newton, 1993). Traditionally, LGBTQI+ resorts are strongly associated with male travellers; however, there are resorts and travel destinations that specifically cater to lesbian guests (Vorobjovas-Pinta, 2019). While the LGBTQI+ acronym encompasses many other identities, knowledge about tourism products and services catering to specifically bisexual, transgender, queer/questioning, intersex and others is limited. It is understood that gay and lesbian resorts are usually inclusive of all other identities.

This chapter draws on an ethnographic study of an exclusively gay and lesbian resort, 'Lizard Bay',[1] located in far north Queensland, Australia. It is part of a larger research project examining the notion and symbolic value of gay space (see Vorobjovas-Pinta, 2018a, 2018b; Vorobjovas-Pinta & Dalla-Fontana, 2018; Vorobjovas-Pinta & Robards, 2017). In this chapter, I explore how employees make sense of working at the exclusively gay and lesbian resort by drawing upon notions of organisational socialisation and sensemaking. Due to the remoteness of the resort, the majority of the employees live on-site, blurring the lines between work and leisure. Hospitality workers are known not only to be employed to perform their daily duties but are also inadvertently tasked with manufacturing resort leisure for guests and contributing towards a positive holiday ambience (Adler & Adler, 1999). With this in mind, I examine the ways in which resort staff negotiate their work and leisure. I also consider employees' relationships with one another as well as with resort guests.

Literature Review

Organisational socialisation and sensemaking

Organisational socialisation refers to 'the process by which one is taught and learns "the ropes" of a particular organisational role' (Van Maanen & Schein, 1979: 211). It plays a crucial role in terms of managing employees' motivation and enthusiasm, as well as relationships with co-workers. While the classic theorisation of organisational socialisation is concerned with the development and application of organisational tactics on socialisation (see, for example, Ashforth & Saks, 1996; Cooper-Thomas & Anderson, 2002), more recent studies suggest that an organisation's culture is dependent upon the socialisation of employees as they learn and adapt to the ways in which an organisation functions (Matuszewski & Blenkinsopp, 2011). Indeed, Chao et al. (1994: 730) characterise socialisation as 'the learning content and process by which an individual adjusts to a special role in an organisation'. As such, it could be understood that organisational socialisation is imbued with the notions by which an individual comes to appreciate the expected behaviours, and the social knowledge required to assume a particular role within an organisation (Louis, 1980). Inadvertently, this is also required to maintain functional relationships with other employees. Arguably, employees who live at their workplace are even more exposed to the particularities of organisational socialisation, especially when it extends into their private, off-duty lives. And as such, this might affect and even mandate a certain style of leisure.

Louis' (1980) work on organisational socialisation has synergies with Weick's (1995) notion of 'sensemaking', whereby the identities of employees are constructed in the context of others, relying on retrospective experiences that help to develop plausible images for prospective action, indicating that sensemaking is 'driven by plausibility rather than accuracy' (Weick, 1995: 17). There seems to be a broad consensus that the term 'sensemaking' means what it says, i.e. the process of making sense. Theoretically, sensemaking is born out of the necessity to work through uncertain and/or ambiguous situations, such as starting a new job and entering a new workplace (Blenkinsopp & Zdunczyk, 2005; Matuszewski & Blenkinsopp, 2011). Resort hotels offer a valuable arena to explore the interplay between work and leisure, because such employment is likely to evoke sensemaking in light of organisational socialisation. Resort workers are at the centre of the leisure–work nexus as they produce and service leisure for their customers and experience their own leisure in the same space. Here sensemaking might imply that we do not have access to an 'objective' reality that can serve as an ultimate reference for assessing the accuracy of our sensemaking efforts (Rosness *et al.*, 2016).

Negotiating the blurred lines of work and leisure

A small body of tourism research has examined situations where staff live at the place of their employment. For example, the literature has explored: the mobilities of young budget travellers and their engagement with work at ski resorts (e.g. Duncan, 2008); organisational socialisation and sensemaking in the context of cruise ship employment (e.g. Gibson & Perkins, 2015; Matuszewski & Blenkinsopp, 2011); the divergence of characteristics between backpackers and working holidaymakers (e.g. Brennan, 2014); as well as the layered vulnerability of the seasonal harvest workforce (e.g. Underhill & Rimmer, 2016).

The dichotomy of work and leisure is generally understood to be a product of industrial capitalism. There are clear boundaries between these two constructs on our social lives. Each construct is bound by specialised space and time (Barry *et al.*, 2019; Guerrier & Adib, 2003). Work is usually defined by routines, procedures and codes of conduct, whereas leisure denotes freedom, pleasure and enjoyment. The two constructs seem to be in opposition with one another and, perhaps, they should counterbalance each other in order to maintain a healthy lifestyle. Indeed, Urry (2002: 2) emphasises that leisure activities presuppose their opposite – 'regulated and organised work'. The constant negotiation of our work and leisure defines the notion of work-life balance. The work-life balance has long been a topic of contemporary interest (Sharpley, 2018). However, this might not seem as clear cut as it first appears. Sharpley (2018) suggests that different types of work produce different levels of satisfaction and, as such, our indi-vidual wants and needs are defined by the relationship between work and leisure. For some these two facets stand in stark juxtaposition to one another, for others leisure might be an extension of work, and some others might seek the neutrality between their work and leisure times. But what if you live at work? How does one negotiate leisure at work?

In this chapter, I explore some of the questions posed above. Drawing upon the theories of organisational socialisation and sensemaking, I seek to understand how gay and lesbian resort workers make sense of their employment and how they relate to leisure while they are 'on the job'.

I also examine the effects of extended social interactions between colleagues at the resort. In this case, extended social interactions are the result of the remoteness of the resort. Compared with other traditional tourism and hospitality jobs, workers at this particular gay and lesbian resort are obliged to work and socialise in close proximity to other workers and guests.

Research Background and Context

The fieldwork took place in an exclusively gay and lesbian resort in far north Queensland, Australia, over six weeks between the months of September and October 2014. The resort lies within a remote area of tropical rainforest, approximately 45 km from Cairns Airport, and 5 km away from the closest township. The resort has 30 rooms accommodating 80–100 guests at capacity. Amenities include an outdoor swimming pool, a hot tub, bar, dining area and gym. These amenities extend onto a secluded and otherwise undisturbed beachfront which, in the absence of any competition, the resort confidently claims as its own. Staff bungalows are located right next to the main building of the resort, and there is no clear separation/divide between the two types of accommodation.

The business agreed to my conducting fieldwork in exchange for voluntary and unremunerated work. This unique situation allowed me to blend into the natural setting of the everyday resort culture. My duties were diverse; among other tasks, I drove the company car to deliver goods, worked at the resort reception, conducted marketing and social media work and helped occasionally in the kitchen. These tasks themselves offered multiple points of engagement in my professional role as researcher, not only with the resort's visitors but also with its staff – my colleagues – which translated into an opportunity rigorous and rich data-collection process.

Method

This chapter draws on a larger study that I conducted as part of my PhD (see Vorobjovas-Pinta, 2017). The overall research aim was to gain a better understanding of the role and symbolic value of gay space by studying the motivations and behaviours of gay travellers. The resort workers play a crucial role in manufacturing the leisure space and, as such, they are an inseparable part of the experience creation process. Sometimes, they are the experience. Ethnographic research facilitated the achievement of these aims by promoting the embeddedness of myself as the researcher, in the environs of gay tourism. Indeed, the social world cannot be researched without being part of it, and this stands as a core tenet of this study (Tedlock, 2003).

Reflexivity and the insider positionality

Ethnography is both an epistemology and a methodology. As an epistemology, it is aligned to the constructivism/interpretivism paradigm (Agar, 2006; Creswell & Poth, 2018). The ways in which we, scholars, engage with individual ethnographic research accounts rests on various theoretical and disciplinary perspectives navigating our logic-in-use (Green *et al.*, 2012). On an epistemological level, I took a subjectivist stance as this study required close communication with research participants. Such communication allowed me to maintain close proximity to the participants and to learn about their perceptions and their individual sets of circumstances (Creswell & Poth, 2018).

As a member of the LGBTQI+ community, I adopted an insider position. I was already familiar with the vernacular of gay culture and the experience of being a gay man in a predominantly heteronormative society. The insider approach yielded in an emic perspective which conveys the meaning of the internal language, symbols and a defined culture (Vorobjovas-Pinta & Robards, 2017). An emic perspective adopts a stance as if looking 'at things through the eyes of members of the culture being studied' (Willis, 2007: 100) and endeavours to capture particular group's 'indigenous meanings of real-world events' (Yin, 2016: 16).

Data collection

This research adopted two distinct modes of data collection: semi-structured interviews and participant observation.

The flexibility of semi-structured interviews in eliciting facts and knowledge about the day-to-day routines at the resort was supported by the demands of the observational data (Patton, 2002). Although there are no fixed guidelines as to what is the right number of interviews that should be conducted, a certain emphasis should be put on the depth, nuance and roundness of the data generated. Arguably, data collection can continue until the point of informational saturation (Guest *et al.*, 2006; Mason, 2010). In the course of conducting this research, an assumption was made that semi-structured interviews with seven employees at the resort would be sufficient to ensure the richness of the data, as well as to attain theoretical saturation (Gold, 1997; Guest *et al.*, 2006). Seven staff members represented roughly one-half of the staff working at the resort. The private nature of semi-structured interviews enabled participants to volunteer ideas that might be personal or emotionally charged without feeling the need to provide a socially acceptable rationale (Stokes & Bergin, 2006). The saturation became evident, as no new themes emerged from the data towards the end of the study. As this research is qualitative in nature, the number of participants was based foremost upon the maximum feasibility within the timeframe of this project. This study used a convenience-based sample; that is, selection included any individual available and willing to participate in the study (Onwuegbuzie & Leech, 2007). All staff members were invited to participate. None of the potential participants was rejected from the interview process. All interview participants were introduced to the project by providing them with a research information sheet establishing the purpose of the interview, and of the study. Participation was on an entirely voluntary basis, and no financial compensation or other incentive was provided for their time. The interviews were recorded digitally, and later transcribed for thematic analysis using NVivo software.

The second method employed in this study was participant observation. No special recruitment method was required: all resort staff, as well as resort guests and visitors were observed over the duration of the field trip. The very presence of these people at the resort made them qualified to be part of this study; they indeed formed a part of the prevailing ethnographic milieu (Patton, 2002). Arguably, the most complete form of sociological datum is that collected by the participant observer as it provides a holistic explanation of a phenomenon as opposed to a point-in-time view (Becker & Geer, 1957).

Participants

In total, seven interviews with staff members were undertaken: five of them identified themselves as gay and two of them identified as heterosexual. The interview schedule comprised three sections: the first section pertained to the employees' perceptions of their work; the second section referred to the employees' understanding about the resort customers' needs and wants; and the third section of the interview schedule aimed to collect demographic data. All interview participants were assigned an alias to ensure the data was non-identifiable (see Table 8.1).

Participants were advised that they had the right to decline to answer any question or to withdraw from the interview at any time. In order to protect participants further, each was permitted to view and amend the transcripts of their own interviews; no participant expressed the need or

Table 8.1 List of interview participants

Name	Age	Sexual identity	Living arrangement
Shaun	30	Gay male	On-site
Andrew	33	Gay male	Off-site
Tim	24	Gay male	On-site
Albert	64	Heterosexual male	On-site
Frank	68	Gay male	On-site
Joseph	27	Gay male	On-site
Alex	24	Heterosexual male	On-site

desire to do so. Participants were never asked questions that could reveal their identities in the transcripts. In this chapter I also refer to employees who were not interviewed but who were part of my observations. These data also remain non-identifiable.

Findings and Discussion

As I entered the reception area I was greeted with a warm salutation: 'Welcome to the family, we've been waiting for you'. Although the tiny building housing the reception desk, and its welcoming occupant, sat right behind the main hotel building towering above it, this space felt distinctly like an inviting gateway to a truly idyllic resort life.

These were my very first impressions and observations noted in my fieldwork journal as I arrived at the resort back in early September 2014. I was indeed curious about this new place not only in terms of research but also in terms of who my new fellow colleagues and, perhaps, friends would be. After all, I was to spend six weeks here. From the very first moment I attempted to make sense of the new reality, confirming the idea that sensemaking is triggered by events that are new and unexpected (Weick *et al.*, 2005). Situations such as starting a new job or moving to a new place evoke the notion of sensemaking and stimulate a search to answer the question: What's the story?' (Matuszewski & Blekinsopp, 2011). My role as an employee who lived on the premises provided me with an opportunity to observe resort employees' attempts to make sense of their work–leisure dichotomy. Staff at the resort represented a variety of social, cultural and occupational backgrounds. Their upbringing, lifestyles, worker-employer interactions and cultural values varied with regard to their orientation towards work and leisure.

I discuss the findings under three major themes that emerged from the analysis: (1) negotiating the workplace environment; (2) negotiating the relationship with guests; and (3) negotiating leisure time at the resort.

Negotiating the workplace environment

The perception that gay people are being discriminated against in workplaces should their superiors or colleagues become aware of their sexual identity is prevalent (Denier & Waite, 2019; Rumens, 2016; Rumens & Ozturk, 2019). Anecdotally, such assumptions still hold true for many LGBTQI+ people. This is particularly evident in rural and regional Australia, where LGBTQI+ individuals are known to experience increased levels of anxiety and higher incidences of depression and suicide (Bowman *et al.*, 2020). Enclavic workspaces, such as the exclusively gay and lesbian resort, offer an escape from the traditional perceptions of the heteronormative workplace. These spaces are open, inclusive and welcoming. Indeed, these qualities formed the basis for the motivation to work at a gay and lesbian resort. Shaun (30)[2] observes:

> My motivation for coming was, I suppose, because I previously worked at a gay restaurant. So, I thought I would have more of a chance of getting a job here if I had that background.

Friendships, intimacy and networking clearly matter in the lives of the gay resort workers. Some employees see their employment at the resort as an opportunity to expand their professional network and build a further career. For example, Tim (24) reflects:

> I guess, well, firstly being gay probably did help [to get a job at this resort]. [...] I guess I also wanted to network with some gay people who are in the industry. That could potentially help with a career progression, networking, and just a bit of a change of lifestyle.

Career opportunities are perceived to be associated with a common sexual orientation, with a perception that a gay camaraderie between colleagues is beneficial. This has synergies with Rumens' (2008: 24) findings that gay employees may gain pleasure from taking steps in establishing 'friendships with instrumental or networking goals in mind'.

Camaraderie among the staff at the resort is pivotal to the successful running of resort operations, particularly because almost all staff members live on the premises of the resort. Frank (68), a resort manager, describes the need for a healthy camaraderie as a control tool:

> This is not just to control the staff. [...] if the staff are good enough you don't need to control.

Workplaces are important discursive arenas in which gay men's friendships are formed (Rumens, 2010). However, crossing over from the identity category of 'co-worker' to 'friend' can pose a significant dilemma in terms of professionalism. From my observations, the boundaries of a 'co-worker' and a 'friend' have been constantly straddled, and as the time went by, I came to realise that perhaps this is indeed the work culture at this resort. It seemed to work well. Frank's idea of employees getting along for both professional and personal gain was generally supported by the rest of the staff. Shaun (30) observes:

> I think the staff in general do get along very well with each other. We do help and support each other. We know quite a bit about each other's jobs but we also socialise a lot.

The camaraderie, respect and support for one another at the resort was evident in the everyday routines, both at the resort and off-site. For example, on our day off, Tim (24), Lafayette (26)[3] and myself went to Cairns for some lunch. Lafayette is an effeminate gay man who has a colourful personality and, consequently, attracts a lot of attention. While the resort offered him a sense of freedom and support from other staff and guests, the general public are not always as supportive as people at the resort. On this occasion Lafayette suffered some serious verbal abuse. Tim and I stepped in just in time to avoid any further confrontation. However, this situation reminded us that we work and live in a bubble, where being a minority essentially means being a majority. In societies where heterosexuality is the prevailing norm, marginal spaces within which minorities recast them-selves as local, ephemeral majorities become an essential conduit of collec-tive social imagination (Vorobjovas-Pinta, 2018b). In this instance, the resort enables alternative norms to be realised through mutual assent. Furthermore, this socialisation process in turn has implications on the for-mation of identity and an individual's 'sensemaking' (Weick, 1995).

Negotiating the relationship with the guests

The value of employee-guest interaction in the hospitality settings has attracted a fair amount of attention in academic research (e.g. Prayag & Ryan, 2012; Yaoyuneyong *et al.*, 2018). Yaoyuneyong *et al.* (2018) suggest that the overall quality of service and guest experiences are primarily evaluated on the basis of employee-guest interaction. This is particularly pertinent for resort operations, where a resort functions as a getaway focused on vacation-related experiences, such as leisure and relaxation. This is where guests expect a high level of service. As such, the employee-guest interactions are at the centre of experience development and execu-tion. Albert (64), Frank (68) and Tim (24) elaborate:

Albert (64):   I didn't realise that the guests feel, what's the word … they like me having dinner with them or sitting down with them. This is part of their experience […].

Frank (68):   […] we want to have a good time. And that is what I am trying to create here. Guests see it. Well, you seen it. Because I told you at the beginning you will be surprised how I interact with the guests. This is pure entertainment. And that is not because I want to be a smart ass, it's purely to say to them, hey when you're at home with your other half, or with a little party with your friends, you laughing, you making fun, because you're allowed to do it.

Tim (24):   You're definitely there [for the guests], serving them but at the same time entertaining them, making them feel welcome. We always stay happy and positive because, I mean, they're on a holiday themselves, so you want to keep the mood and the vibe very happy.

Evidently, the resort provides guests with a sense of relaxation and comfort. Because of the nature of the resort, the sense of relaxation, safety and understanding is first and foremost delivered by the members of the staff. The resort is a distance away from the mainstream properties, so the guests can be open about their sexuality and feel protected. The general feeling at the resort is that the management and staff allow guests to be what they are, to look for what they want and to say what they feel. After all, guests at the resort are just like the staff – members of the LGBTQI+ communities or their allies. Shaun (30) observes:

> But yeah it's busy, people work hard but people are relaxed and we try to be relaxed, then the guests are relaxed.

Shaun's (30) comments indicate that, to some extent, he is also manufacturing a 'personality' for the benefit of the resort guests. This has led to some resort workers finding it hard to juggle their interactions with the guests in their leisure time. Because of the relatively small size of the property, even on their days off employees are exposed to the resort guests, and as such the employee-guest interaction is extended. From my observations, some employees chose to stick around in their rooms and the nearby bungalows to have a break from their work. For them, work entailed constant interactions with the resort guests. The prolonged exposure to the guests could potentially result in burnout. Cordes and Dougherty (1993: 628) have argued that burnout is greatest in the helping professions 'because of the high level of arousal from direct, frequent, and rather intense interactions with clients'. This has parallels with the high demands for interaction with guests at the resort.

Negotiating leisure time at the resort

Leisure, in its connection to work, has been theorised in two opposing ways: as either an extension or 'spillover' of work activities and relationships, or as compensation for the stressors and dissatisfaction associated with work (Adler & Adler, 1999; Guerrier & Adib, 2003). It is widely suggested that conscious identity work occurs in situations that call for 'a higher level of awareness of the precarious nature of people's sense of self' (Winkler, 2018: 122). While some resort workers aimed to escape the employee-guest interactions during their leisure time by simply spending the day inside their room, the majority of them enjoyed their leisure within the resort, mingling with the guests and other staff members. They had chosen to give up their free leisure time and seemed to prefer to engage in this ambiguous mix of leisure consumption and work. Andrew (33) and Tim (24) reflect:

Andrew (33): I spend most of my time among the guests, so I actually don't feel like I shouldn't be down there [in the pool and bar area] or I shouldn't talk to guests or I shouldn't be randomly seen around enjoying myself [...].

Tim (24): If I'm down there for breakfast, and I am not on my shift, I'm not a rude person, like I probably won't go up and have a huge conversation because I want my own space. But I'll always make sure I wave to someone or say good morning,

> it's the way I'd like to be treated. I don't think you should work at a resort and then also live there and [...] after you've finished your shift to, sort of you don't talk to them.

Similarly, whenever the resort management organised parties at night (some of them are rather spontaneous), the role of the staff is not only to run the 'show' but also to take part as they would if they were patrons at the resort. Resort employees are traditionally assigned status and honour by guests (Selwyn, 2000) and it may be that resort employees valued being the centre of attention. This has synergies with organisational socialisation and sensemaking as resort employees come to appreciate the expected behaviours as well as the social knowledge required to engage with their work (Louis, 1980; Rosness *et al.*, 2016). As such, it could be understood that the fulcrum of hosting a party is the contribution towards 'forming or consolidating relationships with strangers' (Selwyn, 2000: 34). Therefore, such parties can be used to improve and cement relationships between staff and guests. Shaun (30) elaborates:

> I think the guests generally [...] have been more than happy to have you around or even invite you to come and join them. So, it does make living here easier.

On the other hand, the sense of wanting to escape the resort, especially after prolonged interactions with guests, is palpable. There is no doubt that the work of resort employees involves emotional labour. The range of emotions that resort employees display is immense. They not only need to be courteous and happy during the day-to-day activities at the resort, but also sympathetic to guests' problems, and sometimes strict and assertive to guests and other employees who misbehave. Therefore, some employees opt to escape the resort at least for a day in order to enjoy and reclaim their leisure time – leisure that is not consumed by the realities of the resort life. Shaun (30) and Alex (24) elaborate:

Shaun (30):	It does get to a point when you do need to get off the resort. And, I think, it's important to do that, because I've seen some people who have worked here just become disconcerted with the place, because it becomes their life. And because they don't get away from it, because they don't have a car or friends or family or something like that it can start to eat away at them. So, I think it is important for them to have some means of escape or some means of exit.
Alex (24):	And your major problem is that your life will become what's happening at the resort.

The comments from Shaun (30) and Alex (24) highlight the intrinsic dichotomy between work and leisure. It has synergies with Guerrier and Adib's (2003: 1399) research which argues 'there are specialised spaces and times in which we work and other spaces and times put by for leisure'.

And because the resort has the unique challenge of being a remote property, there is an innate need to 'forcibly' separate leisure and work times.

Conclusion

In this chapter, I explored the ways in which gay and lesbian resort employees negotiate their work, life and leisure by drawing upon notions of organisational socialisation and sensemaking. The notion of sensemaking emerges through negotiation of three distinctive facets: workplace environment; relationships with resort guests; and leisure time at the resort.

In this study, individuals working at the resort have constructed their identity in the context of others (i.e. their fellow employees), which affected the way in which they made sense of themselves and their work-leisure environment. Indeed, employees at the resort can be open about themselves and bring their own personalities and idiosyncrasies to work. The process of socialisation with fellow colleagues and guests influences the way in which identity and an individual's sensemaking is formed (Weick, 1995).

The constant negotiation of work and leisure time is a highly emotional matter. This is because the boundaries between work and leisure are blurred. This is evident in the everyday realities of resort employees, whose leisure activities are incorporated into work, and whose work activities spill over into leisure time. As such, work and leisure are inextricably linked.

Acknowledgment

Parts of this chapter appeared in 'Gay Neo-tribes: An Exploration of Space and Travel Behaviour' (Doctoral dissertation) by Oskaras Vorobjovas-Pinta, University of Tasmania, Sandy Bay, Australia, 2017.

Notes

(1) Pseudonym used to avoid making reference to the name of the resort.
(2) All names used in this publication are aliases. Participants' ages are shown in brackets.
(3) Lafayette (26, gay male), an employee at the resort, was not interviewed in this study.

References

Adler, P.A. and Adler, P. (1999) Resort workers: Adaptations in the leisure-work nexus. *Sociological Perspectives* 42 (3), 369–402.

Agar, M. (2006) An ethnography by any other name ... *Forum Qualitative Sozialforschung/ Forum: Qualitative Social Research* 7 (4). See http://www.qualitative-research.net/ index.php/fqs/article/view/177/396.

Ashforth, B.E. and Saks, A.M. (1996) Socialization tactics: Longitudinal effects on newcomer adjustment. *Academy of Management Journal* 39 (1), 149–178.

Barry, B., Olekalns, M. and Rees, L. (2019) An ethical analysis of emotional labor. *Journal of Business Ethics* 160, 17–34.

Becker, H. and Geer, B. (1957) Participant observation and interviewing: A comparison. *Human Organization* 16 (3), 28–32.

Blenkinsopp, J. and Zdunczyk, K. (2005) Making sense of mistakes in managerial careers. *Career Development International* 10 (5), 359–374.

Bowman, S., Nic Giolla Easpaig, B. and Fox, R. (2020) Virtually caring: A qualitative study of internet-based mental health services for LGBT young adults in rural Australia. *Rural and Remote Health* 20 (1), 5448.

Brennan, C. (2014) Backpackers or working holiday makers? Working tourists in Australia. *Qualitative Sociology Review* 10 (3), 94–114.

Chao, G.T., Leary-Kelly, A.M., Wolf, S., Klein, H.J. and Gander, P.D. (1994) Organisational socialisation: Its contents and consequences. *Journal of Applied Psychology* 79 (5), 730–743.

Collins, J.C. (2012) Identity matters: A critical exploration of lesbian, gay, and bisexual identity and leadership in HRD. *Human Resource Development Review* 11 (3), 349–379.

Cooper-Thomas, H. and Anderson, N. (2002) Newcomer adjustment: The relationship between tactics. *Journal of Occupational and Organizational Psychology* 75, 423–437.

Cordes, C.L. and Dougherty, T.W. (1993) A review and an integration of research on job burnout. *Academy of Management Review* 18 (4), 621–656.

Creswell, J.W. and Poth, C.N. (2018) *Qualitative Inquiry & Research Design: Choosing among Five Approaches*. Thousand Oaks, CA: Sage.

Denier, N. and Waite, S. (2019) Sexual orientation at work: Documenting and understanding wage inequality. *Sociology Compass* 13 (4), e12667.

Duncan, T. (2008) The internationalisation of tourism labour markets: Working and playing in a ski resort. In C.M. Hall and T. Coles (eds) *International Business and Tourism* (pp. 181–194). London: Routledge.

Gibson, P. and Perkins, L. (2015) A question of equilibrium: Cruise employees at sea. *Tourism in Marine Environments* 10 (3–4), 255–265.

Gold, R.L. (1997) The ethnographic method in sociology. *Qualitative Inquiry* 3 (4), 388–402.

Green, J., Skukauskaite, A. and Baker, B. (2012) Ethnography as epistemology: An introduction to educational ethnography. In J. Arthur, M.I. Waring, R. Coe and L.V. Hedges (eds) *Research Methodologies and Methods in Education* (pp. 309–321). London: Sage.

Guerrier, Y. and Adib, A. (2003) Work at leisure and leisure at work: A study of the emotional labour of tour reps. *Human Relations* 56 (11), 1399–1417.

Guest, G., Bunce, A. and Johnson, L. (2006) How many interviews are enough?: An experiment with data saturation and variability. *Field Methods* 18 (1), 59–82.

Hughes, H.L. (2006) *Pink Tourism: Holidays of Gay Men and Lesbians*. Wallingford: CABI.

Hughes, H.L., Monterrubio, J.C. and Miller, A. (2010) 'Gay' tourists and host community attitudes. *International Journal of Tourism Research* 12 (6), 774–786.

Louis, M.R. (1980) Surprise and sense making: What newcomers experience in entering unfamiliar organisational settings. *Administrative Science Quarterly* 25 (2), 226–251.

Mason, J. (2010) *Qualitative Researching* (2nd edn). London: Sage.

Matuszewski, I. and Blenkinsopp, J. (2011) 'New kids on the ship': Organisational socialisation and sensemaking of new entrants to cruise ship employment. *Journal of Hospitality and Tourism Management* 18 (1), 79–87.

Mendoza, C. (2013) Beyond sex tourism: Gay tourists and male sex workers in Puerto Vallarta (Western Mexico). *International Journal of Tourism Research* 15 (2), 122–137.

Monterrubio, J.C. (2008) Identity and sex: Concurrent aspects of gay tourism. *Tourismos: An International Multidisciplinary Journal of Tourism* 4 (2), 155–167.

Newton, E. (1993) *Cherry Grove, Fire Island: Sixty Years in America's First Gay and Lesbian Town*. Boston, MA: Beacon Press.

Onwuegbuzie, A.J. and Leech, N.L. (2007) A call for qualitative power analyses. *Quality & Quantity* 41 (4), 105–121.

Patton, M.Q. (2002) *Qualitative Research & Evaluation Methods* (3rd edn). Thousand Oaks, CA: Sage.

Prayag, G. and Ryan, C. (2012) Visitor interactions with hotel employees: The role of nationality. *International Journal of Culture, Tourism and Hospitality Research* 6 (2), 173–185.

Rosness, R., Evjemo, T.E., Haavik, T. and Wærø, I. (2016) Prospective sensemaking in the operating theatre. *Cognition, Technology & Work* 18, 53–69.

Rumens, N. (2008) Working at intimacy: Gay men's workplace friendships. *Gender, Work and Organization* 15 (1), 9–30.

Rumens, N. (2010) Firm friends: Exploring the supportive components in gay men's workplace friendships. *The Sociological Review* 58 (1), 135–155.

Rumens, N. (2016) *Queer Company: The Role and Meaning of Friendship in Gay Men's Work Lives*. Milton Park: Routledge.

Rumens, N. and Ozturk, M.B. (2019) Heteronormativity and the (re)construction of gay male entrepreneurial identities. *International Small Business Journal: Researching Entrepreneurship* 37 (7), 671–688.

Selwyn, T. (2000) An anthropology of hospitality. In C. Lashley and A. Morrison (eds) *In Search of Hospitality: Theoretical Perspectives and Debates* (pp. 18–37). Oxford: Butterworth-Heinemann.

Sharpley, R. (2018) *Tourism, Tourists and Society* (5th edn). London: Routledge.

Stokes, D. and Bergin, R. (2006) Methodology or 'methodolatry'? An evaluation of focus groups and depth interviews. *Qualitative Market Research* 9 (1), 26–37.

Tedlock, B. (2003) Ethnography and ethnographic representation. In N.K. Denzin and Y.S. Lincoln (eds) *Strategies of Qualitative Inquiry* (2nd edn) (pp. 165–213). Thousand Oaks, CA: Sage.

Van Maanen, J. and Schein, E.H. (1979) Toward a theory of organizational socialization. *Research in Organizational Behavior* 1, 209–264.

Vorobjovas-Pinta, O. (2017) Gay neo-tribes: An exploration of space and travel behaviour. Doctoral dissertation, University of Tasmania.

Vorobjovas-Pinta, O. (2018a) 'It's been nice, but we're going back to our lives': Neo-tribalism and the role of space in a gay resort. In A. Hardy, A. Bennett and B. Robards (eds) *Neo-Tribes: Consumption, Leisure and Tourism* (pp. 71–87). Cham: Palgrave Macmillan.

Vorobjovas-Pinta, O. (2018b) Gay neo-tribes: Exploration of travel behaviour and space. *Annals of Tourism Research* 75, 1–10.

Vorobjovas-Pinta, O. (2019) Resorts. In H. Chiang (ed.) *Global Encyclopedia of Lesbian, Gay, Bisexual, Transgender, and Queer (LGBTQ) History* (pp. 1379–1383). Farmington Hills, MI: Charles Scribner.

Vorobjovas-Pinta, O. and Dalla-Fontana, I.J. (2018) The strange case of dating apps at a gay resort: Hyper-local and virtual-physical leisure. *Tourism Review* 74 (5), 1070–1080.

Vorobjovas-Pinta, O. and Hardy, A. (2016) The evolution of gay travel research. *International Journal of Tourism Research* 18 (4), 409–416.

Vorobjovas-Pinta, O. and Hardy, A. (2021) Resisting marginalisation and reconstituting space through LGBTQI+ events. *Journal of Sustainable Tourism* 29 (2–3), 448–466. doi:10.1080/09669582.2020.1769638

Vorobjovas-Pinta, O. and Robards, B. (2017) The shared oasis: An insider ethnographic account of a gay resort. *Tourist Studies* 17 (4), 369–387.

Underhill, E. and Rimmer, M. (2016) Layered vulnerability: Temporary migrants in Australian horticulture. *Journal of Industrial Relations* 58 (5), 608–626.

Urry, J. (2002) *The Tourist Gaze* (2nd edn). London: Sage.

Weick, K.E. (1995) *Sensemaking in Organizations*. Thousand Oaks, CA: Sage.

Weick, K.E., Sutcliffe, K.M. and Obstfeld, D. (2005) Organizing and the process of sensemaking. *Organization Science* 16 (4), 409–421.

Willis, J.W. (2007) *Foundations of Qualitative Research: Interpretive and Critical Approaches*. Thousand Oaks, CA: Sage.

Winkler, I. (2018) Identity work and emotions: A review. *International Journal of Management Reviews* 20, 120–133.

Yaoyuneyong, G., Whaley, J.E., Butler, R.A., Williams, J.A., Jordan Jr., K.L. and Hunt, L. (2018) Resort mystery shopping: A case study of hotel service. *Journal of Quality Assurance in Hospitality & Tourism* 19 (3), 358–386.

Yin, R.K. (2016) *Qualitative Research from Start to Finish*. New York: Guilford Press.

9 Sensual and Sexual Experiences Come First: An Analysis of Gay Patrons' Comments on Gay Saunas, Spas and Cruising Clubs in the Asia Pacific Region

Bình Nghiêm-Phú and Jillian Rae Suter

Introduction

The LGBT (lesbian, gay, bisexual and transgender) market is often regarded as a powerful one. In America alone, the spending power of this market is estimated to be around US$1 trillion (Witeck Communications, 2016). Therefore, considerable research has been attempted to understand this market's general preferences for and attitudes towards certain products and services, particularly in the hospitality, leisure and tourism sectors (Hattingh & Spencer, 2017, 2020; Monterrubio & Barrios, 2016). A few studies have been implemented to reveal LGBT consumers' evaluation of product and service quality (Poria, 2006). However, the lack of studies on LGBT consumers' perceptions of product and service attributes is insufficient for the management of LGBT-related businesses.

This chapter, therefore, aims to examine the attributes of certain LGBT products and services which are salient to LGBT consumers while travelling. Specifically, this chapter focuses on gay customers' experiences at saunas, spas and cruising clubs in order to identify their perceptions of the attributes of two particular servicescapes: massage and sauna (or cruising). The reasons for this emphasis are threefold. Firstly, previous studies have chosen to investigate the main element of LGBT travel: accommodation (Berezan *et al.*, 2015; Poria, 2006). The supporting components of saunas, spas and cruising clubs have been largely neglected. Secondly, visiting gay saunas, spas and cruising clubs can be considered

an important leisure act which is meaningful to the creation and maintenance of the gay identity (Hughes & Deutsch, 2010; Rupp *et al.*, 2014).
Yet, which attributes are important to gay customers when using such
products and services remains unknown. Thirdly, the types of gay saunas,
spas and cruising clubs differ among countries, and the purposes of use
also differ by venues and users. Therefore, instead of analysing each type
of venue (sauna, spa and cruising club), the examination of each type of
service (massage and sauna) is more appropriate. The outcomes of this
study will help deepen the understanding of gay customers' preferences
and evaluations, especially of those products and services directly related
to the sexual identity of such customers.

Literature Review

In the late 1970s, Devall (1979) argued that gay leisure is representative of gay culture, and that leisure activities can help create and maintain
the social identities of gay men. Later, Clift and Forrest (1999) studied and
discovered three dimensions of English gay residents' holiday motivations,
which are gay social life and sex, culture and sights, and comfort and
relaxation. Pritchard *et al.* (2000: 279) found in the contexts of Wales and
the Netherlands that 'some gays and lesbians use holidays to assert their
cultural power and to escape those forces which attempt to control and
constrain their behavior and identity'. Herrera (2003) added that travelling was a strategy used by gay men to cope with their homosexuality, to
gain new relationships and to learn how to live a more peaceful life after-
wards. Thus, leisure has provided many benefits for gay individuals.

On the other hand, there are many factors that can negatively affect
gays' leisure, such as the lack of diverse opportunities to meet co-participants,
in-group diversity, rejection, discrimination and oppression (Browne &
Bakshi, 2011; Harper & Schneider, 2003; Herrera, 2003). However, the
most important constraining factors are sensitivity to being in the minority
and being of the same-sex sexual orientation (Hughes *et al.*, 2010; Pritchard
et al., 2000). Nevertheless, it was found in a study in Mexico that local
residents had a relatively positive attitude towards gay tourism and gay
tourists (Hughes *et al.*, 2010). The situation in many other places is similar
as societies are becoming friendlier and more tolerant towards gay individuals and their behaviours (Hartal, 2019; Squires, 2019).

In summary, previous studies have identified several motivations for gay
people to travel, including sexual encounters. The sites for actual sexual
activities are numerous. They range from common and mixed spaces such
as bars and hotels (Hughes & Deutsch, 2010; Rupp *et al.*, 2014) to specific
venues such as massage parlours, saunas, spas and cruising clubs (Chen,
2018; Prior & Cusack, 2010). However, compared to the research about the
macro environment of gay cities and villages, studies on the micro spaces
and venues of gay and gay-related businesses are very limited.

Among the abovementioned sites, massage parlours have long been regarded as sexual venues (Armstrong, 1978; Bryant & Palmer, 2010). They provide job opportunities for many local and migrant workers as well as recreation options for travellers and tourists. However, the original and primary purpose of massage parlours is to provide tactile and aroma treatments and relaxation in order to release the physical and mental tensions of customers, and consequently to improve the quality of their lives (Wilkie *et al.*, 2017). Similarly, the ultimate purpose of saunas or bathing facilities is to create a sense of wellbeing for their users (Sorri, 1988). Yet, in certain places, saunas have been transformed into sexual areas (Lee *et al.*, 2012; Tattelman, 1997; Valtakari, 1988). In both cases, massage parlours and saunas are the main businesses in and of themselves. Consequently, customer satisfaction and customer loyalty are very important to their success or failure. In a larger sense, massages and saunas, as well as other additional or supporting products and services, can help increase the enjoyment that travellers and tourists may experience at a given place (Wang, 2011). Thus, understanding the major attributes of massage and sauna products and services is significant not only to the management of the micro businesses of the parlours but also to the development of the macroeconomic activities of the destinations.

Massage and sauna products and services are provided in a variety of venues, such as hotels, resorts and spas, among others. The types of venue are diverse, as are the specific types of offerings and treatments. Yet generic services, and thus the overall experience, of massage and sauna may be defined similarly by members of a consumer group. For gay patrons in particular, a massage service and experience often involves body treatments (and, in certain cases, sexual encounters) provided by masseurs and the like in and around a massage parlour. Furthermore, a sauna service and experience often includes bathing, steaming and, most importantly, making out with other patrons inside a venue with limited instruction or control from the venue's staff. These services and experiences are highly compatible with gay customers (Hughes & Deutsch, 2010; Rupp *et al.*, 2014; Tattelman, 1997).

Method

Sample selection

The gay population is a somewhat hidden one for several reasons. In a narrow sense, many individuals choose to withhold their sexualities from others in order to maintain their privacy and safety (McKeown *et al.*, 2010). In a larger sense, a lack of family support and the conservatism of the local society and religion have prevented the disclosure of an uncountable number of LGBT people (Pastrana, 2015; Siraj, 2012). From a tourism perspective, the openness of a destination may also affect the degree of disclosure by LGBT tourists (Hughes *et al.*, 2010; Wong & Tolkach, 2017).

In order to recruit participants from hidden populations, various snowball sampling methods have been invented (Kendal *et al.*, 2008). Qualitative methods (e.g. interview and observation-participation) are then adopted to collect in-depth information from the participants (Monterrubio & Barrios, 2016). However, these combinations are only powerful for an already-identified population. In recent studies, the advantages of social media platforms and internet-based survey tools have been utilised to approach both the open and hidden groups of the gay population (Hattingh & Spencer, 2017, 2020). Yet, the rigid nature of the structured or quantifiable questionnaire definitely limits the variability and flexibility of the answers. An alternative, which freerides on the strengths of both the qualitative and quantitative methods, is to data mine user-generated content. Nevertheless, the data-mining method has rarely been used in LGBT-related research, regardless of its merits (Nghiêm-Phú, 2018).

Nowadays, gay customers can contribute their opinions (user-generated content) on a lot of gay-related sites. For gay travellers in particular, travelgayasia.com is one of the most popular options. This site is ranked third among approximately 489 million gay travel related sites as suggested by Google Search (as of March 2019). However, unlike other sites that may be mainly considered as news portals (e.g. gaytravel.com, travelgay.com), travelgayasia.com is an interactive environment where users can write reviews about the venues they have been to or post questions to ask the opinions of other members.

In consideration of the difficulty of approaching gay travellers and the weaknesses of traditional research methods, this chapter opts to target users (reviewers) of travelgayasia.com as its population and to employ users' reviews posted on the site as the data. Information encoded in the reviews is salient to service providers given the fact that users must make the effort to write and post such content (Cadotte & Turgeon, 1988). However, the sample of travelgayasia.com reviewers is not necessarily a perfect representation of the whole gay traveller population. Instead, this sample consists of the most active and probably the most open gay travellers, both online and in the real world (Hammick & Lee, 2014). Those gay travellers who have no knowledge of this site and those who choose not to openly discuss their experiences are unfortunately excluded. Similarly, gay individuals who do not or cannot use much English, the lingua franca of travelgayasia.com, are not included in the sample.

Setting selection

This chapter purposely opts to emphasise gay venues in the Asia Pacific region, since the existing literature has mainly focused on Western gay cultures (Vorobjovas-Pinta & Hardy, 2016). However, the purpose of this chapter is not to examine the behaviours of Asian and Pacific gay people at saunas, spas and cruising clubs in the region. Instead, the chapter investigates how travellers in or to the region perceive the attributes of such servicescapes. This means that the travellers may come from any part of the world. However, due to the lack of background information (users of review platforms do not have to nor are inclined to report their personal profile), the origins of such travellers (e.g. inside or outside the Asia Pacific region) are unknown. Also, the actual diversity in the gay community cannot be detected. In a general sense, there are masculine gay individuals alongside feminine ones (Caceres & Rosasco, 1999). In addition, there are confident gay consumers who are more likely to complain about their dissatisfactions alongside guarded gay consumers who are less inclined to do so (Olson & Ro, 2015). The sample collected from travelgayasia.com, nevertheless, cannot represent that heterogeneity either. It should be noted that non-gay individuals who are curious about or who opt to use services at gay venues (Mayo, 2004) and have posted something on the site might be also included in the sample.

Furthermore, the whole region is treated as one setting in accordance with the divisions of travelgayasia.com (the other regions include Europe, the United States and Canada, Central and South America, and Africa). In other words, 'Asia Pacific' is considered as a single destination, despite the fact that it consists of many large and small destinations which greatly differ in terms of sociocultural conditions. Regarding the gay community in particular, Asia still is considered a conservative region. In many countries (e.g. Indonesia, Malaysia, Singapore, the Middle East), same-sex acts are still illegal (Chua, 2012; Goh, 2011). Gay activities and gay-related businesses have been hidden or have remained in a grey environment. Religious regulations (e.g. Confucianism, Muslim) and social characteristics (e.g. close-knit communities) are some of the reasons behind this state of affairs. However, in other countries and territories (e.g. Hong Kong, Taiwan, Thailand), gay rights have been better regarded, and gay businesses (including saunas, spas and cruising clubs) have become somewhat open (Hsu & Yen, 2017; Kong, 2012; Moussawi, 2013). This is the result of more powerful gay-advocate movements across the region (Horton et al., 2015; Offord, 2013). Constrained by the abovementioned issues, the examination of gay saunas, spas and cruising clubs in this chapter can only focus on those units that have, to some extent, opened to the public in general, and to the gay audience in particular.

Furthermore, at the time of data collection, gay saunas, spas and cruising clubs could only be found in 40 cities of 14 countries in the region (according to travelgayasia.com's collection). Thus, activities at and perceptions of the gay-related sites in the remaining countries are unrecognised. Those with hidden units are also overlooked. However, the limited number of active and open gay saunas, spas and cruising clubs encourages the aggregation of all the sites rather than the separation of sites according to countries and cities. As a consequence of this practice, the differences in the business activities and in the perceptions of gay patrons among countries in the region could not be taken into account.

Data collection and analysis

All the reviews posted in 2017 on travelgayasia.com about gay saunas, spas and cruising clubs in Asia Pacific were manually collected by one of the researchers in April 2018. The initial sample includes 1493 units of reviews, and all of them were written in English. There were some reviews outside the sample written in other languages (e.g. Chinese, Japanese). However, the non-English reviews were eliminated due to their limited number, their sporadic distribution and the complexity of the consequent analysis.

From the initial sample, two sub-samples that directly relate to massage experiences ($n = 706$, 47.3%) and sauna or cruising experiences ($n = 224$, 15.0%) were extracted and recruited as the databases for the study. The remaining reviews were excluded since the reviewers did not openly mention any specific experiences that they had. It should be noted again that the built-in categorisation on travelgayasia.com was not referred to, since the types of products or services differ among the listed countries, and many venues are used differently by different users.

Examination of the data began with an analysis of the frequency of the keywords that appeared in the reviews. This was done automatically on Voyant Tools (https://voyant-tools.org) (Sinclair & Rockwell, 2012). After the frequency lists were generated, the two researchers selected 19 keywords relating to the massage experience and 25 keywords concerning the sauna experience. The reasons are twofold. Firstly, these keywords were mentioned by at least 5% of the reviewers in each category of data; thus, they are more meaningful than the remaining keywords. Secondly, these keywords reflect the potential attributes of a servicescape, which are important to the evaluation of service quality of the users (Bitner, 1992; Nghiêm-Phú, 2017). However, a consequent examination of the reviews suggested that some keywords did not have significant meanings when they were returned to their original contexts. In addition, several keywords had to be extended or adjusted to properly represent the attributes that the reviewers mentioned in their reviews. This process reduced the message attributes to 13 and the sauna attributes to 15.

Thenceforth, the data were coded manually in an Excel file. Each attribute was given a column in the Excel file. Its appearance within a review was given a value of 1, and its non-appearance a value of 0. Initially, one researcher worked on all the data independently. This researcher coded the data twice in order to ensure intra-coder reliability (Kassarjian, 1977). Later, approximately 10% of the data of each category was randomly selected by IBM SPSS and sent to the other researcher to cross-check. As a consequence, minor disagreements were found in four massage attributes (1.5%) and three sauna attributes (4.0%). The inter-coder reliability indices were then calculated for such attributes (the platform was available at http://dfreelon.org/; Freelon, 2010). Results show that all the values of Scott's pi, Cohen's kappa and Krippendorff's alpha exceeded 0.83. Therefore, the coding of the first researcher can be considered highly reliable (Hayes & Krippendorff, 2007). After that, the two sets of data were analysed in IBM SPSS to understand the frequency of and the correlations (co-occurrences) among the attributes.

Findings

The final 13 massage attributes and 15 sauna attributes are presented in Table 9.1. Accordingly, 'masseur's skill' was considered the most important attribute of a massage parlour in Asia Pacific by more than 90% of the reviewers. In addition, 'co-patrons (crowd)' was regarded as the most important attribute of a sauna venue in the region by more than 77% of

Table 9.1 Massage and sauna attributes

Massage attributes (n = 706)	Frequency	Percent	Sauna attributes (n = 224)	Frequency	Percent
Masseur's skill (M1)	638	90.37	Co-patrons (crowd) (S1)	174	77.68
Facility and location (M2)	317	44.90	Staff (S2)	100	44.64
Price, tip and value (M3)	254	35.98	Cleanliness (S3)	100	44.64
Friendliness, politeness, welcomeness and kindness (M4)	221	31.30	Dark and cruising area (S4)	85	37.95
Massage time (M5)	212	30.03	Steam room (S5)	72	32.14
Masseur's appearance and age (M6)	204	28.90	Price and tip (S6)	65	29.02
Cleanliness (M7)	187	26.49	Shower (S7)	50	22.32
Manager and receptionist (M8)	134	18.98	Clothing mode (S8)	37	16.52
Shower (M9)	124	17.56	Jacuzzi (S9)	31	13.84
Conversation (M10)	99	14.02	Locker room (S10)	31	13.84
Oil therapy (M11)	91	12.89	Gym and pool (S11)	29	12.95
Website and social media platform (SMP) (M12)	71	10.06	Massage (S12)	28	12.50
Thai massage (13)	37	5.24	Dry room (S13)	28	12.50
			Towel (S14)	26	11.61
			Water (S15)	15	6.70

the contributors. Both massage parlour and sauna venue only share three similar attributes: 'price and tip', 'cleanliness' and 'shower facility'.

The correlations among the massage attributes and the sauna attributes are displayed in Tables 9.2 and 9.3, and are visualised by Figures 9.1 and 9.2. In the first case, the strongest correlations are those between 'facility and location' and 'cleanliness', 'oil therapy' and 'Thai massage', and 'facility and location' and 'shower'. In the second case, the robust associations can be observed between 'steam room' and 'dry room', 'steam room' and 'Jacuzzi', and 'shower' and 'water'.

Discussion

Each servicescape is attached to certain attributes that are important for its customers' experiences. Basically, Bitner (1992) defined three major elements of a servicescape, including the ambient conditions, space and function, and signs, symbols and artefacts. Among these, the first is a sensory element while the second and the third represent the physical components.

The findings of this study, however, suggested that patrons at gay saunas, spas and cruising clubs in the Asia Pacific region perceived a more diverse range of servicescape attributes. In the sauna experiences, the most important attributes are those of the people element: co-patrons and staff. A sensory attribute of 'cleanliness' (through the senses of sight and smell) is also present and was ranked third. The remaining attributes are of a physical nature, including 'price and tip', 'dark and cruising area', 'steam room', 'shower', 'Jacuzzi', 'locker room', 'gym and pool', 'dry room' and 'towel', among others.

In terms of the massage experiences, the categorisation is even more diverse. There is one sensory attribute of 'cleanliness' and four physical attributes of 'facility and location', 'shower', 'website and social media platform' and 'price, tip and value'. The people element ('masseur's appearance and age' and 'manager and receptionist'), although less important than that of the sauna experiences, was also mentioned. However, the most important attribute of 'masseur's skill' is that of the technical element. The other technical attributes are 'massage time', 'conversation', 'oil therapy' and 'Thai therapy'. In addition, there is one atmospheric attribute of 'friendliness, politeness, welcomeness and kindness'. The mention of Thai massage, in particular, although it was the least popular attribute, helps create a somewhat Asian atmosphere for the massage parlours in the region.

The abovementioned observations have suggested that the attributes of servicescapes are not limited to the sensory and physical elements (Bitner, 1992) or the physical and atmospheric components (Nghiêm-Phú, 2017). For gay saunas, spas and cruising clubs in Asia Pacific, the people and technical categories also play important roles in providing meaningful

Table 9.2 Correlations among massage attributes

	M1	M2	M3	M4	M5	M6	M7	M8	M9	M10	M11	M12
M2	-0.024											
M3	-0.145**	0.065										
M4	-0.018	0.042	-0.099**									
M5	-0.100**	0.036	0.217**	-0.029								
M6	-0.057	0.040	0.023	0.055	-0.009							
M7	-0.054	0.375**	0.058	0.031	-0.029	-0.014						
M8	-0.124**	0.050	0.081*	0.117**	0.045	0.106**	0.037					
M9	-0.001	0.249**	0.112**	0.018	0.169**	0.059	0.204**	0.080*				
M10	0.035	0.029	0.003	0.132**	-0.015	0.121**	0.007	0.127**	0.017			
M11	-0.018	0.018	0.099**	0.032	0.200**	0.063	-0.020	0.040	0.111**	0.064		
M12	0.013	0.077*	0.103**	0.028	0.058	0.078*	0.045	0.006	0.081*	0.163**	0.040	
M13	0.034	0.069	0.036	0.143**	0.137**	0.046	-0.069	0.081*	0.075*	0.106**	0.308**	0.006

Notes: **Correlation is significant at the 0.01 level (2-tailed); *Correlation is significant at the 0.05 level (2-tailed).

Table 9.3 Correlation among sauna attributes

	S1	S2	S3	S4	S5	S6	S7	S8	S9	S10	S11	S12	S13	S14
S2	−0.101													
S3	0.028	0.006												
S4	0.242**	0.019	0.131											
S5	−0.021	0.016	−0.060	0.250**										
S6	0.059	0.198**	0.059	0.088	0.087									
S7	0.056	0.079	0.036	0.222**	0.274**	−0.036								
S8	0.065	−0.013	−0.037	0.098	−0.023	0.007	0.021							
S9	0.029	0.082	0.004	0.219**	0.278**	0.000	0.189**	0.031						
S10	0.091	0.160*	−0.022	0.140*	0.167*	0.285**	0.251**	0.100	0.027					
S11	−0.081	0.001	0.055	0.109	0.076	−0.071	0.081	0.151*	−0.001	0.077				
S12	−0.024	0.231**	−0.014	0.038	0.231**	−0.004	0.089	−0.059	0.279**	−0.034	0.055			
S13	−0.089	0.068	−0.014	0.205**	0.289**	0.056	0.089	−0.059	0.279**	0.044	0.055	0.184**		
S14	−0.007	0.095	0.151*	0.205**	0.168*	0.168*	0.174**	0.214**	0.097	0.218**	−0.015	0.032	−0.011	
S15	−0.157*	0.047	0.047	0.048	0.198**	0.025	0.285**	−0.023	0.255**	0.100	0.056	0.061	0.007	0.070

Notes: **Correlation is significant at the 0.01 level (2-tailed); *Correlation is significant at the 0.05 level (2-tailed).

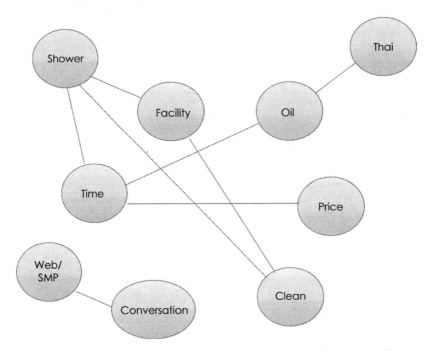

Figure 9.1 Correlations among certain massage attributes (coefficients ≥ 0.15)

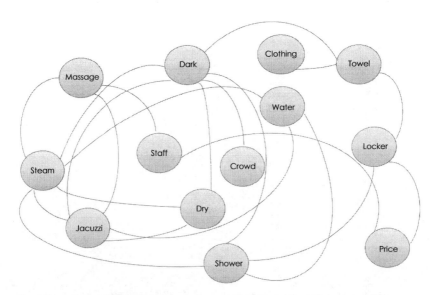

Figure 9.2 Correlations among certain sauna attributes (coefficients ≥ 0.20)

experiences to customers. However, only a few of them can be used as hints to say that those servicescapes are gay oriented. The first is an attribute of the massage servicescape: the appearance and age of the masseurs. Non-gay patrons at non-gay massage parlours may also perceive this particular attribute since there are many direct encounters between customers and masseurs. Yet gay users are more specific about this attribute since they have high expectations and requirements of physical body condition (Hutson, 2010). The quote below illustrates one reviewer's perception of his masseur's appearance.

> Nickname Ju.:   My guy is a beefy muscly bear, manly with tattoos and goatee, not at all what I expected they would have. (Reviewed on 30 October 2017 about a venue in Hong Kong)

The following gay-oriented attributes are those of the sauna servicescape: 'co-patrons', 'dark and cruising area' and 'clothing mode'. Since saunas and similar venues have been employed as sexual areas (Lee *et al.*, 2012; Valtakari, 1988), the presence of such salient attributes is predictable. Interestingly, 'co-patrons' and 'dark and cruising area' share a positive correlation. The 'dark and cruising area', in particular, has several positive associations with other physical attributes, including 'steam room', 'shower', 'Jacuzzi', 'gym and pool' and 'dry room'. Together, these attributes create a sensual area which is important to the sexual encounters of those who visit gay saunas, spas and cruising clubs in the Asia Pacific region. In such areas, one or more clothing modes (e.g. nude, towel and underwear) may be applied to maximise the eroticism of the experiences (Tattelman, 1997). The following quote describes the perception of one reviewer of the co-patrons.

> Nickname De.:   There were mostly Asians in the sauna at the time I went, around a dozen or so, with maybe one or two other Westerners, but everyone was friendly and enjoying the place. (Reviewed on 19 September 2017 about a venue in Hong Kong)

However, the gay-related attributes alone cannot represent the gay massage and sauna servicescapes. Other non-gay attributes are also very important to gay users' experiences, especially in the Asia Pacific region. This observation suggests that gay customers, with the exclusion of their sexual identity, are similar to non-gay customers in terms of preference and evaluation of service quality (Poria, 2006). Treating gay customers differently may be considered an explicit, although possibly unintended, discrimination act.

On an additional note, the Asian atmosphere of the gay massage and sauna servicescapes in the region may help differentiate them from those in the West (Moussawi, 2013). The potential differences stem from the people

(Asian staff and patrons), the technique (Thai massage) and the friendliness and the welcoming atmosphere. In this context, the exoticness of the Western patrons may be better appreciated, and the Western patrons may be given more privileges than when they frequent gay venues in their own cultures (Scuzzarello, 2020). The following quote exemplifies this point:

> **Nickname Ma.:** I'm white, 36 with a 'kind-of' gym toned body. In saunas in Europe or the States I usually find fun but I'm certainly not the center of attention. That was completely different at [the venue's name]. (Reviewed on 29 September 2017 about a venue in Shanghai)

Managerial implications

Generally, gay saunas, spas and cruising clubs are tailored for gay customers. Therefore, the gay-related servicescape attributes should be managed with special care, especially the promotional activities. Specifically, pictures posted on websites and other social media platforms should be real. Any mismatches (see the quote from nickname An.) will consequently lead to customers' dissatisfaction and negative future intentions (Oliver, 1980). This holds true for other service factors, such as price and massage time.

> **Nickname An.:** Allowed to choose from 4 trainers. None of trainers with pictures on the website are there. All the trainers are not hot. (Reviewed on 8 April 2017 about a venue in Seoul)

On an additional note, the positive correlations between 'masseur's appearance and age' and 'manager and receptionist' or 'conversation' suggest that the 'masseur's appearance and age' attribute may be improved with a customised approach when the manager or receptionist selects the masseur per request, or with some friendly conversation with their customers before, during and after the main service. As evidence, 'conversation' was found to have positive associations with 'friendliness, politeness, welcomeness and kindness' and 'manager and receptionist'.

For the sauna servicescape, the management of the two internal attributes of 'dark and cruising area' and 'clothing mode' is easier than that of the external attribute of 'co-patrons'. Regarding the first internal attribute, managers at gay saunas, spas and cruising clubs in Asia Pacific should take care about the level of darkness or lightness and the cleanliness conditions (see the quote from nickname Le.). Concerning the second internal attribute, managers should make sure that the dressing theme is effectively enforced (see the quote from nickname ha.).

> **Nickname Le.:** The place was all very clear, even the dark room got lights. Very dirty and stains everywhere. (Reviewed on 26 June 2017 about a venue in Hong Kong)

Nickname ha.:   I went there on Sunday night which is the nude night and I confirm with the receptionist before I go, but nobody was controlling the towel and is just like a normal Sauna evening. … Not my cup of tea and may be is not my lucky day. (Reviewed on 12 February 2017 about a venue in Hong Kong)

For the third external attribute, the current situation in Asia Pacific suggests two management strategies: one involves nationality (no entrance or higher price for foreign customers, especially Westerners) and the other involves age or weight (higher entrance fees for older and heavier customers) (see the quotes from nicknames Au. and St.). As a consequence, customers who were denied due to the nationality issue felt internally discriminated (within the gay community). In the other case, non-local, older or heavier customers have to pay a higher price to enter the venues yet may eventually be happy. Otherwise, younger and fitter customers must endure undesired audiences and thus become unhappy. In order to avoid conflicts and dissatisfaction, the entrance regulations must be overtly stated (on the website or on site) and consistently implemented (no case-by-case rule). In addition, the gay customers in or to the region should not be treated as a homogeneous market. They indeed are heterogeneous (Hattingh & Spencer, 2020; Olson & Ro, 2015) and therefore should be selectively targeted.

Nickname Au.:   If you are not local, standard $22 per visit. It is a bit off putting to see others paying $10 or whatever. Definitely do not like this aspect. (Reviewed on 10 November 2017 about a venue in Singapore)
Nickname St.:   My biggest issue was that dependent on your age, determines how much [customers] have to pay to get in. … Discrimination in another form … (Reviewed on 1 September 2017 about a venue in Singapore; review unused for the analysis)

In addition to the gay-related attributes, other common elements must be taken care of. For example, customers of both the massage and sauna servicescapes in Asia Pacific prioritise price and cleanliness. The price element of the massage servicescape can be guaranteed by the satisfactory fulfilment of the service-time length and the friendly and kind appearance of managers and receptionists. That of the sauna servicescape can be assured by the proper provision of locker room and towels. Moreover, cleanliness should be given particular attention in the shower area of the massage servicescape and with the towels of the sauna servicescape.

The findings of this study are meaningful not only to the management of micro gay-related businesses but also to that of each destination as a macro entity. Specifically, gay and non-gay customers have similar preferences for and evaluations of product and service attributes. Differences, if there are any, originate from and relate to the sexual orientation of the individual customers. When targeting the gay customer market, destinations in the Asia Pacific region, in particular, should be aware of and approve the attributes and businesses that cater to that particular need. An active and supportive managerial approach is required in order to fully exploit the potential of such activities. Otherwise, gay-related businesses may hide themselves in the dark or grey areas. In such cases, fees and taxes may be lost while negative consequences still need to be dealt with.

However, it should be noted that the above discussions only hold true under an assumption that all the practices at the gay-oriented venues are open and legal. Unfortunately, this is not the real situation in certain countries, for example, Malaysia, Singapore and Vietnam (Chua, 2012; Goh, 2011). In addition, the attitude of the local population, which is not always positive and supportive (Manalastas *et al.*, 2017), has not been taken into account. Therefore, the management of gay venues in the Asia Pacific region should be implemented with the utmost care and respect in order to avoid conflicts with administrative representatives and the public at large. Promotional activities on websites and other social media platforms should consider the fact that anyone can gain access to these sites if restrictions and directions are not in force. In addition, management of the crowd before and after they enter the venues should acknowledge the fact that the appearance and behaviours of these customers may create distress and irritation for the surrounding local residents.

Conclusion

Massage and sauna venues have long been regarded and used as sexual areas for gay men. For gay patrons at such venues, sensual and sexual experiences are important. However, the analysis of comments about gay saunas, spas and cruising clubs in the Asia Pacific region has added that gay patrons do care about multiple servicescape elements, including the physical, technical, people and atmospheric or emotional ones. In terms of the massage servicescape, the most important attribute is applicable to all types of guests: the skills of the masseurs. However, for the sauna servicescape, the most important attribute is gay related: the co-patrons. In both cases, the gay-related servicescape attributes are less salient than the common attributes in terms of their frequencies. This outcome advocates a more balanced and less extreme approach in servicing gay customers. Specifically, when isolating the sexual orientation factor (which is not always overt), gay and non-gay customers tend to have similar expectations and evaluations of products and services.

In addition to its fruitful undertakings and outcomes, the study reported in this chapter could not avoid some limitations. Firstly, as mentioned in the previous sections, the sample of this study is not representative, the diversity of the gay population was not taken into account and the differences in the perceptions of gay customers among countries and venues were not considered. A series of studies, including those adopting the traditional questionnaire-based survey method, are necessary to tackle these issues. Secondly, due to its exploratory nature, only the frequency of the attributes was coded. Consequently, the actual evaluations of such attributes (good or bad) could not be detected. To address this shortcoming, future studies may apply the sentiment analysis technique to capture the level of positivity or negativity that reviewers gave to each attribute (Liu, 2010). The outcome of such analysis would provide information about gay patrons' satisfaction and dissatisfaction, which is useful for service and product quality management. Thirdly, only gay saunas, spas and cruising clubs in the Asia Pacific region were targeted in this study. Thus, the situations in America, Europe and other regions could not be identified. As an advanced step, future research may apply the coding scheme developed in this study to analyse and compare the situations in different regions. Such findings are generalisable in a worldwide context. Moreover, researchers could make more efforts to employ user-generated content to investigate those sensitive topics involving the LGBT populations. The reviews are an important source of information given the fact that gay users also have to contribute their time and probably risk their privacy to post them (Cadotte & Turgeon, 1988). In the reviews, the opinions about the products and services are expressed in an overt yet anonymous way.

Furthermore, several side observations of this study may be further validated or elaborated in future research. For example, some reviewers mentioned discrimination within the gay customer community. This discrimination may originate from both the providers and the co-users. The managerial and psychological consequences of such acts could be addressed in a detailed manner. Another interesting topic involves the openness of the gay customer population regarding conventionally sensitive conversations. Researchers may want to investigate how the openness of certain gay figures, with the help of social media platforms, has affected their followers' preferences and evaluations. In addition, researchers should examine the attitudes of the other related stakeholders among the public (e.g. local residents, administrators) towards the operation of gay-oriented venues and the visibility of gay-sexuality content on the internet. The understandings generated from such attempts would be helpful for the management of gay-related attributes of products and services in the future.

References

Armstrong, E.G. (1978) Massage parlors and their customers. *Archives of Sexual Behavior* 7 (2), 117–125.

Berezan, O., Raab, C., Krishen, A.S. and Love, C. (2015) Loyalty runs deeper than thread count: An exploratory study of gay guest preferences and hotelier perceptions. *Journal of Travel & Tourism Marketing* 32 (8), 1034–1050.

Bitner, M.J. (1992) Servicescapes: The impact of physical surroundings on customers and employees. *Journal of Marketing* 56 (2), 57–71.

Browne, K. and Bakshi, L. (2011) We are here to party? Lesbian, gay, bisexual and trans leisurescapes beyond commercial gay scenes. *Leisure Studies* 30 (2), 179–196.

Bryant, C.D. and Palmer, C.E. (2010) Massage parlors and 'hand whores': Some sociological observations. *Journal of Sex Research* 11 (3), 227–241.

Caceres, C.F. and Rosasco, A.M. (1999) The margin has many sides: Diversity among gay and homosexually active men in Lima. *Culture, Health & Sexuality* 1 (3), 261–275.

Cadotte, E.R. and Turgeon, N. (1988) Dissatisfiers and satisfiers: Suggestions from consumer complaints and compliments. *Journal of Consumer Satisfaction, Dissatisfaction & Complaining Behaviors* 1, 74–79.

Chen, B.-W. (2018) Touching intimacy: Bodywork, affect and the caring ethic in erotic gay massage in Taiwan. *Gender Work Organ* 25 (6), 637–652.

Chua, L.J. (2012) Pragmatic resistance, law, and social movements in authoritarian states: The case of gay collective action in Singapore. *Law and Society Review* 46 (4), 713–748.

Clift, S. and Forrest, S. (1999) Gay men and tourism: Destinations and holiday motivations. *Tourism Management* 20 (5), 615–625. doi:10.1016/S0261-5177 (99)00032-1

Devall, W. (1979) Leisure and lifestyle among gay men: An exploratory essay. *International Review of Modern Sociology* 9 (2), 179–195.

Freelon, D.G. (2010) ReCal: Intercoder reliability calculation as a web service. *International Journal of Internet Science* 5 (1), 20–33.

Goh, J.N. (2011) Balanced genitals – YouTube confessional disclosures and signposts for Malaysian gay theologies. *Theology & Sexuality* 17 (3), 279–295.

Hammick, J.K. and Lee, M.J. (2014) Do shy people feel less communication apprehension online? The effects of virtual reality on the relationship between personality characteristics and communication outcomes. *Computers in Human Behavior* 33, 302–310.

Harper, G.W. and Schneider, M. (2003) Oppression and discrimination among lesbian, gay, bisexual, and transgendered people and communities: A challenge for community psychology. *American Journal of Community Psychology* 31 (3–4), 243–252.

Hartal, G. (2019) Gay tourism to Tel-Aviv: Producing urban value? *Urban Studies* 56 (6), 1148–1164.

Hattingh, C. and Spencer, J.P. (2017) Salient factors influencing gay travellers' holiday motivations: A push-pull approach. *African Journal of Hospitality, Tourism and Leisure* 6 (4), 1–25.

Hattingh, C. and Spencer, J.P. (2020) Homosexual not homogeneous: A motivation-based typology of gay leisure travelers holidaying in Cape Town, South Africa. *Journal of Homosexuality* 67 (6), 768–792.

Hayes, A.F. and Krippendorff, K. (2007) Answering the call for a standard reliability measure for coding data. *Communication Methods and Measures* 1 (1), 77–89.

Herrera, S.L. (2003) 'We gotta get out of this place': A qualitative study on the effects of leisure travel on the lives of gay men living in a small community. Unpublished Master's thesis, Texas A&M University.

Horton, P., Rydström, H. and Tonini, M. (2015) Contesting heteronormativity: The fight for lesbian, gay, bisexual and transgender recognition in India and Vietnam. *Culture, Health & Sexuality* 17 (9), 1059–1073.

Hsu, C.-Y. and Yen, C.-F. (2017) Taiwan: Pioneer of the health and well-being of sexual minorities in Asia. *Archives of Sexual Behavior* 46 (6), 1577–1579.

Hughes, H.L. and Deutsch, R. (2010) Holidays of older gay men: Age or sexual orientation as decisive factors? *Tourism Management* 31 (4), 454–463.

Hughes, H., Monterrubio, J.C. and Miller, A. (2010) 'Gay' tourists and host community attitudes. *International Journal of Tourism Research* 12 (6), 774–786.

Hutson, D.J. (2010) Standing OUT/Fitting IN: Identity, appearance, and authenticity in gay and lesbian communities. *Symbolic Interaction* 33 (2), 213–233.

Kassarjian, H.H. (1977) Content analysis in consumer research. *Journal of Consumer Research* 4 (1), 8–18.

Kendal, C., Kerr, L., Gondim, R.C., *et al.* (2008) An empirical comparison of respondent-driven sampling, time location sampling, and snowball sampling for behavioral surveillance in men who have sex with men, Fortaleza, Brazil. *AIDS and Behavior* 12 (4), S97–S104.

Kong, T.S.K. (2012) A fading Tongzhi heterotopia: Hong Kong older gay men's use of spaces. *Sexualities* 15 (8), 896–916.

Lee, S.-S., Lam, A.N.-S., Lee, C.-K. and Wong, N.-S. (2012) Virtual versus physical channel for sex networking in men having sex with men of sauna customers in the city of Hong Kong. *PlosOne.* doi:10.1371/journal.pone.0031072

Liu, B. (2010) Sentiment analysis and subjectivity. In N. Indurkhya and F.J. Damerau (eds) *Handbook of Natural Language Processing* (2nd edn) (pp. 627–665). Boca Raton, FL: Chapman & Hall.

Manalastas, E.J., Ojanen, T.T., Torre, B.A., Ratanashevorn, R., Hong, B.C., Kumaresan, V. and Veeramuthu, V. (2017) Homonegativity in Southeast Asia: Attitudes toward lesbians and gay men in Indonesia, Malaysia, the Philippines, Singapore, Thailand, and Vietnam. *Asia-Pacific Social Sciences Review* 17 (1), 25–33.

Mayo, C. (2004) Queering school communities. *Journal of Gay & Lesbian Issues in Education* 1 (3), 23–36.

McKeown, E., Nelson, S., Anderson, J., Low, N. and Elford, J. (2010) Disclosure, discrimination and desire: Experiences of Black and South Asian gay men in Britain. *Culture, Health & Sexuality* 12 (7), 843–856.

Monterrubio, C. and Barrios, M.D. (2016) Lesbians as tourists: A qualitative study of tourist motivations in Mexico. *Tourismos: An International Multidisciplinary Journal of Tourism* 11 (4), 64–90.

Moussawi, G. (2013) Queering Beirut, the 'Paris of the Middle East': Fractal Orientalism and essentialized masculinities in contemporary gay travelogues. *Gender, Place & Culture* 20 (7), 858–875.

Nghiêm-Phú, B. (2017) User evaluation of airport servicescape characteristics: A quantitative datamining approach. *Proceedings of CAUTHE 2017: Time for Big Ideas? Re-thinking the Field for Tomorrow* (pp. 105–114). Dunedin: University of Otago.

Nghiêm-Phú, B. (2018) Comment and comment response strategies – an analysis of gay hotel guests' comments and managers' responses. *Tourism and Hospitality Management* 24 (1), 1–17.

Offord, B. (2013) Queer activist intersections in Southeast Asia: Human rights and cultural studies. *Asian Studies Review* 37 (3), 335–349.

Oliver, R.L. (1980) A cognitive model of the antecedents and consequences of satisfaction decisions. *Journal of Marketing Research* 17 (4), 460–469.

Olson, E.D. and Ro, H. (2015) Typology of gay consumers' interaction styles on complaining propensity. *Journal of Homosexuality* 62 (5), 664–682.

Pastrana, A. (2015) Being out to others: The relative importance of family support, identity and religion for LGBT Latina/os. *Latino Studies* 13 (1), 88–112.

Poria, Y. (2006) Assessing gay men and lesbian women's hotel experiences: An exploratory study of sexual orientation in the travel industry. *Journal of Travel Research* 44 (3), 327–334.

Prior, J. and Cusack, C.M. (2010) Spiritual dimensions of self-transformation in Sydney's gay bathhouses. *Journal of Homosexuality* 57 (1), 71–97.

Pritchard, A., Morgan, N.J., Sedgley, D., Khan, E. and Jenkins, A. (2000) Sexuality and holiday choices: Conversations with gay and lesbian tourists. *Leisure Studies* 19 (4), 267–282.

Rupp, L.J., Taylor, V., Regev-Messalem, S., Fogarty, A.C. and England, P. (2014) Queer women in the hookup scene: Beyond the closet? *Gender & Society* 28 (2), 212–235.

Scuzzarello, S. (2020) Practising privilege. How settling in Thailand enables older Western migrants to enact privilege over local people. *Journal of Ethnic and Migration Studies* 46 (8), 1606–1628.

Sinclair, S. and Rockwell, G. (2012) Teaching computer-assisted text analysis: Approaches to learning new methodologies. In B.D. Hirsch (ed.) *Digital Humanities Pedagogy: Practices, Principles and Politics* (pp. 241–264). Cambridge: Open Book.

Siraj, A. (2012) 'I don't want to taint the name of Islam': The influence of religion on the lives of Muslim lesbians. *Journal of Lesbian Studies* 16 (4), 449–467.

Sorri, P. (1988) The sauna and sauna bathing habits – a psychoanalytic point of view. *Annals of Clinical Research* 20 (4), 236–239.

Squires, K.K. (2019) Rethinking the homonormative? Lesbian and Hispanic Pride events and the uneven geographies of commoditized identities. *Social & Cultural Geography* 20 (3), 367–386.

Tattelman, I. (1997) The meaning at the wall: Tracing the gay bathhouse. In B. Ingram, A.-M. Bouthillette and Y. Retter (eds) *Queers in Space: Communities, Public Spaces, Sites of Resistance* (pp. 391–406). Seattle, WA: Bay Press.

Valtakari, P. (1988) The sauna and bathing in different countries. *Annals of Clinical Research* 20 (4), 230–235.

Vorobjovas-Pinta, O. and Hardy, A. (2016) The evolution of gay travel research. *International Journal of Tourism Research* 18 (4), 409–416.

Wang, X. (2011) The effect of unrelated supporting service quality on consumer delight, satisfaction, and repurchase intentions. *Journal of Service Research* 14 (2), 149–163.

Wilkie, D.J., Kampbell, J., Cutshall, S., Halabisky, H., Harmon, H., Johnson, L.P., Weinacht, L. and Rake-Marona, M. (2017) Effects of massage on pain intensity, analgesics and quality of life in patients with cancer pain: A pilot study of a randomized clinical trial conducted within hospice care delivery. *The Hospice Journal* 15 (3), 31–53.

Witeck Communications (2016) *America's LGBT 2015 buying power estimated at $917 Billion.* Press release, 20 July. See http://www.witeck.com/pressreleases/2015-buying-power/ (accessed April 2018).

Wong, C.C.L. and Tolkach, D. (2017) Travel preferences of Asian gay men. *Asia Pacific Journal of Tourism Research* 22 (6), 579–591.

10 Away from the Mainstream: Motivations of Travellers Seeking Alternative Forms of LGBT Travel

Stephan Dahl and Ana Margarida Barreto

> For holidays, it was big cities, bars, clubs and so. And maybe the one or other gay resort. But now, I go into the woods with the guys.
>
> Andreas, 39, male[1]

Introduction

Research into LGBT tourism has been criticised for being focused on gay urban tourism, which takes place in either large urban environments like London or in moderately urban seaside resorts like Sitges or Key West (Vorobjovas-Pinta & Hardy, 2016; Weeden *et al.*, 2016), and at occasional LGBT festivals and events, such as Pride events (Johnston, 2005, 2012; Waitt & Markwell, 2014). The tourism literature characterises LGBT tourists as relatively wealthy and as DINKs (double income, no kids) (Köllen & Lazar, 2013), with little attention paid to travellers who do not fit this profile (Casey, 2010). Meanwhile, other forms of LGBT-focused tourism are growing in popularity, although often underreported in the literature. The most glaring example of this is the lack of research into lesbian tourism (Therkelsen *et al.*, 2013). The research question examined in this chapter is, therefore: What are the motivations of LGBT travellers who do not take part in urban and beach-type holiday tourism?

The primary author's experiences inspire this research. He is a gay man who lived for many years in large urban centres, where he participated in a variety of 'alternative' queer culture events, including sports groups, yoga and volunteer organisations. He then moved to Portugal, where access to such groups was limited. This sparked his interest in how LGBT tourism caters for LGBT folk beyond urban and beach-type tourism. Both authors are researchers who are trained marketing researchers with many years' experience in online communities and communications (Barreto, 2014; Dahl, 2006, 2014; Dahl et al., 2009; Eagle & Dahl, 2018). This chapter therefore reflects research approaches in this area, particularly building on netnography (Kozinets, 2010). This approach is supplemented with in-depth interviews with target audience members. Thus, as a first step in the chapter, we identify relevant target audiences before delving deeper into the motivations of travellers taking part in these types of activities, intending to provide insights for future market development.

Diversification and Development of an Alternative LGBT Tourism Market

On the supply side, the diversification of LGBT tourism is driven by tourism operators and destination marketers moving into potentially viable niche markets (Blichfeldt et al., 2013), as well as the wider societal and legal acceptance of LGBT travellers. While LGBT families are not the focus of this chapter, research into their motivations for choosing holidays has shown that motivations in this market segment are more nuanced and diverse than the more singular focus on beach and nightlife explored in traditional research into the motivations of LGBT travellers. For example, Lucena et al.'s (2015) work on LGBT families indicates how families juggle their multiple identities both as families and as members of the LGBT community. Thus, their travel choices reflect the split between the choice of destination and accommodation as an LGBT identity and a family identity. In practice, these travellers try to combine both, but often have to pick one identity. Consequently, the questions arise: Is this limited only to LGBT families? Or are other LGBT travellers trying to combine different identities? What are their motivations in choosing their holidays? Do these motivations express a desire to combine different interests or perceived identities? And are these driving forces reflected in the already noted diversification of the LGBT travel market?

To explore this question, we focus on motivations that LGBT travellers have when they take part in holidays that are explicitly different from the more conventional LGBT-focused urban/beach-type holidays. As a first step, we examined LGBT media, focusing mainly on online media such as personal blogs and online forums, to identify types of 'alternative' LGBT travel experiences. These findings then guided our further research into motivations for these LGBT travellers. We sought out participants in these experiences and explored their motivations to divert from the 'mainstream'.

Therefore this chapter is structured as follows. The next section briefly presents three types of 'alternative' LGBT travel experiences: (1) sports and adventure tourism; (2) volunteering and activism tourism; and

(3) spirituality tourism. This is followed by an exploration of the motivations of travellers choosing these three travel experiences. The chapter concludes with a discussion of the findings of the research.

Types of 'Alternative' LGBT Tourism

To explore the diversification of the LGBT travel market and alternatives to conventional 'urban/beach' tourism experiences for LGBT travellers, we examined LGBT media, including magazines, websites and blogs. This helped us establish which types of holidays are taken and discussed in particular fora. Creating a typology was a fundamental step to help guide our research for the second part of this chapter, in which we then purposefully collected data and explored the motivations of travellers taking part in these experiences based on this typology. For convenience, we grouped the travel experiences into three 'alternative' travel experiences to the conventional LGBT destinations of 'beach and city'.

In the following section, we briefly review the characteristics of each type and provide short examples. Notably, while we used this typology to enable us to explore the motivations of travellers away from the mainstream in the second part of this chapter, these categories are not mutually exclusive, nor exhaustive – and are likely to change over time. Indeed, many travellers partake in and combine different types of holidays, and many tour operators operate several categories of travel experiences, including combinations of beach, urban and some or all of the categories discussed below.

Nevertheless, the broad categorisations help us to appreciate the diversification of the LGBT travel market and examine the target audiences more closely in the second part of the chapter. The three alternative categories we identified were tourism focused on sports and adventure, volunteering and activism not related to LGBT causes and tourism focusing on individual, spiritual development.

Sports and adventure tourism

LGBT-focused sports and adventure tourism, offering hiking, kayaking, running and many other forms of sports and outdoor activities, has grown in popularity following the rise of LGBT-focused athletics associations and events, such as the Gay Games, and a multitude of Gay Ski Weekends (see Johnston, 2012, for an in-depth exploration of an event in New Zealand), among many events held worldwide. For a more detailed review of the rise of gay and lesbian sports organisations and events, see Waitt (2003), Symons (2010) and Watson et al. (2013). The growth in tourism offerings reflects this expansion of sports and athletics organisations and their growing importance as either alternative or complementary to the conventional scene based on bars and clubs for many gays and lesbians, particularly in urban areas. Many organisations also run dedicated holidays, bringing together participants from different partner organisations engaging in the same sports, or in the form of 'national gatherings' of different branches of an association. For example, *Outdoorlads*, a gay men's hiking association in the UK, regularly brings together its members to experience organised hostel weekends and hiking trips.

Dedicated sports and adventure tourism extends the experience of meeting other LGBT folk in an athletic environment and enables socialising with other people outside the individuals' local organisation or association. For others, sports and adventure holidays represent a way of engaging with the gay and lesbian sports movement temporarily, for example, to try out their skills. A further incentive is that such holidays allow LGBT people who do not live within easy reach of an LGBT sports organisation to take part. While we discuss motivations in the next sections, overwhelmingly such holidays are seen as a means to socialise with other LGBT people in a space where the emphasis is not primarily on sexual expression, but rather on performing said activities where sexual expression is a possibility but not a main purpose (Place & Livengood, 2018).

Examples of sports and adventure tourism

Two examples illustrate this category: *Wild Women Expeditions*, focusing on female travellers, and *HETravel*, focusing on male travellers.

Wild Women Expeditions was founded in the early 1990s and today specialises in organising multi-sport adventures, hiking trips and canoe and kayak trips for women. As a tour operator, the company offers tours that combine sports and sightseeing, including to destinations not usually considered welcoming to LGBT travellers, such as Tanzania and Egypt. As commonly encountered in the lesbian travel market, the focus is purely on the gender of the participants, and no overt mention is made of sexual orientation. This company, as well as others such as *Sights and Soul* or *Gutsy Women Travel* are frequently mentioned (and advertise) on lesbian websites and in magazines. On websites, however, there is no mention of sexual orientation.

HETravel similarly operates as a tour operator. In addition to sports and adventure experiences, they also offer some cultural and culinary trips. HETravel was founded in 1973 and over the years has merged with different male-focused adventure travel companies. Similar to Wild Women Expeditions, the focus is on multi-sport adventures, combining hiking, camping, kayaking and biking, and includes destinations that are not usually seen as LGBT friendly. In contrast to the lesbian-focused operators, HETravel and most male-focused travel companies explicitly state that they are for gay/bisexual men only.

Volunteering and activism tourism

Volunteer tourism combines engaging with environmental, cultural and social issues at a destination with a short- or medium-term stay (Wearing, 2001). Volunteers often share meals, sleeping areas and training time, thus creating a uniquely intense experience with opportunities to exchange information and to form ties that might have not developed in more traditional holiday settings or at home (McGehee & Santos, 2005). In comparison with other forms of tourism, LGBT volunteer tourism is a very recent phenomenon. This category reflects the broader move beyond a singular, sexual-orientation focused travel experience in the wider LGBT culture. For example, beyond tourism, there is a growing Ecoqueer movement (e.g. Sbicca, 2012), combining ecological living and activism with LGBT identity.

Examples of volunteering and activism tourism

Global Volunteers is a volunteering organisation which was the first non-LGBT organisation to develop a dedicated programme for LGBT volunteers (http://lgbt.globalvolunteers.org/), in 2014 (Daniel, 2014). Volunteers teach English, renovate buildings, clear trails or provide recreational opportunities in countries such as Cuba or Vietnam. The primary focus is the same as other volunteer holidays offered by the operator; however, the LGBT programme aims to create a positive impact on the broader LGBT community by encouraging a culture of understanding and mutual respect in host communities through awareness-raising of different sexual orientations and gender identities.

The Quinta Project in Portugal is a queer nature and diversity project combining volunteering and environmental activism on a community farm and social enterprise. The project is open to both men and women. Based in the arid Alentejo region, volunteers help with the farm's water retention projects and food production and engage in community education about environmental and social issues. The project also provides accommodation for travellers, together with nature experiences and sustainability education. Uniquely, the Quinta Project offers volunteers assistance in setting up similar social enterprise projects with the help of non-LGBT partner organisations.

Spirituality tourism

Spirituality tourism refers to a significant number of local, frequently male, yoga and spirituality groups. Many of these evolved from the teachings of the Body Electric School (BE), founded in 1984 by Joseph Kramer, who created a blend of Eastern traditions such as Tantra and Taoism as a means of safe(r) sexual expression at the beginning of the AIDS crisis. This original idea has been added to and reinterpreted by different groups, combining original BE ideas with traditional yoga practices and blending in other philosophies. The result is an eclectic mix of different spiritual practices and groups, ranging from the more erotic-focused BE/tantric groups to traditional yoga and meditation practices. While originally restricted to males, some practitioners have extended the offering to different genders, including offering experiences to lesbians and transgender people.

Similar to the sports/adventure organisations referred to above, many local yoga and spiritual groups evolved to become large and popular meeting spaces for gay men (and to a lesser extent lesbians). Many groups also offer holiday or retreat packages, often in cooperation with LGBT-focused hotels.

Examples of spirituality tourism

Kumara Luna, led by Sophia, a queer-identifying woman from California, runs regular classes in San Diego as well as organising a large number of retreats in the United States and India. Some retreats are women-only, others are open to all members of the LGBT community – and a small number have no designated target group, although the website clearly states that the LGBT community is welcome at every retreat.

YogaNu is a nude yoga group from London. The group holds several classes a week aimed at gay and bisexual men. In contrast to BE, the classes are not sexual, focusing on conventional, but nude, yoga practices. The group organises three to four retreats yearly. For example, two-week-long retreats during May 2019 were offered at the Finca La Maroma gay hotel in Spain. Early in the season, these retreats are marketed both to members of the group and to hotel guests, thus extending the season for the hotel as well as giving members of the group the chance to socialise away from the usual London base.

Motivations

Research into travellers' motivations commonly uses the pull/push model (Phau *et al.*, 2013), including for LGBT travellers (Weeden *et al.*, 2016). Pull factors include destination attributes, such as climate and attractions, that 'pull' travellers to the destination, whereas push motivations include considerations such as a desire for relaxation or escape from everyday life, with individual decision making being a dynamic mix of both motivations.

The previously noted emphasis on gay men and a limited choice of destinations (urban or beach) can in part be attributed to specifically selecting LGBT spaces to recruit participants, e.g. visitors to LGBT bars and entertainment establishments (Köllen & Lazar, 2013; Nghiêm-Phú, 2018; Vorobjovas-Pinta, 2018), participants at significant events (de Jong, 2017) or in other specific LGBT spaces such as gay beaches

(Andriotis, 2010), or by interviewing LGBT-focused travel operators (Jarvis & Weeden, 2017). The dearth of research focusing on lesbian travellers has been noted in the literature (Pritchard *et al.*, 2002; Weeden *et al.*, 2016).

Study design

Our study into motivations was conducted in two phases. Firstly, the researchers undertook a netnographic review (Kozinets, 2010), as part of a wider research project, of blogs, forums, websites and social media accounts of LGBT travellers. This review was guided by purposefully seeking out travel websites and blogs focusing on, or written by, travellers who took part in one of the three types of travel described in the first section of this chapter. Our sample included a wide variety of different websites, micro-blogs, forums and groups, including those that are not specifically geared towards LGBT travellers, such as yoga discussion groups and volunteer forums. Based on requests made to those groups, we conducted 27 interviews with travellers who had visited the Iberian Peninsula during the past two years and who had been on at least one of the three types of holiday we examined. Our sample includes participants aged from 23 to 63. The majority of participants were between 35 and 55 years of age, which broadly corresponds to the observed age range discussing this type of holiday online. All interviewed travellers identify as LGBQ, with 16 identifying as male and gay, two as male and bisexual, five as female and lesbian, three as female and bisexual and one participant as genderqueer and queer. No participant identified as transgender or transsexual. Most participants stated that they do not primarily book holidays marketed exclusively as LGBT and perceived as 'mainstream' ($n = 17$). Nevertheless, several participants combine different types of holidays: some chose their activities mainly because of the pursuit involved, whereas others selected their travels explicitly because the holiday was not perceived to be specifically LGBT-focused, despite being marketed as such (for example, a yoga retreat linked to a gay men's yoga group).

Findings

Conflicting motivations and desire for combined identities

The motivations stated by the participants were often complex and multifaceted, even contradictory at times, offering an insight into the interplay of thoughts of belonging to different, sometimes opposing 'groups'. Each group is often perceived to have its own unique behaviours and motivations, and individuals strive to achieve personal coherence among different group allegiances and identities. These conflicting motivations are summed up by Hans:

It's tricky. On the one side I'm gay, I love to see men's bodies, the idea of sex and watching other guys and for that a beach is great. But then, I also like the outdoors, mountains, nature and being active. In one way, I want to like going to the beach, but when I'm there I don't [like it]. And I know what I really want is to hike in a forest and be in nature with other [gay] guys. But [both] it's hard to find. So, I either hike and love what I do and back down on being myself. Or I go on a gay beach holiday, and be me but hate what I do. (Hans, 35, male[1])

Hans is here contrasting the conventional LGBT tourism experience with the type of holiday that he would prefer, which has been less commonly part of 'mainstream' LGBT tourism. He also attests to the complex relationship of travellers identifying as LGBT, although avoiding specifically perceived gay holiday destinations (beach and city). In a similar manner, Nat says:

It depends which of my 'me's I let take the upper hand. (...) it is hard to have all combined. It just isn't there. For me, this is a real gap in the market. I feel it is always a decision. Being the one [lesbian] or the other [adventure tourist] at a time. (Nat, 43, female)

Holidays where identities are perceived as a real 'arrival' are appreciated, as these two quotes illustrate:

... the first time I went on a walk[ing holiday] with this group of other guys I almost cried. It felt amazing, the home I always wanted. (Ian, 37, male)

When I'm with the group [at a spiritual retreat centre], I know I can come out and be me. I can be silly, sad, funny, what I want. It's completely different to going out or going to a regular [spiritual] meeting or class. I drive through the gate, and I'm whole. (Erik, 53, genderqueer)

This desire to reconcile groups and socialise with others belonging to the same interest groups drives the different types of alternative LGBT tourism. Gunther, who frequently chooses LGBT adventure tours, sums up the importance of the social (push) motivations we encountered in participants:

I just can't do the normal [gay beach] holiday thing. I don't want to. I want to have an exciting holiday, escape from my job and life at home. I want to meet new people like me. Spend quality time with them. (Gunter, 49, male)

However, pull motivators such as experiencing new places or nature take precedence for people seeking adventure tourism:

the fact that everyone is also lesbian around me is a great bonus. But the main thing is what we do together. (Heather, 41, female)

Participants in volunteer tourism also often prioritised their motivations for taking part in the activities and the purpose of the organisation, while shared sexual orientation with other volunteers was considered a bonus.

> For me it's important to learn, give back and experience new things. I want to contribute to a worthwhile project. It's a bonus when I bring some queer magic to the country, too. But mainly I want to learn, experience and contribute. (Serat, 29, male)

Motivators for different types of travel

Travellers choosing different types of holidays had diverse foci. Adventure and volunteer tourists predominantly sought a combination of group experiences commonly perceived as mutually exclusive, such as the perceived hedonistic lifestyle centred on urban or beach location with a more rugged and adventurous type of 'straight guys' holiday. On the other hand, participants in spiritual tourism more characteristically sought a holistic experience, describing their experiences as 'evolved' from a perceived conventional LGBT travel experience. Their experience was juxtaposed with their everyday lives, creating a mix of spiritual and sexual-orientation and identity push motivation:

> Going to a sanctuary [retreat centre] feels like entering a different live to me. When I'm there, I'm liberated from the society and their views of what I should do or how I should behave. I can be me in every aspect. (...) The worst part about going is having to leave. And knowing that out there, I need to hide myself and the experiences I have. (Seth, 38, male)

This juxtaposition is also reflected in the terminology, using terms like 'sanctuary' and 'retreat'. Experiences related to spiritual tourism are regularly described as incorporating a different approach to the touristic experience itself, and to other aspects of the self and relationships with others.

For all travellers, different emphases can be seen as a continuum, ranging from an intense focus on the self and self-actualisation to focusing on reaching beyond the immediate community. In terms of such a continuum, spiritual tourism emphasises the self and self-actualisation. While this does not mean that bonding with the group around the traveller is not part of the experience, the group is often seen as primarily supporting the individual's personal journey. The expression 'holding the space' often appears in this context, with the implied meaning that the group supports each individual on their particular journey.

In terms of relating to others, for adventure tourists, social bonding among like-minded group members emerges as a very common motivator:

> The best thing about going on these holidays is meeting other guys like me. (...) friendships from the time away can turn into friendships at home. ... Or we see each other again on another trip. (Marko, 36, male)

Thus, the emphasis for adventure travellers lies within the group, including the possibility of extending the group beyond the trip.

For volunteer tourism, the intentions are the most outward-looking, and can be located at the other extreme of the suggested continuum. Although participants value socialising with their co-volunteers, reaching beyond the immediate peer group is essential and valued. As this volunteer describes:

> ... we spent a lot of time with locals, and learn much about their daily lives, their struggles and how they manage. We can then bring what we have seen back to the group [of co-volunteers]. (Abbie, 28, female)

Reflecting this outward focus, outreach programmes are explicitly part of volunteer tourism, emphasising the importance of this motivational factor. In practice, outreach can incorporate local LGBT organisations or extend well beyond the community. Some programmes include meetings with local LGBT groups, whereas others focus primarily on the volunteer purpose, such as education or activism.

Specifically, for volunteer tourism, activism was an important aspect of the experience. Both activism related to LGBT causes, such as networking with or supporting LGBT causes in countries where LGBT rights were less advanced, or activism in other areas such as sustainability and ecology, are common. Activism was also mentioned in relation to adventure tourism, although only a few travellers noted that their actions would advance LGBT acceptance at their holiday destinations. As one traveller puts it:

> We went to this little mountain village in Extremadura. Something like 50 gay men, you can imagine! The locals didn't know what had hit them. But in the end, we had a massive big party at a local bar and everyone had fun. I don't think they will ever think of gay men in the same way as before. (Juan, 36, male)

Being yourself in a community as a common motivator

Common to all respondents was a desire to find non-judgmental community support, similar to the push motivations discussed in the literature relating to LGBT tourism. An environment in which travellers feel that they can be themselves is an attraction for seeking out these forms of holidays. However, within such an environment, finding a community beyond sexual orientation is a strong motivator. Reflecting on this, Thomas puts this more differentiated approach down to age and social developments:

> When I was young, being gay was the thing that united us. But things have changed, and I don't think guys just want to be with other guys because anymore just because they are gay. Now we want to have something else in common, do things and stuff that brings us together. (Thomas, 49, male)

A number of travellers also identified that they started to engage with these forms of LGBT travelling, and meeting other gay people in the process, as a perceived alternative to the gay scene. Travelling represented a different approach to finding people to socialise with, sometimes irrespective of the actual purpose of the holiday:

> For me, it was a way to meet other women. I didn't really hike before, but now, because most of my friends do it, we all do it all the time. (Jana, 43, female)

> For me things changed when I hit 40. I suddenly realised how shallow the scene was. Once I had that stuck on my mind, it felt uncomfortable going out. (…) I looked for other things to do and found out about a sports group (…). Of course, I went to the gym before, but that was to have a body good for the scene. I was not interested in running or hiking or stuff like that. But once I started to go there [the group], I felt that people can be totally different [than on the commercial gay scene] and from there it became something I do all the time. I really jumped into that if you so want. I train with them. I go on holidays with them. I guess, I replaced the one scene with another, but this one feels more like it is me now. (Martin, 42, male)

Several travellers found the 'commercial' scene, including beach and city LGBT travel options, as something juxtaposed to the type of scene, and by extension holiday, they frequented. Other travellers alternated different types of LGBT holidays, while some travellers felt that once they had discovered alternative forms of LGBT travelling, and socialising, they abandoned the perceived 'commercial' scene altogether. This behaviour mirrors the sometimes cynical relationship and feeling of disconnection reported elsewhere in the literature, for example concerning the gay shame movement (see Halperin & Traub, 2009, for an in-depth review of the gay shame movement).

Travellers frequently noted the central role that their participation had in finding new social contacts and in maintaining contacts they had previously made:

> Every time I go on a [hiking] holiday, I meet one or two new people. But I also meet a lot of people I know from before. Some of us have actually become quite close, like, we do things together between holidays and go out together. (Saran, 27, female)

The role of (possible) sexual encounters

Differences also emerged around the question of sex or the potential for finding sex partners as motivational factors. Going on alternative LGBT holidays served on the one hand as a possible way to find sexual partners, while on the other hand sex was not usually the primary motivator. This contradictory relationship becomes clear in the way Peter describes his involvement in tantric retreats. During tantric retreats, sex with other participants is part of the programme, although referred to in other terms:

> When I'm at a retreat, we do a lot of bodywork. But that is not the same as wham bam boom. And we don't pick our sacred intimate [person

giving a massage] because of their six-pack or looks. We develop connections beyond the bodily forms and enter in a spiritual stage. (Peter, 62,
male)

Others describe sex as something that occurred 'naturally' when on
holidays. In relation to hiking holidays, Raul puts it as follows:

What else would happen when six guys sleep together in a room? Of
course, not always and not everyone joins. Nothing has to happen, but I
yet have to find a time when nothing happened. (Raul, 44, male)

A surprising aspect of the answers was how travellers thought about
the challenges faced by LGBT people visiting destinations not usually perceived as LGBT friendly. Most travellers seemed surprised they were
accepted and welcomed. Maybe because many live and work in bigger
cities, their initial expectations had been that they would be met with
significant homophobia. Instead, many reflected on their surprise that,
while they encountered occasional curiosity, they experienced no perceived homophobia. As a hiker puts it:

Most of the negativity was in my head. For the first few trips I was always
surprised when people were friendly to us. But then I got it. They were
just being normal. And it was me who imagined they would be really
homophobic. (Narciso, 45, male)

However, interaction with locals was often limited and so the experiences recounted should not be interpreted as there being no
homophobia.[2]

Discussion

In the first section we identified several 'alternative' forms of LGBT
holidays which, so far, have not been extensively explored in the literature.
This typology of holidays then guided our further exploration of motivations for LGBT travellers seeking to holiday away from the urban/beach-
type holiday choices.

We used these types of holidays as a basis to explore travellers' motivations, reflecting on the complex nature of juggling multiple desires for
group membership. This finding is complementary to findings from the
lesbian and gay cruise vacation market (Weeden et al., 2016) as well as
previous research into the LGBT family segment (Lucena et al., 2015).
This chapter, together with previous research, highlights the complex
interplay of motivations for LGBT travellers. Previous research, often conducted in LGBT-identified spaces, has presumed the notion that an LGBT
identity is highly influential when choosing a holiday destination (Melián-
González et al., 2011). As Köllen and Lazar (2013) criticised, the motivation of gay travellers in the extant literature has focused on gay-specific
push factors such as escapism and anonymity, living out a gay identity and

looking for sex, while pull factors included gay friendliness and gay events. Consequently, LGBT tourism marketing often emphasises the availability of bars, clubs and events as the main selling argument (Horner & Swarbrooke, 2016). In contrast, we found that travellers seeking the travel options described here often prioritise social and adventure aspects, seeing bars, events, opportunities for sex, etc., as complements rather than main motivations. This echoes research into lesbian travel (Therkelsen *et al.*, 2013), which showed a more complex set of pull and push factors than those described in gay male-focused research.

While our sample was necessarily small and specific, our research points towards a subtle shift away from what are perceived as mainstream 'urban and beach' gay holidays. The shifting focus of the travellers we interviewed led to push motivations that downplay those emphasised in the literature (anonymity, identity-seeking and sex). Instead, offerings centred around areas outside the 'mainstream' city and beach-centric options, not normally regarded as open-minded and welcoming places, are becoming increasingly embraced by LGBT tourists.

Our participants indicate that the key to successful growth lies in incorporating non-LGBT activities, and therefore providing more pull motivations – in other words, combining both an appeal to an LGBT identity and other pull motivators such as sports, activism or personal well-being. This may lead to a more diversified LGBT travel scene, potentially resembling the varied offerings in non-LGBT tourism.

Using this combination approach to innovate in the LGBT travel market, there is ample opportunity for further growth. For example, LGBT families are still not well catered for. Of all the presented examples, The Quinta Project was the only one that specifically mentioned families.

Similarly, in line with previous research, it was notable that fewer lesbian travel options exist. This observation extends to both destinations, speciality lodgings as well as tour operators, that are explicitly marketing to a lesbian/bisexual market.

In tandem with fewer offerings, there is also less in the way of websites and social media or traditional media about lesbian holidays. Compared to the myriad of websites, magazines and social media influencers targeting the gay male market, the lesbian market is significantly less visible. There are examples of highly successful publications, such as the lesbian-oriented website *Globetrotter Girls*, which also has a significant social media presence. However, the social media following of this blog on Instagram is significantly less (20,000) than that of a comparable, although much younger gay traveller blog (*Nomadic Boys*, 100,000).

Even fewer options appear to exist for transsexual/transgender travellers. There are relatively few blogs for trans travellers and we have not encountered any tour operators explicitly targeting the trans market. Similarly, few LGBT options embrace both male and female (and other gendered) travellers. Only the volunteer tourism operators appeared to openly market to people identifying as any gender. With increasing recognition of gender diversity, there is certainly more scope for development in these areas.

Concluding Remarks

Emerging forms of LGBT tourism are more diverse than conventional forms, which have previously relied heavily on travel where the main focus has been on urban nightlife or beach holidays, and often a mixture of the two. The common motivator discussed in the literature was sexual orientation, and the conventional holiday forms allowed for a 'safe space' to live openly (cf. Coon, 2012, for a discussion of the balance between the importance of safe spaces and visibility in predominantly gay tourism). Emerging forms of alternative tourism embrace a more nuanced version of the traveller, combining different interests which include, but are not restricted to, sexual orientation. Thus, travellers see meeting like-minded people sharing common interests as the primary motivator. The types of tourism discussed in this chapter empower travellers to express and experience multiple facets of their personality – and combine these to create a new type of holiday experience.

From a practical and professional perspective, this chapter indicates pathways for future LGBT tourism development. For example, Paradela *et al.* (2014) report on the efforts by Galacia, a region usually associated with spectacular landscapes, to become gay friendly. At the time, the region paid little attention to alternative forms of travel as discussed in this chapter. For example, nature and adventure travel might be viable pathways to enter the LGBT tourism market. In short, tourism operators are encouraged to think beyond the conventional urban/beach focus, and develop more diverse forms of tourism to cater for a growing and diverse audience.

For researchers in this area, the discussions in this chapter show that future research should embrace more nuanced , diverse and multifaceted views of LGBT tourism. Exploring other motivators and newly emerging forms of LGBT tourism, including how holidaymakers navigate the combination of different motivations, are possible future avenues for research.

Disclosure

Stephan Dahl is a founder member of The Quinta Project.

Notes

(1) Because of space restrictions, we only include the English translation of the interviews. Names are changed to preserve anonymity. The gender is as self-defined by the participant.

(2)   While travellers often reflected on all of their experiences, including in different countries, travellers were interviewed because of their travels to Spain or Portugal, two countries with generally fairly liberal views towards LGBT travellers. See, for example, the International Lesbian, Gay, Bisexual, Trans and Intersex Association (ILGA, 2018), which ranks both countries as within the top 10 countries of 49 European countries included in the report.

References

Andriotis, K. (2010) Heterotopic erotic oases. *Annals of Tourism Research* 37 (4), 1076–1096.

Barreto, A.M. (2014) The word-of-mouth phenomenon in the social media era. *International Journal of Market Research* 56 (5), 631–54.

Blichfeldt, B.S., Chor, J. and Milan, N.B. (2013) Zoos, sanctuaries and turfs: Enactments and uses of gay spaces during the holidays. *International Journal of Tourism Research* 15 (5), 473–483.

Casey, M. (2010) Even poor gays travel: Excluding low income gay men from understandings of gay tourism. In Y. Taylor (ed.) *Classed Intersections: Spaces, Selves, Knowledges* (pp. 181–198). New York: Routledge.

CMI (2017) *22nd Annual LGBTQ Tourism & Hospitality Survey*. San Francisco, CA: Community Marketing & Insights. See https://www.communitymarketinginc.com/documents/temp/CMI_22nd-LGBT-Travel-Study-Report2017.pdf.

Coon, D.R. (2012) Sun, sand, and citizenship: The marketing of gay tourism. *Journal of Homosexuality* 59 (4), 511–534.

Dahl, S. (2006) Peer support via the internet: What kind of online support is sought by individuals with chronic medical conditions? *Journal of Medical Marketing* 6 (4), 268–275.

Dahl, S. (2014) *Social Media Marketing: Theories and Applications*. London: Sage.

Dahl, S., Eagle, L. and Baez, C. (2009) Analyzing advergames: Active diversions or actually deception. An exploratory study of online advergames content. *Young Consumers* 10 (1), 46–59.

Daniel, D. (2014) A new volunteer program for L.G.B.T. travelers. *New York Times*, 31 July. See https://intransit.blogs.nytimes.com/2014/07/31/a-new-volunteer-program-for-l-g-b-t-travelers/

de Jong, A. (2017) Unpacking Pride's commodification through the encounter. *Annals of Tourism Research* 63, 128–139.

Eagle, L. and Dahl, S. (2018) Product placement in old and new media: Examining the evidence for concern. *Journal of Business Ethics* 147, 605–618.

Halperin, D.M. and Traub, V. (eds) (2009) *Gay Shame*. Chicago, IL: University of Chicago Press.

Horner, S. and Swarbrooke, J. (2016) *Consumer Behaviour in Tourism* (3rd edn). Abingdon and New York: Routledge.

ILGA (2018) *Rainbow Europe 2018*. Brussels: ILGA Europe. See https://www.ilga-europe.org/rainboweurope/2018.

Jarvis, N. and Weeden, C. (2017) Cruising with Pride: The LGBT cruise market. In R. Dowling and C. Weeden (eds) *Cruise Ship Tourism* (2nd edn) (pp. 332–347). Wallingford: CABI.

Johnston, L. (2005) *Queering Tourism: Paradoxical Performances at Gay Pride Parades*. London and New York: Routledge.

Johnston, L. (2012) Queering skiing and camping up nature in Queenstown: Aotearoa New Zealand's gay ski week. In J. Caudwell and K. Browne (eds) *Sexualities, Spaces and Leisure Studies* (pp. 43–58). London: Routledge.

Köllen, T. and Lazar, S. (2013) Gay tourism in Budapest: An exploratory study on gay tourists' motivational patterns for traveling to Budapest. *American Journal of Tourism Management* 1 (3), 64–68.

Kozinets, R.V. (2010) *Netnography: Ethnographic Research in the Age of the Internet.* Thousand Oaks, CA: Sage.

Lucena, R., Jarvis, N. and Weeden, C. (2015) A review of gay and lesbian parented families' travel motivations and destination choices: Gaps in research and future directions. *Annals of Leisure Research* 18 (2), 272–289.

McGehee, N.G. and Santos, C.A. (2005) Social change, discourse and volunteer tourism. *Annals of Tourism Research* 32 (3), 760–779. doi:10.1016/j.annals.2004.12.002

Melián-González, A., Moreno-Gil, S. and Araña, J.E. (2011) Gay tourism in a sun and beach destination. *Tourism Management* 32 (5), 1027–1037.

Nghiêm-Phú, B. (2018) Comment and comment response strategies – an analysis of gay hotel guests' comments and managers' responses. *Tourism and Hospitality Management* 24 (1), 1–17.

Paradela, A.B.O., González, M.E.A. and Vila, T.D. (2014) Turismo LGTB. Una aproximación al caso de Galicia. *Revista Galega de Economía* 23 (1), 79–98.

Phau, I., Lee, S. and Quintal, V. (2013) An investigation of push and pull motivations of visitors to private parks: The case of Araluen Botanic Park. *Journal of Vacation Marketing* 19 (3), 269–284.

Place, G. and Livengood, J. (2018) Motivation to participate in recreation/sport for gay athletes. *Journal of Physical Education and Sports Management* 5 (1), 1–9.

Pritchard, A., Morgan, N. and Sedgley, D. (2002) In search of lesbian space? The experience of Manchester's gay village. *Leisure Studies* 21 (2), 105–123.

Sbicca, J. (2012) Eco-queer movement(s): Challenging heteronormative space through (re) imagining nature and food. *European Journal of Ecopsychology* 3, 33–52.

Symons, C. (2010) *The Gay Games: A History.* London and New York: Routledge.

Therkelsen, A., Blichfeldt, B.S., Chor, J. and Ballegaard, N. (2013) 'I am very straight in my gay life': Approaching an understanding of lesbian tourists' identity construction. *Journal of Vacation Marketing* 19 (4), 317–327.

Vorobjovas-Pinta, O. (2018) Gay neo-tribes: Exploration of travel behaviour and space. *Annals of Tourism Research* 72, 1–10.

Vorobjovas-Pinta, O. and Hardy, A. (2016) The evolution of gay travel research. *International Journal of Tourism Research* 18 (4), 409–416.

Waitt, G. (2003) Gay games: Performing 'community' out from the closet of the locker room. *Social & Cultural Geography* 4 (2), 167–183.

Waitt, G. and Markwell, K. (2014) *Gay Tourism: Culture and Context.* London: Routledge.

Watson, R., Tucker, L. and Drury, S. (2013) Can we make a difference? Examining the transformative potential of sport and active recreation. *Sport in Society* 16 (10), 1233–1247.

Wearing, S. (2001) *Volunteer Tourism: Experiences that Make a Difference.* Wallingford and New York: CABI.

Weeden, C., Lester, J.-A. and Jarvis, N. (2016) Lesbians' and gay men's vacation motivations, perceptions, and constraints: A study of cruise vacation choice. *Journal of Homosexuality* 63 (8), 1068–1085.

Part 4

Gay Tourism: Spatial Discourses

11 Marketing and Communicating Gay-Friendly Hospitality Spaces: The Case of Rainbow Tasmania Tourism Accreditation

Oscar Vorobjovas-Pinta and Louise Grimmer

> In the mid to late nineties, Tasmania became a by-word around the
> world for homophobia, intolerance and bigotry. In fact, [...]
> Tasmania was referred to as 'Bigot's Island'. Now Tasmania has
> become another word for tolerance, inclusion and social justice.
> Rodney Croome AM (Kirk, 2003)

Introduction

Tasmania is an island state 240 km south of mainland Australia with a population of just over half a million (Australian Bureau of Statistics, 2016). At 68,000 square km, Tasmania is less than one-third the area of the state of Victoria (Australia) and is similar in size to the Republic of Ireland, West Virginia (USA) and Hokkaido (Japan). Like many other destinations, the island state has endeavoured to attract tourists as part of its economic growth programme (Tasmanian Government, 2020). One of these initiatives is the Rainbow Tasmania Tourism Accreditation Program launched in 2013 by the Tourism Industry Council Tasmania and Rainbow Communities Tasmania. The programme was designed as an add-on module to the national Australian Tourism Accreditation Program (*Tasmanian Times*, 2013) to encourage and welcome LGBTQI+ visitors to Tasmania.

The opening quote from Rodney Croome AM, founder of Australian Marriage Equality, taken from an interview with a local radio station in 2003, describes the great metamorphosis Tasmania underwent in legitimising LGBTQI+ voices. For many years Tasmania had been perceived, certainly by mainland Australia and perhaps indeed by the rest of the world, as a backward state where homophobia, bigotry and discrimination against LGBTQI+ individuals and communities thrived. This is not surprising, given that it took nearly a decade of debate, and the involvement of the United Nations Human Rights Committee, the federal government, the High Court and Amnesty International, before homosexuality was finally decriminalised in 1997 (Croome, 2006). Historic attitudes towards LGBTQI+ people in Tasmania were recently highlighted by Hannah Gadsby in her critically acclaimed show *Nanette* (Gadsby *et al.*, 2018):

> From the years 1989 to 1997, right? This is ten years. Effectively my adolescence. Tasmania was at the centre of a very toxic national debate about homosexuality and whether or not it should be legalised. And I'm from the northwest coast of Tasmania, the 'Bible Belt'. Seventy percent of the people, I lived amongst, believed that homosexuality should be a criminal act. Seventy percent of the people who raised me, who loved me, who I trusted, believed that homosexuality was a sin, that homosexuals were heinous, sub-human paedophiles. Seventy percent. (Gadsby *et al.*, 2018)

Despite being the last state in Australia to decriminalise homosexuality, today Tasmania stands at the forefront of LGBTQI+ rights. It has some of the world's best anti-homophobia school programmes and anti-discrimination laws, and in 2004 it became the first state in Australia to permit same-sex relationship registration (Croome, 2006). In the 2017 Australian Marriage Law Postal Survey (aka the Same-sex Marriage Plebiscite), 63.6% of Tasmanians voted in support of same-sex marriage, which was above the national average (Australian Bureau of Statistics, 2017).

In light of broader moves designed to improve LGBTQI+ civil rights and societal acceptance, gay-friendly symbols such as rainbow stickers and flags started appearing on the shopfronts of 'regular' (i.e. not LGBTQI+ -focused) businesses. The display of such symbols signifies a business's support for and alliance with people identifying as LGBTQI+ and their allies through providing gay-friendly spaces as part of the business. While this can be understood as a sign of solidarity and willingness to improve the social fabric of the society, it can also be perceived as a marketing tool attracting the 'pink dollar'. It should also be noted that 'gay' and 'gay-friendly' spaces are inherently different – one is set up specifically for LGBTQI+ clientele and the other welcomes LGBTQI+ people. Members of LGBTQI+ communities often seek spaces that are inclusive, supportive and free of discrimination (Vorobjovas-Pinta & Hardy, 2021).

This chapter presents the case of the Rainbow Tasmania Tourism Accreditation Program and examines its role in supporting the development and communication of gay-friendly spaces and in the evolution of

LGBTQI+ tourism more broadly in Tasmania. Using the lens of an accreditation programme, the authors examine the role of gay-friendly hospitality spaces and the way business owners construct and communicate their spaces for LGBTQI+ patrons, their allies and others.

The Gay Travel Market

The definitions of 'LGBTQI+ traveller' and 'LGBTQI+ tourism market' are highly problematic. Given that LGBTQI+ communities are characterised by their sexuality – the most intimate form of human behaviour – the identification of 'gay', 'lesbian' or any other individuals represented under the LGBTQI+ banner, including their own self-perceptions, is both difficult and complex. As such, there are several dilemmas associated with identifying and understanding the LGBTQI+ tourism market. Firstly, early research questioned the very existence of an LGBTQI+ market, suggesting that sexual orientation, in itself, should not constitute a market segment (Fugate, 1993). And while Gluckman and Reed (1997) and Peñaloza (1996) support the existence of an LGBTQI+ market segment(s), on the grounds of the relationship between market segments and social movements, there is no clear understanding as to how large or diverse these markets might be (Vorobjovas-Pinta & Hardy, 2016). Consequently, many organisations still have not figured out how to communicate with LGBTQI+ consumers, particularly from a marketing, communication and advertising standpoint (Bellis, 2018). Similarly, Ciszek (2020: 6) argues that, just like LGBTQI+ communities, diverse publics are not homogeneous: 'for organisations to build trusting relationships with diverse publics, they need to recognise the complexity of these publics and develop efforts that account for the multiple identities within a diverse public'.

Secondly, there are no clear numbers on the size of the LGBTQI+ population. LGBTQI+ people are often termed as the non-heterosexual population, which includes those who identify as gay, lesbian, bisexual, transgender, questioning/queer or intersex or who construct their sexuality in other ways using non-heterosexual terminology. In his landmark works, *Sexual Behaviour in the Human Male* (1948) and *Sexual Behaviour in the Human Female* (1953), Alfred Kinsey postulated that approximately 10% of human society are homosexual or have 'homosexual tendencies'. Both works, commonly known as the Kinsey Reports, were highly controversial not only among the public due to the sensitive nature of the topic but also within the scientific community, who questioned the methodological rigour and the scientific validity of the findings. While Kinsey's claims are still being disputed some 70 years after their publication, the figure of 10% has been legitimised by the public and remains widely quoted. Anecdotally, only 2–3% of the population outwardly embrace their sexuality. Australia's non-heterosexual population aged 18 and over in 2016 is thought to be over 592,000; 3.2% of the total adult population in Australia describe themselves as non-heterosexual. In Tasmania, this number is lower; 2.7% of the total Tasmanian population identify themselves as non-heterosexual (Wilson & Shalley, 2018). According to 2016 Census data, there are just under 46,800 same-sex couples living in Australia, which represents a 39% increase since the 2011 Census. In Tasmania, same-sex couples account for only 0.8% of all couples living together. It should be noted that the Census only measures relationships in each household, which means that it does not take into account those relationships that extend beyond the household.

Lastly, there are problems associated with understanding the demographic particularities of the LGBTQI+ travel segments. In the last 30 years, academic research pertaining to gay tourism has sought to address issues arising from societal and political changes, not only in Australia but also around the world (Vorobjovas-Pinta & Hardy, 2016). In particular, researchers have focused on the impacts of those changes on the LGBTQI+ travel market. However, both the substantial body of academic literature and the common terminology relating to LGBTQI+ individuals have used somewhat morphed and homogeneous terminology, such as 'the gay market' and 'the gay community', to portray the consumption behaviour of these groupings (Vorobjovas-Pinta, 2018). Nonetheless, while the term 'gay' technically refers to gay men and lesbians, it is also used broadly to include all other sexual orientations or gender identities under the LGBTQI+ banner. The term 'gay tourism' has been established as a more recognisable and user-friendly term than 'LGBTQI+ tourism' (Southall & Fallon, 2011). Gay travellers have often been conceptualised as high-spending travellers with significantly higher rates of disposable income than their heterosexual counterparts due to their status as DINKs (double income, no kids). However, these myths have since been debunked, acknowledging that there is a great diversity within the LGBTQI+ communities (Vorobjovas-Pinta & Hardy, 2016). Indeed, it has been discovered that that gay individuals have often suffered from salary discrimination and that using statistical salary data 'to describe all lesbian and gay people is misleading and, in many cases, deliberately deceptive' (Badgett, 1997: 66).

The collection of observations above raises the question as to whether the integration and acceptance of LGBTQI+ communities in the wider intra- and international global psyche have contributed to changes in the travel motivations of LGBTQI+ travellers. If we agree that sexual orientation is one of the core composing elements of societal demographics, then when combined with the fact that sexual orientation is no longer 'hidden' in many societies, we can argue that the gay travel segment has evolved, and continues to evolve. It therefore follows that, as a demographic grouping, the needs, and the desired tourism experiences, of this market segment represent one of the influences existing in the macro-environment of the market.

Understanding Gay-Friendly Spaces

The tourism sector has played a pivotal role in supporting LGBTQI+ people in the workplace and in welcoming LGBTQI+ customers (UNWTO, 2017). In instances where policies and legislation have lagged in promoting equal rights for LGBTQI+ people, the international business community has often stepped in to support and promote gay-friendly policies for employees and customers, and this includes in countries in which LGBTQI+ people face significant discrimination and/or harsh penalties.

The term 'LGBTQI+ -friendly' is also commonly known as 'gay-friendly'. It can be argued that the term 'gay-friendly' is more recognisable and user-friendly. In broad terms, the notion 'gay-friendly' implies a space such as a bar, a restaurant or a hotel that is welcoming and inclusive of all LGBTQI+ individuals (not just gay men or women) and that attempts to eradicate homophobia and heterosexism. Guaracino (2007: 108) suggests that the definition of 'gay-friendly' is very subjective and that it 'is not solely scientific [...] but an experience and an environment that someone just feels'.

Since its conception in 1978 by the artist Gilbert Baker, the symbol of the pride rainbow has been increasingly used to represent lesbian, gay, bisexual, transgender and questioning/queer, intersex and other identities' pride and solidarity (Dreyfus, 2015). Today, the pride rainbow in the form of stickers and flags is used to identify certain areas as safe from bullying, discrimination and hostility (Wolowic *et al.*, 2017). These spaces either cater specifically to the LGBTQI+ communities and are known as 'gay spaces', or they signify a welcome and inclusive environment for all sexualities and identities, signalling a 'gay-friendly space'. The qualities of a gay-friendly space are safety, a sense of belonging, free expression of one's identity, feeling comfortable and welcome and acceptance (Barbosa *et al.*, 2017). The rainbow flag on street signs and pedestrian crossings can also mark geographically defined spaces for LGBTQI+ communities (Ghaziani, 2015).

Tourism and hospitality businesses display a 'rainbow flag' as a symbol to indicate their support for the LGBTQI+ community. Today, many businesses around the globe display either a rainbow flag or a rainbow sticker on their doors to signal their identity and association. Unsurprisingly, this is not just about the social justice and equality that drives these businesses to offer more inclusive services, but it is also associated with the 'pink dollar' – the name given to money spent by members of the LGBTQI+ communities. For example, LGBTQI+ residents of the United States spent US$63.1bn on travel in 2018, representing a 1.9% average annual growth rate; in Australia this number was US$6.9bn, representing a 2.8% annual growth rate (Out Now, 2018). Moussawi (2018) suggests that places that market themselves as 'gay-friendly' are increasingly becoming more expensive compared with those that do not. This, in turn, excludes those on lower incomes and reinforces the notion that social class plays a central role in people's access to 'gay space'. As such, some gay and gay-friendly spaces have been reported as 'completely unattainable and meaningless to many' (Field, 2016: 130).

The realisation that LGBTQI+ people might possess distinct purchasing behaviour has also resulted in the 'pinkwashing' phenomenon, whereby companies, destination management organisations and even politicians engage in a variety of marketing strategies to promote products, destinations or ideas by publicising gay friendliness and inclusivity. As such, they hope to be perceived as progressive, modern and tolerant. 'Pinkwashing' is problematic as it can appropriate the LGBTQI+ movement to promote a corporate or political agenda (Dahl, 2014). 'Pinkwashing' is a disservice to the businesses and other organisations, which authentically believe in social justice and do not necessarily use their 'gay-friendliness' as a marketing tool. There is therefore an ongoing tension existing between different actors in promoting gay-friendly businesses, destinations, places and spaces.

Rainbow Tasmania Tourism Accreditation Program

This chapter presents the results of a small pilot study which involved interviews with two different hospitality businesses, owned and operated by members of the LGBTQI+ communities in Hobart, Tasmania, Australia. In-depth, semi-structured interviews provided rich insights into how restaurants and café owners create safe and welcoming spaces for LGBTQI+ patrons as well as non-members of the LGBTQI+ community, how business owners marketed and communicated the gay-friendly nature of their spaces, and the role of the Rainbow Tasmania Tourism Accreditation Program in assisting with marketing and communication efforts.

In line with societal and political changes, in 2013 a local non-governmental organisation 'Rainbow Tasmania', along with Tourism Tasmania, the Tourism Industry Council Tasmania and the Office of the Anti-Discrimination Commissioner, developed and launched the Rainbow Tasmania Tourism Accreditation Program for tourism and hospitality businesses. The programme introduced quality assurance standards for visitors to Tasmania identifying as LGBTQI+. The Tasmanian tourism industry became the first tourism industry in Australia to introduce standards around what constitutes a 'gay-friendly' tourism and hospitality business, with the purpose of making Tasmania the most inclusive and inviting tourism destination in the country (*Tasmanian Times*, 2013). Accreditation is available for businesses to become a LGBTQI+ -friendly business (Tourism Industry Council Tasmania, 2019). In return, The Rainbow Tasmania Tourism Accreditation provides tourism businesses with:

• the authorisation to display the Rainbow Tasmania Tourism Accreditation logo at point of business and on all promotional and advertising material;

- the confidence you and your staff need to deal with LGBTI clientele effectively;
- greater LGBTI client satisfaction;
- assurance that your business is compliant with the Anti-Discrimination Act 1998 (Tas); and
- a marketing edge when communicating with this group.

To qualify, a gay-friendly accredited business must comply with rigorous criteria, and will then gain the right to display the Rainbow Tasmania Tourism Accreditation logo (see Figure 11.1) on their businesses premises as well as in all of their marketing collateral, signalling to LGBTQI+ customers that they deliver LGBTQI+ -friendly services. In addition to the formal accreditation system, many businesses show solidarity with LGBTQI+ communities and independently display rainbow stickers.

Creating Gay-Friendly Space

The ability to create a gay-friendly space through setting up a hospitality business such as a café or restaurant was considered important by respondents in enabling them to provide a 'safe' space for customers, as well as for themselves and the people they employ. This has synergies with prior research exploring the notion of gay space (e.g. Blichfeldt *et al.*, 2013; Vorobjovas-Pinta, 2018).

Figure 11.1 The logo of Rainbow Tasmania Tourism Accreditation
Source: Tourism Industry Council Tasmania.

> I think there was an acknowledgement that one of the reasons you set up a gay friendly business when you're gay, it's because you want a safe space. And it's not just for your customers, which of course you do, but it's for you as well. And you open your own business because you're saying to people if you don't like what we do, don't come. (Business 2/ Participant 3)

By providing safe spaces for LGBTQI+ patrons and staff, business owners can in some ways take control of their own space and try to prevent discrimination for the people who interact in that space.

> You set up a business because you probably felt when you've worked for other people, you've been discriminated against or you can't really be who you are. You set up your own business and you say this is who we are. If you like that, come and be supportive. (Business 2/Participant 3)

> And I suppose when you set yourself up in business, if people don't like how you identify, they don't come. (Business 2/Participant 3)

> And when people arrive at your business you make no judgment about them. … You take people at face value but when people come to your business whether it's in a restaurant or café, you suspend your judgement. You welcome everyone regardless of how they look or act. And, I'd like to say that sometimes you positively affirm their identity once they say something and because we identify too and you make a connection and of course you'd hope that you are warm to everyone but there is that connection. So that people feel a little bit safe without saying, oh we've got the same characteristics. I suppose that's what you do. (Business 2/Participant 3)

Through providing, and therefore controlling, a gay-friendly space, business owners also have the opportunity to provide 'safe' employment for their staff, many of whom identify as gay.

> We employed about 10 people and I was just looking back at the photos and about half of them would have identified as gay. So what happens is, you set up a business and people go, those two girls are running a business. So other people feel that you'd be a good employer as well and that they would be safe. (Business 2/Participant 3)

A hospitality business also provides an opportunity for members of the broader public to show their support for not only an individual business, but also for members of the LGBTQI+ community who own, work in or frequent the space.

> But it also became a really interesting and exciting place for straight people to go to because it was a bit challenging and different. So, you're gay owned and you're gay friendly and then before you know it you're attracting people from communities who are accepting of differences. (Business 2/Participant 3)

> I think one of the things that marriage equality has done for the community that I'm a part of, is at least start a conversation. So now normal

everyday Australians – more and more of them realise, they know that more people are gay and that we are okay. We're just like everyone else. So I think there's going to be more education but I think we need formal means. And that's why I think accreditation is important, for businesses to say that this is what we need to think of. (Business 2/Participant 3)

In turn, gay-friendly hospitality spaces become welcoming places for people of different sexual identities and sexual orientation, and spaces can help promote tolerance and acceptance of the LGBTQI+ community where everyone is safe and welcome.

People who are already open to other ideas [*come to the business*]. So that's really good, and people who are interested in trying different foods etc. So it sort of has a snowballing effect. I think people who are tolerant and think, 'Oh this is an exciting place to be. Who are these people?' But there were never overt conversation about it's a café full of gays. It was not like that, it was just a café where everyone was welcomed. (Business 2/Participant 3)

I use to see lots of younger straight couples, they'll be holding hands across the table and I thought well I think it is important for a gay couples to do that if they wanted to as well and feel comfortable about that. You know lots of different couples mixed up in the room here together and there's never been a problem. (Business 1/Participant 2)

I used to think that it was totally unfair that a straight couple could do it [*publicly demonstrate romantic behaviour*] but a gay couple couldn't if they wanted to. (Business 1/Participant 2)

So yeah just in terms of the general behaviour you know, somewhere they can relax and be themselves I suppose. So I think it may be important from that point of view to know that there's that. I don't know how important it is any more but I use to feel that it was important back then. (Business 1/Participant 2)

However, one respondent noted that there are still issues with tolerance, judgment and acceptance for LGBTQI+ people and despite the legalisation of gay marriage in Tasmania in 2017, there are still broader challenges for the community that did not disappear with the advent of new legislation.

That's an interesting thing because I think particularly since we've had marriage equality and you might have seen this too, everyone wants to be 'seen'. All of a sudden we're ok and we're accepted and people want our money and they all of a sudden think they're really tolerant, and you think you could have been like that 20 years ago! And I know attitudes have changed but I be suspicious about people's motivation, and do people who don't identify actually understand the barriers that are still in place? You can't just change the law and think that people are tolerant and accepting. Doesn't happen overnight. (Business 2/Participant 3)

> I think some of those people who are still vulnerable, particularly young people, we need to say that this is safe place to be, where you feel that you can be safe. I think cafes and hospitality and tourism businesses, all of them have always been pretty good. (Business 2/Participant 3)

Respondents highlighted the importance of gay-friendly space and acknowledged that there are still places that are not welcoming for LGBTQI+ people.

> I think there is a little stigma out there. You know there is still a lot of people who didn't want to support our marriage. You know you're talking about a large percentage of the Australian population and I mean that's not to say they are not gay friendly. (Business 1/Participant 1)

> I know there'll be places in Hobart that I feel not comfortable doing that [*visiting*]. (Business 1/Participant 1)

Communicating Gay-Friendly Space

Respondents acknowledged that in addition to providing safe spaces, it was also vitally important that business owners effectively *communicate* that they offer gay-friendly spaces. Two key measures that can assist in sharing this information with the LGBTQI+ community, as well as a broader cross-section of their customers, were identified in the interviews as word-of-mouth and the use of 'gay-friendly' imagery (e.g. the rainbow business sticker).

Word-of-mouth

One of the most effective ways in which communication about gay-friendly hospitality businesses is spread is through friends, customers and other supporters sharing information via word-of-mouth. Word-of-mouth has been confirmed in the literature as a very effective method for businesses, particularly small operators, to promote their business. Studies have shown that this method of marketing communication is most effective for hospitality businesses such as restaurants and cafés (Litvin *et al.*, 2008, 2018; Longart, 2010; Zhang *et al.*, 2010), and respondents noted that word-of-mouth was very important in promoting their café or restaurant, especially when they first opened the business.

> Because before Facebook and the Internet, you had to rely on word-of-mouth ... to know where you'll be welcomed and where you'll be safe. (Business 2/Participant 3)

> ... a hairdresser who still runs a business in that street [*where the business was located*], he came and supported us and he brought all his friends and before you know it you've got people who are like-minded that want to support your business and your business grows. (Business 2/ Participant 3)

So I was thinking that this man [*name removed*]. He owned a restaurant called [*business name removed*]. So he put us in contact with other people. So before you know it, there's a whole network of gay people who want you to succeed. Then you realise that you're part of a community and they are some of my best friends now … there's this whole community of gay people who want you to succeed and help. (Business 2/Participant 3)

Through word-of-mouth, businesses are able to reinforce the message that they are members of a community, and in turn strengthen connections between members of the community.

So one of the things that happens if you are, if you are a gay owned business. What happens is that you become part of a community of connections. (Business 2/Participant 3)

You have people who think these girls are trying to do good stuff and they're a part of our community, how can we help? So that happens. (Business 2/Participant 3)

The rainbow sticker

In 2013 gay-friendly stickers started to appear on the shopfronts of Tasmanian businesses. The stickers were part of a movement aimed at improving LGBTQ+ civil rights and societal acceptance. While this can be understood as a sign of solidarity and willingness to improve the social fabric of the society, the fact that non-identifying businesses were also displaying the sticker indicated that it was also a marketing tool for attracting the 'pink dollar'.

Respondents noted the importance of displaying the rainbow sticker on their business premises, especially when they first started their businesses.

We set up a business and because we had friends who were gay and who were quite active in the gay community, we had a little rainbow sticker on the window of the café. (Business 2/Participant 3)

We opened [*café name removed*] and by then we were active in that community and it felt like it was appropriate to do that [*display the sticker*]. And lots of our customers at [*café name removed*] were identifying as part of that community and so it was the natural thing to do. (Business 2/Participant 3)

Tasmania was the last state to decriminalise homosexuality in 1997 and the rainbow sticker was a tangible way for business owners to publicly identify as a gay business but also to show members of the gay community that the business offered a safe and welcoming space.

Because I suppose Tasmania had just legalised homosexuality and just making something legal doesn't mean people accept you. It was still pretty taboo to be out publicly, and publicly out. And you wanted to support people who were in your community. (Business 2/Participant 3).

On the flip side, the rainbow sticker also acted as a signal and deterrent for people who might not be supportive of the community or gay-friendly businesses.

> ... and if there's a little rainbow sticker on the window, if people aren't tolerant and accepting then go somewhere else to get their coffee. So and it seems to work for us, you know. (Business 2/Participant 3)

> It [*the rainbow sticker*] was a political and a social stance. And it was saying if you don't like it, fuck off and go somewhere else. (Business 2/Participant 3)

> And it never, ever worked against us that I know ... there was an understanding that there was pink dollars to be had. And if you supported that community, they would support you too and they do. (Business 2/Participant 3)

Concluding Remarks

This chapter discussed the case of the Rainbow Tasmania Tourism Accreditation Program. The programme enables tourism and hospitality businesses to communicate that their businesses treat all people in the same non-discriminatory manner, and provide a safe and comfortable environment for LGBTQI+ customers. While previously many tourism and hospitality businesses in Tasmania were formally accredited, today the programme appears to have become somewhat obsolete. In many ways, the very reason why the programme was initiated also made it redundant. Increased levels of tolerance and acceptance resulted in less need to actively show support for the LGBTQI+ communities. This sentiment strengthened after the Australian Marriage Law Postal Survey in 2017. Of note, the official tourism website 'Discover Tasmania', which promotes Tasmania to visitors, no longer contains information for LGBTQI+ travellers.

Although the official accreditation process appears to be somewhat redundant, businesses in Tasmania continue to display gay-friendly stickers on their shopfronts. This pilot study uncovered that businesses continue to display gay-friendly stickers for several reasons, such as the willingness to create gay-friendly spaces and to communicate those spaces. The ability to create a gay-friendly space through setting up a hospitality business is considered important, as it enables owners to provide a 'safe' space for customers; similarly, the communication of gay-friendly spaces is also vitally important. While societal attitudes towards LGBTQI+ communities have become more positive, there still remain those who continue to promote hateful and inaccurate information and material about LGBTQI+ people (Sargeant, 2017). Displaying simple visual signifiers of safe and inclusive spaces for LGBTQI+ people therefore continues to be essential.

References

Australian Bureau of Statistics (2016) *2016 Census QuickStats*. See http://quickstats.census-data.abs.gov.au/census_services/getproduct/census/2016/quickstat/6?opendocument.

Australian Bureau of Statistics (2017) *1800.0 Australian Marriage Law Postal Survey, 2017*. See https://www.abs.gov.au/ausstats/abs@.nsf/Lookup/by%20Subject/2071.0~2016~Main%20Features~Same-Sex%20Couples~85.

Badgett, L. (1997) Beyond biased samples: Challenging the myths on the economic status of lesbians and gay men. In A.R. Gluckman and B. Reed (eds) *Homo Economics: Capitalism, Community and Lesbian and Gay Life* (pp. 65–71). New York: Routledge.

Barbosa, B., De Moraes, T.C. and Rocha, A. (2017) Rio de Janeiro as a gayfriendly destination: The gay tourists' perspective. *Revista Turismo & Desenvolvimento* 27–28 (2), 181–183.

Bellis, R. (2018) Brands still haven't figured out how to talk to LGBTQ consumers. *Fast Company*, 14 March. See https://www.fastcompany.com/40543299/brands-still-havent-figured-out-how-to-talk-to-lgbtq-consumers.

Blichfeldt, B.S., Chor, J. and Milan, N.B. (2013) Zoos, sanctuaries and turfs: Enactments and uses of gay spaces during the holidays. *International Journal of Tourism Research* 15 (5), 473–483.

Ciszek, E. (2020) We are people, not transactions: Trust as a precursor to dialogue with LGBTQ publics. *Public Relations Review* 46 (1), 101759.

Croome, R. (2006) Homosexuality. In A. Alexander (ed.) *The Companion to Tasmanian History*. Hobart: Centre for Tasmanian Historical Studies, University of Tasmania.

Dahl, S. (2014) The rise of pride marketing and the curse of 'pink washing'. *The Conversation*, 27 August. See https://theconversation.com/the-rise-of-pride-marketing-and-the-curse-of-pink-washing-30925.

Dreyfus, E. (2015) Here's where the rainbow flag came from. *Wired Magazine*, 26 June. See http://www.wired.com/2015/06/fly-rainbow-flag-high-sex-marriage-ruled-right/.

Field, N. (2016) *Over the Rainbow: Money, Class and Homophobia*. London: Dog Horn Publishing.

Fugate, D.L. (1993) Evaluating the US male homosexual and lesbian population as a viable target market segment. *Journal of Consumer Marketing* 10 (4), 46–57.

Gadsby, H., Olb, J. and Parry, M. (2018) *Hannah Gadsby: Nanette*. Collingwood: Guesswork Television.

Ghaziani, A. (2015) *There Goes the Gayborhood?* Princeton, NJ: Princeton University Press.

Gluckman, A. and Reed, B. (1997) The gay marketing moment. In A.R. Gluckman and B. Reed (eds) *Homo Economics: Capitalism, Community and Lesbian and Gay Life* (pp. 3–9). London: Routledge.

Guaracino, J. (2007) *Gay and Lesbian Tourism: The Essential Guide for Marketing*. Oxford: Butterworth-Heinemann.

Kinsey, A.C., Pomeroy, W.B. and Martin, C.E. (1948) *Sexual Behaviour in the Human Male*. Philadelphia, PA: W.B. Saunders.

Kinsey, A.C., Pomeroy, W.B., Martin, C.E. and Gebhard, P.H. (1953) *Sexual Behaviour in the Human Female*. Philadelphia, PA: W.B. Saunders.

Kirk, A. (2003) Tasmania passes law that recognises same-sex relationships. *Australia Broadcasting Corporation*, 29 August. See http://www.abc.net.au/pm/content/2003/s935245.htm.

Litvin, S., Goldsmith, R. and Pan, B. (2008) Electronic word-of-mouth in hospitality and tourism management. *Tourism Management* 29 (3), 458–468.

Litvin, S., Goldsmith, R. and Pan, B. (2018) A retrospective view of electronic word-of-mouth in hospitality and tourism management. *International Journal of Contemporary Hospitality Management* 30 (1), 313–325.

Longart, P. (2010) What drives word-of-mouth in restaurants? *International Journal of Contemporary Hospitality Management* 22 (1), 121–128.

Moussawi, G. (2018) Queer exceptionalism and exclusion: Cosmopolitanism and inequalities in 'gay-friendly' Beirut. *The Sociological Review* 66 (1), 174–190.

Out Now (2018) Out Now's global LGBT2030 research program. See https://www.outnowconsulting.com/.

Peñaloza, L. (1996) We're here, we're queer, and we're going shopping! A critical perspective on the accommodation of gays and lesbians in the U.S. marketplace. *Journal of Homosexuality* 31 (1–2), 9–41.

Sargeant, C. (2017) Melbourne venues are putting up rainbow stickers to show they're LGBTQI+ safe spaces. *Special Broadcasting Service*, 28 August. See https://www.sbs.com.au/topics/pride/agenda/article/2017/08/28/melbourne-venues-are-putting-rainbow-stickers-show-theyre-lgbtqi-safe-spaces.

Southall, C. and Fallon, P. (2011) LGBT tourism. In P. Robinson, S. Heitmann and P. Dieke (eds) *Research Themes for Tourism* (pp. 218–232). Wallingford: CABI.

Tasmanian Government (2020) *Economic Growth*. See https://www.stategrowth.tas.gov.au/?a=85382.

Tasmanian Times (2013) New 'LGBTI friendly' standards for Tasmanian tourism. *Tasmanian Times*, 23 April. See https://tasmaniantimes.com/2013/04/new-lgbti-friendly-standards-for-tasmanian-tourism/.

Tourism Industry Council Tasmania (2019) *Rainbow Tasmania Tourism Accreditation*. See https://tict.com.au/documents/22/Rainbow_Accreditation_Info_Kit_and_Criteria_Digital_Form.pdf.

UNWTO (2017) *Second Global Report on LGBT Tourism*. Affiliate Members Global Reports Vol. 15. Madrid: World Tourism Organization. See https://www.e-unwto.org/doi/pdf/10.18111/9789284418619.

Vorobjovas-Pinta, O. (2018) Gay neo-tribes: Exploration of travel behaviour and space. *Annals of Tourism Research* 72, 1–10.

Vorobjovas-Pinta, O. and Hardy, A. (2016) The evolution of gay travel research. *International Journal of Tourism Research* 18 (4), 409–416.

Vorobjovas-Pinta, O. and Hardy, A. (2021) Resisting marginalisation and reconstituting space through LGBTQI+ events. *Journal of Sustainable Tourism* 29 (2–3), 448–466. doi:10.1080/09669582.2020.1769638

Wilson, T. and Shalley, F. (2018) Estimates of Australia's non-heterosexual population. *Australian Population Studies* 2 (1), 26–38.

Wolowic, J.M., Heston, L.V., Saewyc, E.M., Porta, C. and Eisenberg, M.E. (2017) Chasing the rainbow: Lesbian, gay, bisexual, transgender and queer youth and pride semiotics. *Culture, Health & Sexuality: An International Journal for Research, Intervention and Care* 19 (5), 557–571.

Zhang, Z., Ye, Q., Law, R. and Li, Y. (2010) The impact of e-word-of-mouth on the online popularity of restaurants: A comparison of consumer reviews and editor reviews. *International Journal of Hospitality Management* 29 (4), 694–700.

12 Is Porto a Gay-Friendly Travel Destination? A Tourism Supply Analysis

Helena Andrade, Zélia Breda and Gorete Dinis

Introduction

Sexual orientation has an important role in an individual's identity, motivating choices about carrying out specific leisure and tourism activities and making the gay community a niche market (Hughes, 1997). The attitude of the local community towards this segment limits its destination experience perspective, making it relevant to analyse the destination's openness towards the gay community.

Portugal fulfils 66% of LGBTQ+ human rights obligations (ILGA Europe, 2020) and is regarded as one of the top 10 gay-friendly countries in Europe, being placed at the 8th position in 2020 (Rainbow Europe, 2020). This followed the government's approval of the 'National Strategy for Equality and Non-discrimination 2018–2030'. This long-term vision was translated into three action plans that define concrete measures and targets until 2021, one of them being the 'Plan to combat discrimination on the grounds of sexual orientation, gender identity and expression, and sexual characteristics' (Comissão para a Cidadania e Igualdade de Género, 2018). Studies analysing the gay community in Portugal and the difficulties it encounters to interact with society at large are still scarce. One of the few studies is that of Costa *et al.* (2017), which concludes that young adults are those that most support homosexuality and same-sex adoption.

Porto is located in the north of Portugal and is the second-largest city in the country. It is experiencing booming tourism demand, especially since 2010, when it started to attract more foreign tourists, standing out in the international market. Since then it has become a trendy tourism destination, voted Best European Destination in 2012, 2014 and 2017 and nominated for Europe's Leading City Break Destination in 2018 by the World Travel Awards. This contributed to enormous international notoriety and tourism growth.

Despite Porto's popularity, the local gay community perceive it as a conservative city, where most of its LGBTQ+ community is still anonymous. Nonetheless, there are a few gay-oriented or gay-friendly establishments (PortugalGay, 2016). The city intends to attract this market segment, for instance through the development of initiatives such as the 'Porto Gay' circuit, since LGBTQ+ tourists represent 10% of international tourism flows and 15% of the turnover of companies operating in the tourism sector (dezanove, 2016). Porto is also expected to benefit from EuroPride, the biggest gay pride event in Europe. Portugal aims to host the event in 2022 and spread diversity across the country by not focusing on a single city. It is expected that the opening session will be in Porto, and the final celebration will be in Lisbon, with the EuroPride march (Agência Lusa, 2019).

Although acceptance of same-sex couples has increased, Portugal is a conservative Catholic country where homosexuality is still outside the norm. Despite the relatively inclusive legal framework, there is nevertheless the need for concrete implementation measures to promote inclusion, safety and a non-discriminatory mind-set. According to ILGA Portugal (2018), a significant proportion of reported discriminatory situations occurred in Lisbon (23.81%), followed by Porto (18.52%). Therefore, this study aims to explore whether accommodation service providers in Porto treat potential tourists differently depending on their sexual orientation, due to overt or subtle prejudice, contributing to determining whether Porto can be associated with an image of acceptance, inclusion and diversity (UNWTO, 2017). For this, a qualitative study was carried out in which emails were sent through the accounts of fictional couples (homosexuals and heterosexuals) in order to verify whether responses were similar or if there were signs of preconception based on the sexual orientation of tourists. In addition to presenting the empirical study results, this chapter starts by looking into key concepts related to sexual diversity, prejudice, and discrimination to link them to the tourism sector and introduce some characteristics of gay tourists. A brief description of Porto as a tourism destination for the gay community is also presented.

Sexual Diversity, Prejudice and Discrimination

According to Lawler (2008), there is no comprehensive definition of identity, nor of how it develops in an individual. However, it can be pointed out that identity incorporates dimensions such as race, nationality, social class and gender, and is a social construction developed with a focus on the outside world.

While sexual identity is based on individuals' views about themselves as sexual beings, that is, which gender they create for themselves, homosexual identity includes political and collective issues – that is, cultural and social affiliation to homosexual communities (Hughes, 1997). The more the homosexual community is exposed to stigmas, the more individuals feel excluded and believe themselves to be of a lower social identity (Stenger & Roulet, 2018), leading them to be unable to express their sexuality or to secretly meet people with the same sexual orientation (Visser, 2003), since an identity, especially a sexual identity, needs to be validated by others.

Sexual identity influences how individuals introduce themselves to the community they are part of (Hughes, 1997). However, despite self-identity resulting from the environment where they are situated, individuals do not always relate to what society expects from them. When they do not fit in with these expectations, they may face situations of stigma and prejudice – created by sociodemographic, psychological or religious beliefs (Brown & Henriquez, 2008; Herek, 2002, 2015; Norton & Herek, 2013; Schope & Eliason, 2000; Stenger & Roulet, 2018; Walters & Moore, 2002; Worthen et al., 2017). Individuals can also be treated as minorities and discriminated against in terms of the acquisition of services (Poria, 2006), leading to a decrease in the consumers' self-esteem and a feeling of humiliation (Walsh, 2009). There is almost an imposition of a sense of abnormality in the gay community, because when it is said that homosexuals are 'normal' it seems that it is analogous to some sort of disability.

Market discrimination refers to different treatment given to consumers based on their characteristics – sexuality, age, disability, race and nationality (Walsh, 2009). When gay consumers attempt to acquire services and are discriminated against or denied access, this leads to the inhibition of consumption practices (Poria, 2006), since they avoid going to places where they do not feel welcome (Gremler et al., 1994). When the service is not what one expects, it is known that one spends less money than initially planned, in addition to not returning in the future, not recommending the service, or even passing on a negative image of it (King et al., 2006).

When negative word-of-mouth (WOM) is provided due to poor service delivery, it implies poor publicity about the customer experience passed on to potential service customers – and today it spreads faster through the online community (eWOM). When gay consumers are exposed to discrimination, they may even file formal complaints to expose it to the whole community (Munar & Jacobsen, 2014) in order to reduce market share and create a negative public image (Walters & Moore, 2002).

Service experience greatly influences loyalty. Staff are usually not trained to assimilate information when they react to or change their behaviour towards same-sex clients (Poria, 2006). To not feel discriminated against, gay tourists opt, for example, not to ask for a double bed at check-in (Lucena et al., 2015). This, in particular, explains the need for accommodation establishments to provide training to their staff to raise awareness and ensure a better service experience for their guests (Berezan *et al.*, 2015). The establishments do not have to call themselves 'gay-friendly'; what is essential is non-discriminatory policies for employees and guests, training on diversity and sensitivity, involvement with the gay community and partnerships with agencies working with gay people (IGLTA, 2012).

Homosexuality and Tourism

Homosexuals have created a particular way of being in life, regarding dressing and leisure activities and, in particular, attending places with a high concentration of gay-oriented or gay-friendly establishments, such as bars and clubs, shops, saunas, cafés and public spaces, which create a sense of belonging and self-identification (Meneses, 2000). Vacations have the ability to form and consolidate an identity, regardless of sexuality – they are the opportunity for the gay community to validate its identity and not worry about prejudices or stigmas, or be harassed or imprisoned (Herrera & Scott, 2005; Hughes, 1997). Tourism thus offers an opportunity for homosexuals to express themselves, without reservations (Hughes, 2006).

According to Pritchard *et al.* (2000), sexuality plays an important role in the choice of a tourism destination, allowing the identification of the motivations and preferences of tourists, with most studies in the literature focusing on the homosexual community (Monterrubio, 2019; Monterrubio & Barrios, 2016). These tourists have a profile with specific characteristics, such as high income (Walters & Moore, 2002), high education level (Badgett, 2000, 2001), good professional positions (Hughes, 1997, 2005) and sophisticated tastes (Hughes, 2006), spending large amounts of the 'pink pound' (Pritchard *et al.*, 2000). However, the lesbian market is not considered to be as relevant as the gay market on an economic level (Trihas, 2018).

Regarding the motivations that lead to the practice of tourism, these are the same as for people with other sexual orientations (Hughes, 1997; Monterrubio & Barrios, 2016). Sharpley (1994) points out that gay tourists seek relaxation, socialisation (Monterrubio & Barrios, 2016), self-realisation (Pritchard *et al.*, 2000) and 'switching off' from work for a while (Sharpley, 1994). Visser (2003) studied the South African homosexual market and stated that gay tourists' travel is motivated by natural, cultural and historical attractions.

Despite these characteristics being identified in several studies, the homosexual market is not a homogeneous one. Wong and Tolkach (2017) have critiqued the treatment of LGBT travellers as a single market by identifying a high diversity of travel preferences among Asian gay men. Ro *et al.* (2017) also suggest differences in travel psychographics, with the results of their study showing that gay couples display higher allocentricity than single gay men; the same occurs among white/Caucasian gay men compared with gay men from other ethnic minorities. Psychocentricity was higher for lower-income gay men than higher-income gay men.

Pritchard *et al.* (2000) point out that gay tourists are more likely to choose holidays linked with culture, whereas lesbian tourists have a greater need to be in an accepting, non-judgmental environment. Monterrubio and Barrios (2016) add that the tourism industry regards lesbians as having less economic power, not socialising in bars or at gay events and preferring to maintain their privacy. Although there are differences between the gay and lesbian markets, there is something in common in their holiday choices: they seek safety and socialisation with other people who share the same ideas, choosing destinations where homosexuality is not an issue (Pritchard *et al.*, 2000). On the other hand, contrary to some authors' claims, Clift and Forrest (1999) reveal that gay tourists' motivations to travel do not include searching for opportunities for sexual activity during vacations.

Sexuality is also a determinant in the way tourists choose their destination and book their trip (Pritchard *et al.*, 2000). Hughes (2006) states that destination choice depends on factors such as disposable income, ethnicity, age group, and whether tourists are effectively in a relationship. In the same author's opinion, gay tourists appreciate destinations with sun, landscapes, culture, heritage, sport or entertainment.

A study conducted by Community Marketing & Insights (2016) found that gay and bisexual men enjoy cities with great energy and nightlife. In 2017, the same study showed that gay and bisexual men prefer to choose a destination that is promoted as being LGBTQ-friendly, and lesbians and bisexual women prefer places of natural beauty and good landscapes (CMI, 2017). Kyriakaki and Abanoudis (2016) and Pritchard *et al.* (2000) corroborate the same view, stating that this community avoids visiting destinations where homosexuality is illegal, but rather look for a destination that is friendly and that accepts the LGBTQ+ community (Kyriakaki & Abanoudis, 2016).

Figure 12.1 shows the motivations that lead the homosexual community to the practice of tourism, classified as consumer aspirations, which are similar to those of other sexualities, specific motivations related to their sexual identity, and the choice of destination.

The tourism services most commonly used by this market segment vary according to the destination and the type of trip. Specifically, concerning accommodation, Community Marketing & Insights (CMI, 2016, 2017) reveals that the location of accommodation establishments is the main factor, followed by the price: quality ratio and the low cost of accommodation, the reputation of being LGBTQ-friendly and, finally, customer loyalty. The recommendations of other visitors are also pointed out by Rodrigues *et al.* (2017) as being important in accommodation choice. On the other hand, Berezan *et al.* (2015) emphasise a concept of accommodation that embraces diversity, a good relationship between price and

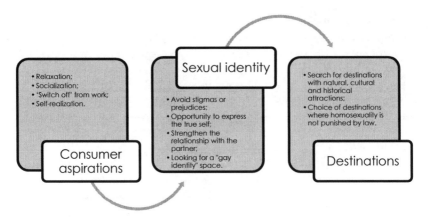

Figure 12.1 Main tourism motivations of the homosexual community

Source: Based on Clift and Forrest (1999), Herrera and Scott (2005), Hughes (1997, 2005, 2006), Köllen and Lazar (2012), Kyriakaki and Abanoudis (2016), Monterrubio and Barrios (2016), Pritchard et al. (2000) and Visser (2003).

quality, and the existence of quiet rooms, comfortable beds and late breakfast.

According to Hughes (2005), homosexual and heterosexual tourists share common travel motivations. However, gay tourists want to have the opportunity to be themselves and to not feel oppressed, to be sure that they will not be subjected to any kind of prejudice or stigma, to be able to enjoy their vacations to deepen their sexual identity, and to ensure the existence of 'gay spaces' in the destination. However, this does not appeal to all gay tourists (Pritchard et al., 2000). The choice of destination is not necessarily linked to their sexuality since, when necessary, gay tourists are willing to leave their sexuality aside to visit specific destinations that are not so receptive to homosexuality (Blichfeldt et al., 2011). Areas that call themselves 'gay spaces' can be regarded as positive, as a result of greater equality and the cohesion of heterosexual and homosexual lifestyles, which contributes to the reduction of homophobic attitudes; on the other hand, these spaces can be seen as negative by their threat to gay culture. Since these spaces allow homosexuals to have their own lifestyle and define themselves as people, interaction with heterosexuals can lead to degaying (Pritchard et al., 2000).

Porto as a Destination for Gay Travellers

Porto, located in the north of Portugal, is the second-largest city in the country and has been voted 'Best European Destination' three times recently, which has contributed to enormous international notoriety and tourism growth. Portugal is a country with a liberal society, fulfilling 69% of the human rights for the gay community (ILGA Europe, 2020). It sanctions the acceptance of an alternative lifestyle and incorporates and supports it in the legislative norms. Same-sex marriage has been legal in Portugal since 2010 (LGBT, 2018), bringing tangible and intangible benefits to Porto (Jordan & Traveller, 2018).

Its acceptance of the gay community, in the opinion of TwoBadTourists (2015), contributes to Porto being one of the most popular tourism destinations in Europe for this market segment. Porto, however, despite respecting the rights of this community, is still a conservative city and does not promote openly gay-oriented tourism supply through official channels. For this reason, and given the increasing interest of the gay community in visiting Porto, a private company has created a travel guide entitled *Porto Gay Circuit* (Publituris, 2016), allowing Porto, in the year of the launch of this project, to be considered a 'gay-friendly' destination (Queer Feed, 2016). Figure 12.2 illustrates the gay-oriented or gay-friendly services mentioned in the guide.

Another way to ascertain the interest of the gay community in a destination is through the events being held there (Jordan & Traveller, 2018). In 2018 the LGBTQ+ Pride March was organised in Porto in July (PortugalGay, 2018), as well as seven other activities classified as pride events (Sixth Porto Drag Festival; Training in Sexual Orientation and Gender Identity; Eros Porto – X Porto Erotic Show; First Ex Aequo Conference; LGBTI Cinema Cycle of the network Ex Aequo; Fourth Queer Porto; BlerghFest – festival commemorating the first anniversary of the collective Blergh).

Bars and discos	• Zoom; Fabrik; Invictus; Club 1906; Conceição 35; Café Lusitano.
Restaurants	• Arte da Baixa; The Lingerie Restaurant; Mão Travessa.
Accommodation	• Hotel Cristal Porto; The Late Birds Porto; Douro Royal Valley Hotel & Spa; Douro Palace Hotel Resort & Spa.
Culture	• Maus Hábitos; Queer Porto.
Shops	• Much Underwear; The Portuguese Cock.
Saunas	• Sauna Camões; Sauna Termas 205.
Tours	• Fresh Lobster Tours; Douro First; Alethea Travel Tours; Rumo Norte - Tours e Viagens.
Other services	• Anjos Urbanos; Rok Fotografia; Abraço; APF; Associação Plano I; Centro Gis; Aliança da Diversidade (ADD); Médicos do Mundo.

Figure 12.2 Products and services presented in the 'Porto Gay Circuit'
Source: Adapted from Porto Gay Circuit (2018).

In the opinion of Queer in the World (2018), a blog and online resource for gay and lesbian travellers, Porto can offer the LGBTQ+ community interesting nightlife, cultural events, museums, art galleries, and wine cellars and beaches, among others. The existing attractions and tourist services have allowed the development of this market segment in Porto, although it is still small when compared to other European cities such as Amsterdam, Paris or Berlin. Even though the existing gay-oriented or gay-friendly supply is not large, tourists feel happy and safe, given that the local gay community is supported through the organisation of segment-specific events and the recognition of equal rights, as well as the existence of a support centre for the LGBTQ+ community in Matosinhos, which became the best helpline in 2017, mainly for the transsexual community (Diário de Notícias, 2018).

Methodology

This study aims to determine whether accommodation service providers treat potential tourists differently depending on their sexual orientation due to overt or subtle prejudice. More specifically, it intends to evaluate whether there is a denial of access or a lower service quality offered to homosexual couples in the process of accommodation reservation. This was done through email messages sent in January 2018 from fictional newlywed couples, both homosexual and heterosexual, to request a reservation at a stratified random sample of 336 accommodation establishments located in Porto. The sample was designed to consider the various types of accommodation typologies (including gay-friendly establishments) and address the four types of couples: gay couple; lesbian couple; heterosexual couple with the man writing the email; and heterosexual couple with the woman writing the email. The response rate was 41.1%, with a maximum response time of 16 days.

The email messages allowed the 'use of deception' by creating an opportunity to collect data. The participants were not aware that their behaviour was under analysis, and had no pressure to answer according to what is socially acceptable or even desirable (Howerton et al., 2012). The aim was to get an answer from the participants, who naturally acted as if it were a real situation.

According to Howerton et al. (2012), personal contact motivates people to be more friendly and more favourable to requests than impersonal contact, whether it is made by telephone or email. Thus, impersonal contacts are more likely to instigate prejudicial attitudes and lack of motivation to convert negative attitudes into positive behaviour. Kurtzberg et al. (2006) corroborate that people tend to respond in a much more negative way when they are contacted by email than through personal contact.

In the email addressed to each establishment, the fictional couples enquired about accommodation availability and requested accommodation information to celebrate their honeymoon. The British market is one of the top tourist markets in the north of Portugal (INE, 2017); therefore, the couples' identities were created with this nationality in mind (Table 12.1).

Based on Howerton *et al.* (2012), the text sent was as follows (using the gay couple as an example):

Hello!

My name is Christopher and I was hoping to get a little information regarding your establishment. My fiancé, Thomas, and I are planning our wedding ceremony for the spring of this coming year. We were thinking about honeymooning in your area and were curious if you have any availability over any of the weekends in April. If you would, please e-mail me back with some information about your rooms as well as whether or not you have availability.

Thanks so much and have a great day!

Sincerely,

Christopher Smith

Following Howerton *et al.*'s (2012) study, the acceptance of the accommodation request was registered (a lack of response was considered a refusal of accommodation), and subtle behaviours were measured: friendliness (e.g. use of questions that deviate from professional interest, such as asking about the ceremony date, size or location); warmth (e.g. use of congratulatory remarks); thoughtfulness (e.g. use of additional information such as the surrounding area, honeymoon packages and romantic outings); and hospitality (e.g. use of phrases such as 'we would love to have you stay with us') (Howerton *et al.*, 2012: 148). In the aforementioned study, the subtle behaviour variables were coded by three researchers on a 5-point scale (with lower scores indicating lower perceived levels), and then the three evaluations were analysed in order to test the consistency between them. Similarly, in our study, each email was blindly rated by three people (a researcher and two non-researchers of different sexual orientation) on a 5-point scale.

Finally, sentiment analysis was performed with the assistance of IBM Watson™ Tone Analyzer, software that uses linguistic analysis to detect

Table 12.1 Fictional couples

	Gay couple	Lesbian couple	Heterosexual couple (man as addresser)	Heterosexual couple (woman as addresser)
Addresser	Christopher Smith	Sarah Johnson	Mark Williams	Emma Davies
Fiancé(e)	Thomas Jones	Rachel Smith	Laura Taylor	Steven Brown

emotional and language tones in written text: joy, fear, sadness, anger, analytical, confident and tentative tones. The result of the analysis of the emotions varies between 0 and 1: below 0.5 represents inexistent emotions; between ≥0.5 and <0.75 represents neutral emotions; and 0.75 upwards represents strong emotions. The data resulting from this methodology were analysed through univariate and bivariate statistical analyses with the support of IBM SPSS Statistics 24.

Results

More than half of the sample did not respond to the email request. As Howerton *et al.* (2012) state, this shows a lack of interest; however, it is not possible to conclude whether it can be considered an act of discrimination. The low response rate (41.1%) and the maximum response time (16 days) to a reservation request in a city that is a top tourist destination might seem somewhat surprising. However, this might be related to the fact that the contacts for the establishments were collected from the National Tourism Registry, and, in some cases, the contacts provided by the owners were personal email addresses. They might have been suspicious about how a British tourist had obtained their email address, since most of the establishments only advertise on online platforms such as Airbnb or Booking, which guarantee data privacy.

From the responses, it can be observed that there was no service denial or behaviour bias that could indicate inferior treatment of homosexual tourists, or differences regarding the participants' sexuality. This translates into no less availability being offered to homosexual couples, as they did not receive more 'no answer' or 'negative answers' than heterosexual couples (Table 12.2), as predicted (Howerton *et al.*, 2012; Walsh, 2009; Walters & Moore, 2002). On the contrary, heterosexual men had more 'no answers' or 'negative answers'. Women got more affirmative answers, especially homosexual women in relation to homosexual men, corroborating the results of Howerton *et al.* (2012) and Rodrigues *et al.* (2017).

Table 12.2 Reactions to the messages of the fictional couples

	Positive	Neither positive nor negative	Negative	No reply
Homosexual	10.5%	10.2%	0.6%	28.9%
Male	20.2%	19.0%	1.2%	59.5%
Female	21.4%	21.4%	1.2%	56.0%
Heterosexual	9.9%	8.7%	1.5%	30.1%
Male	20.2%	11.9%	3.6%	64.3%
Female	19.0%	22.6%	2.4%	56.0%
Total	20.2%	18.8%	2.1%	58.9%

Female staff members were the ones that responded to a greater number of emails, as happened in the study of Rodrigues *et al.* (2017), and men gave a greater number of affirmative answers to men, regardless of their sexual orientation, contrary to the study of Howerton *et al.* (2012).

The staff members who answered the most were those who did not define their position in the accommodation establishment. These provided a greater number of positive responses to heterosexual couples, but without any interference observed between the position occupied and the affirmative answers according to gender or sexual orientation. Concerning the waiting time for responses, contrary to the study of Howerton *et al.* (2012), in which men got answers faster, women received messages in a shorter period of time, similar to the study by Rodrigues *et al.* (2017). As in the study of Howerton *et al.* (2012), heterosexual couples obtained answers faster than homosexual couples.

In the analysis aiming to detect how subtle behaviour was expressed, it was observed that the same type of treatment exists regarding gender and sexual orientation. Nevertheless, it is possible to observe a more careful treatment of homosexual couples. Moreover, contrary to the study of Howerton *et al.* (2012), no inferior treatment was observed of homosexual couples compared to heterosexual couples. Also, contrary to Herek's (2002) study, no more negative attitudes towards gay couples were perceived than those received by lesbian couples; in addition, fewer negative attitudes were observed towards heterosexual women than towards heterosexual men (Norton & Herek, 2013; Schope & Eliason, 2000). It is believed that there is an increasing need to express a positive attitude towards the gay community (Lewis *et al.*, 2017), showing more sympathetic attitudes (Stenger & Roulet, 2018). As attitudes are apprehended and resistant to change and perpetuated by social forces (Walters & Moore, 2002), it can be seen that the staff members of Porto's accommodation establishments are increasingly on the way to enabling the gay community in the municipality of Porto in terms of not perceiving prejudice nor feeling that they are in a climate of discrimination. It is further believed that religion, which condemns same-sex relationships and is strongly rooted in the Portuguese culture, may gradually relax and abandon the belief that the only aim of sexual relationships is procreation (Costa *et al.*, 2019; Schope & Eliason, 2000; Worthen *et al.*, 2017), allowing the reversal of hostility towards homosexual couples.

Regarding the sentiment analysis, there were no emotions linked to prejudice showing anger or fear (Herek, 2015); only joy, sadness, analytical, confident and tentative tones were displayed. Therefore, there was no evidence of prejudice in relation to emotions, regardless of gender or sexual orientation. It was observed that homosexual men received messages where confident and tentative emotions were prominent; more joy and analytical tones were present in the messages sent to heterosexual men. Messages sent to women displayed a lower level of emotional expression.

All in all, the statistical analysis of the email responses to the request for accommodation was able to verify that the variables had no type of association and, as such, they demonstrate that there is no interference with gender discrimination or sexual orientation.

Conclusion

Sexual identity influences the way people engage with others (Hughes, 1997). Although this results from the environment in which they are embedded, individuals do not always relate to what society expects of them. It is difficult for the gay community to achieve these expectations, as a negative label is often associated with their sexual orientation (Herek, 2015; Stenger & Roulet, 2018). Homosexuals, who do not fit within what is considered 'normal', are perceived to suffer due to stigmas and sexual prejudices. Holidays become an opportunity to self-identify and express their sexuality (Hughes, 2006) in a social space, since there is a need to be validated by others (Meneses, 2000). Holidays are, thus, an escape from the reality of daily life.

Homosexuals can be also discriminated against in the acquisition of services, which leads them to lose self-esteem and end up being humiliated. They can react in different ways, inhibiting their consumption practices and/or passing on a negative image of the service that has received them badly.

From this empirical study conducted in the city of Porto, it is possible to conclude that there are neutral emotions and attitudes towards the homosexual community, with some differences found between accommodation establishments characterised as gay-oriented, gay-exclusive or gay-friendly and other establishments. Employees take longer to respond to emails from homosexual couples and are more concerned about the responses they provide, which suggests that they are more careful when obtaining information about the couples' needs and do not provide an affirmative or negative answer to their requests.

Heterosexual men had a more significant number of 'no responses' and/or 'negative responses'. Male staff members gave the same number of affirmative answers to homosexual men and to heterosexual men. Women were those who got the answers to their emails faster. Moreover, no more negative attitudes towards homosexual men were perceived than towards homosexual women. In the statistical analysis, all variables show that there is no association between them, and, as such, there is no discrimination considering gender or sexual orientation. The results indicate that none of the establishment staff who responded to the email had discriminatory practices towards the homosexual community.

By presenting the gay market in a holistic way, namely its different features and consumption practices, the study allows us to draw the attention of accommodation establishments to the importance of the market and how they can deal with it, highlighting the need for non-discriminatory policies for employees and guests, training in diversity and sensitivity, involvement with the gay community and partnerships with agencies working with gay people. Since this study targeted accommodation service providers, the findings do not represent the whole local community of Porto. Tourism professionals have commercial interests, seeing the members of the gay community as customers. Therefore, it would be interesting to extend the study to Porto's residents to assess their openness towards the homosexual community.

References

Agência Lusa (2019) Portugal candidata-se para receber em 2022 maior celebração de orgulho gay na Europa. *Agência Lusa*, 15 January. See https://www.dnoticias.pt/pais/portugal-candidata-se-para-receber-em-2022-maior-celebracao-de-orgulho-gay-na-europa-XA4233132 (accessed 18 February).

Badgett, L. (2000) The myth of gay & lesbian affluence. *Gay & Lesbian Review Worldwide* 7 (2), 22.

Badgett, L. (2001) *Money, Myths and Change: The Economic Lives of Lesbians and Gay Men*. Chicago, IL: University of Chicago.

Berezan, O., Raab, C., Krishen, A.S. and Love, C. (2015) Loyalty runs deeper than thread count: An exploratory study of gay guest preferences and hotelier perceptions. *Journal of Travel & Tourism Marketing* 32 (8), 1034–1050.

Blichfeldt, B.S., Chor, J. and Milan, N.B. (2011) 'It really depends on whether you are in a relationship': A study of 'gay destinations' from a tourist perspective. *Tourism Today* 11, 7–26.

Brown, M. and Henriquez, E. (2008) Sociodemographic predictors of attitudes towards gays and lesbians. *Individual Differences Research* 6, 193–202.

Clift, S. and Forrest, S. (1999) Gay men and tourism: Destinations and holiday motivations. *Tourism Management* 20 (5), 615–625. doi:10.1016/S0261-5177 (99)00032-1

CMI (2016) *CMI's 21st Annual Survey on LGBT Tourism & Hospitality*. San Francisco, CA: Community Marketing & Insights.

CMI (2017) *22nd Annual LGBTQ Tourism & Hospitality Survey*. US Overview Report 2017. San Francisco, CA: Community Marketing & Insights.

Comissão para a Cidadania e Igualdade de Género (2018) *Governo aprova Estratégia Nacional para a Igualdade e Não Discriminação 2018–2030 'Portugal + Igual'*. See https://www.cig.gov.pt/2018/01/governo-aprova-estrategia-nacional-igualdade-nao-discriminacao-2018-2030-portugal/ (accessed 29 March 2018).

Costa, P.A., Carneiro, F.A., Esposito, F., D'Amore, S. and Green, R.J. (2017) Sexual prejudice in Portugal: Results from the first wave European study on heterosexual's attitudes toward same-gender marriage and parenting. *Sexuality Research and Social Policy* 1 (1), 1–12. doi:10.1007/s13178-017-0292-y

Costa, P.A., Pereira, H. and Leal, I. (2019) Through the lens of sexual stigma: Attitudes toward lesbian and gay parenting. *Journal of GLBT Family Studies* 15 (1), 58–75. doi :10.1080/1550428X.2017.1413474

dezanove (2016) Porto Gay Circuit, o novo guia LGBT do Porto chega em 2017. *dezanove*, 16 November. See http://dezanove.blogs.sapo.pt/porto-gay-circuit-o-novo-guia-lgbt-do-1010840 (accessed 29 November 2017).

Diário de Notícias (2018) Centro de apoio à comunidade LGBT de Matosinhos superou os mil atendimentos em 2017. *Diário de Notícias*, 20 February. See https://www.dn.pt/lusa/interior/centro-de-apoio-a-comunidade-lgbt-de-matosinhos-superou-os-mil-atendimentos-em-2017-9132328.html.

Gremler, D.D., Bitner, M.J. and Evans, K.R. (1994) The internal service encounter. *International Journal of Service Industry Management* 5 (2), 34–56.

Herek, G.M. (2002) Gender gaps in public opinion about lesbians and gay men. *Public Opinion Quarterly* 66 (1), 40–66.

Herek, G.M. (2015) Beyond 'homophobia': Thinking more clearly about stigma, prejudice, and sexual orientation. *American Journal of Orthopsychiatry* 85 (5), 29–37.

Herrera, S. and Scott, D. (2005) 'We gotta get out of this place!': Leisure travel among gay men living in a small city. *Tourism Review Internacional* 8 (3), 249–262. doi:10.3727/154427205774791564

Howerton, D.M., Meltzer, A.L. and Olson, M.A. (2012) Honeymoon vacation: Sexual-orientation prejudice and inconsistent behavioral responses. *Basic and Applied Social Psychology* 34 (2), 146–151. doi:10.1080/01973533.2012.655638

Hughes, H. (1997) Holidays and homosexual identity. *Tourism Management* 18 (1), 3–7. doi:10.1016/S0261-5177 (96)00093-3

Hughes, H. (2005) A gay tourism market: Reality or illusion, benefit or burden? *Journal of Quality Assurance in Hospitality & Tourism* 5 (2/4), 57–74.

Hughes, H. (2006) Pink tourism: Holidays of gay men and lesbians. *Tourism and Hospitality Research* 8 (1), 71–73.

IGLTA (2012) *2012 Annual Report*. International Gay and Lesbian Travel Association.

ILGA Europe (2020) *Rainbow Europe 2020*. See https://www.ilga-europe.org/rainboweurope/2020 (accessed 12 Ferbuary 2021).

INE (2017) *Turismo em números, dezembro 2017*. Lisbon: Instituto Nacional de Estatística.

Jordan, P. and Traveller, G.C. (2018) *Handbook on the Lesbian, Gay, Bisexual, Transgender and Queer (LGBTQ) Travel Segment*. Brussels: European Travel Commission.

King, E.B., Shapiro, J.R., Hebl, M.R., Singletary, S.L. and Turner, S. (2006) The stigma of obesity in customer service: A mechanism for remediation and bottom-line consequences of interpersonal discrimination. *Journal of Applied Psychology* 91 (3), 579–593. doi:10.1037/0021-9010.91.3.579

Köllen, T. and Lazar, S. (2012) Gay tourism in Budapest: An exploratory study on gay tourists' motivational patterns for traveling to Budapest. *American Journal of Tourism Management* 1 (3), 64–68.

Kurtzberg, T.R., Belkin, L.Y. and Naquin, C.E. (2006) The effect of e-mail on attitudes towards performance feedback. *International Journal of Organizational Analysis* 14 (1), 4–21. See https://www.researchgate.net/publication/242347295_The_effect_of_e-mail_on_attitude_towards_performance_feedback.

Kyriakaki, A. and Abanoudis, D. (2016) Investigating the lesbian, gay, bisexual and transgender (LGBT) tourism market in Greece. In P.K. Andriotis (ed.) *Conference Proceedings of the International Conference on Tourism (ICOT1016) 'New Challenges and Boundaries in Tourism'* (pp. 256–267). Aegean: International Association for Tourism Policy.

Lawler, S. (2008) *Identity: Sociological Perspectives*. Cambridge, MA: Polity Press.

Lewis, D.C., Flores, A.R., Haider-Markel, D.P., Miller, P.R., Tadlock, B.L. and Taylor, J.K. (2017) Degrees of acceptance: Variation in public attitudes toward segments of the LGBT community. *Political Research Quarterly* 70 (4), 861–875. doi:10.1177/1065912917717352

LGBT (2018) *Casamento entre pessoas do mesmo sexo*. See https://www.lgbt.pt/casamento-entre-pessoas-do-mesmo-sexo/ (accessed 28 September 2018).

Lucena, R., Jarvis, N. and Weeden, C. (2015) A review of gay and lesbian parented families' travel motivations and destination choices: Gaps in research and future directions. *Annals of Leisure Research* 18 (2), 272–289. doi:10.1080/11745398.2015.1040038

Meneses, I. (2000) Intimidade, norma e diferença: A modernidade gay em Lisboa. *Análise Social* 34 (153), 933–955.

Monterrubio, C. (2019) Tourism and male homosexual identities: Directions for sociocultural research. *Tourism Review* 74 (5), 1058–1069. doi:10.1108/TR-08-2017-0125

Monterrubio, J.C. and Barrios, M.D. (2016) Lesbians as tourists: A qualitative study of tourist motivations in Mexico. *Tourismos: An International Multidisciplinary Journal of Tourism* 11 (4), 64–90.

Munar, A.M. and Jacobsen, J.K.S. (2014) Motivations for sharing tourism experiences through social media. *Tourism Management* 43, 46–54.

Norton, A.T. and Herek, G.M. (2013) Heterosexuals' attitudes toward transgender population: Findings from a national probability sample of U.S. adults. *Sex Roles* 68 (11), 738–753.

Poria, Y. (2006) Assessing gay men and lesbian women's hotel experiences: An exploratory study of sexual orientation in the travel industry. *Journal of Travel Research* 44 (3), 327–334. doi:10.1177/0047287505279110

Porto Gay Circuit (2018) *Porto Gay Circuit.* See http://www.portogaycircuit.com/ (accessed 24 December 2017).

PortugalGay (2016) *Informação sobre a cidade do Porto (PortugalGay.pt).* See http://portugalgay.pt/guide/s_porto.asp (accessed 29 November 2017).

PortugalGay (2018) Agenda do Orgulho LGBT+ preenchida para 2018. *PortugalGay,* 1 May. See https://portugalgay.pt/news/010518A/portugal_agenda_do_orgulho_lgbt_preenchida_para_2018 (accessed 19 July 2018).

Pritchard, A., Morgan, N.J., Sedgley, D., Khan, E. and Jenkins, A. (2000) Sexuality and holiday choices: Conversations with gay and lesbian tourists. *Leisure Studies* 19 (4), 267–282. doi:10.1080/02614360050118832

Publituris (2016) Porto vai ter guia LGBT em 2017. *Publituris,* 28 October. See https://www.publituris.pt/2016/10/28/porto-vai-ter-guia-lgbt-2017/ (accessed 26 January 2018).

Queer Feed (2016) Cidade do Porto se tornará oficialmente gay friendly em 2017. *Queer Feed,* 6 November. See http://www.queerfeed.com.br/cidade-do-porto-gay-friendly/ (accessed 27 September 2018).

Queer in the World (2018) *Gay Porto Guide: The Essential Guide to Gay Travel in Porto Portugal 2018.* See https://queerintheworld.com/gay-porto-travel-guide/ (accessed 5 August 2018).

Rainbow Europe (2020) *Country Ranking.* See https://www.rainbow-europe.org/country-ranking (accessed 12 February 2021).

Ro, H., Olson, E.D. and Choi, Y. (2017) An exploratory study of gay travelers: Sociodemographic analysis. *Tourism Review* 72 (1), 15–27.

Rodrigues, C., Moniz, A.I. and Tiago, F. (2017) Turismo gay: Estão preparados? *Revista Turismo & Desenvolvimento* 27–28, 2255–2264.

Schope, R.D. and Eliason, M.J. (2000) Thinking versus acting: Assessing the relationship between heterosexual attitudes and behaviors toward homosexuals. *Journal of Gay & Lesbian Social Services* 11 (4), 69–92. https://doi.org/10.1300/J041v11n04_04

Sharpley, R. (1994) *Tourism and Tourist Motivation.* Huntingdon: Elm Publications.

Stenger, S. and Roulet, T.J. (2018) Pride against prejudice? The stakes of concealment and disclosure of a stigmatized identity for gay and lesbian auditors. *Work, Employment and Society* 32 (2), 257–273. doi:10.1177/0950017016682459

Trihas, N. (2018) Travel motivations, preferences and perceptions of Greek gay men and lesbians. *Tourism Today* 7, 7–26.

TwoBadTourists (2015) Gay Porto: A gay travel guide to Portugal's second city. *TwoBadTourists,* 23 November. See http://www.twobadtourists.com/2015/07/30/gay-porto-a-gay-travel-guide-to-portugals-second-city/ (accessed 20 September 2017).

UNWTO (2017) *Second Global Report on LGBT Tourism.* Affiliate Members Global Reports Vol. 15. Madrid: World Tourism Organization. See https://www.e-unwto.org/doi/pdf/10.18111/9789284418619.

Visser, G. (2003) Gay men, tourism and urban space: Reflections on Africa's 'gay capital'. *Tourism Geographies* 5 (2), 168–189. doi:10.1080/1461668032000068261

Walsh, G. (2009) Disadvantaged consumers' experiences of marketplace discrimination in customer services. *Journal of Marketing Management* 25 (1–2), 143–169.

Walters, A.S. and Moore, L.J. (2002) Attention all shoppers, queer costumers in aisle two: Investigating lesbian and gay discrimination in the marketplace. *Consumption, Markets and Culture* 5 (4), 285–303.

Wong, C.C.L. and Tolkach, D. (2017) Travel preferences of Asian gay men. *Asia Pacific Journal of Tourism Research* 22 (6), 579–591.

Worthen, M.G.F., Lingiardi, V. and Caristo, C. (2017) The roles of politics, feminism, and religion in attitudes toward LGBT individuals: A cross-cultural study of college students in the USA, Italy, and Spain. *Sexuality Research and Social Policy* (14), 241–258. doi:10.1007/s13178-016-0244-y

13 Buenos Aires: Authentically Straight-Friendly

Heather L. Jeffrey and Martin Sposato

Introduction

The *Second Global Report on LGBT Tourism* by the United Nations World Tourism Organisation (UNWTO, 2017) acknowledges the importance of the authenticity of equal rights and marketing in the creation of lesbian, gay, bisexual and transgender (LGBT) tourism destinations. The report also highlights how the positive impacts of tourism link to respect and an understanding of equality. Authenticity and commodification have a long history of dichotomous theorising in tourism studies (Cole, 2007), and unsurprisingly the same arguments have found a home in the theorising of LGBT tourism. Many researchers argue that the promotion, packaging and marketing of LGBT tourism is both the commodification and sanitisation of sexuality. Indeed, the traditional focus of commercially oriented research towards the 'pink dollar' reduces people, and in turn sexuality, to their buying power.

Research on LGBT tourism has been critiqued for its Western centricity (Waitt *et al.*, 2008), and the dominance of the (re)presentation of the West as gay-friendly risks reifying Other destinations as less liberal backward Others (Binnie & Klesse, 2011). Acknowledging this critique, this chapter presents the case of Buenos Aires as an LGBT tourist destination and discusses marketing in order to explore the concept of authenticity and its importance for LGBT tourism destinations. In doing so, key stakeholders are called upon to explore their own marketing practices through the use of semi-structured interviews. The chapter contributes to the extant literature by evaluating how LGBT tourism marketing can be more than the commodification of homosexuality, highlighting how marketing can be a form of activism.

Authentically Gay or Commodified Sexuality

Queer and gay spaces have been celebrated by geographers (Puar, 2001) and tourism researchers as a validation of gay identity due to affordances of freedom (Vorobjovas-Pinta, 2018). However, increasingly critiques of gay space are centred on commodification, as gay, lesbian and queer spaces are identified as overwhelmingly commercial spaces (Oswin, 2008). Within an exclusionary politics of place, the space gives rise to 'the good homo', who is invariably wealthy, white and male (Puar, 2001). Critiques of this type have at their basis a critique of homonormativity – 'a politics that does not contest dominant heteronormative assumptions and institutions, but upholds and sustains them, while promising the possibility of a demobilized gay constituency and a privatized, depoliticised gay culture anchored in domesticity and consumption' (Duggan, 2003: 50). Yet,

> Commercial spaces for consuming leisure – clubs, bars, restaurants, cafés – are paradoxical sites because they fit neoliberal policy goals but are also conduits of sociality and public culture, and therefore offer a nuanced lens into the specificities and differences, as well as cooption, operable in these urban processes. (Gorman-Murray & Nash, 2017)

Space and place are shaped by myriad factors, but at least one of these is advertising discourse. Advertising renders a place a product to be consumed, a commodity, and Markwell (2002) highlights that while the right to consume and the (re)presentation of LGBT tourists in marketing materials could be understood as inclusion, it is at the cost of exclusion of those who may not identify with the commercial scene. Advertisements understood as discourse are disciplinary (Foucault, 1980); they shape what it is to be an LGBT tourist. Even UNWTO (2017) utilises a discourse of marketing, promoting LGBT tourists as a market segment. Yet, while in the past the notion of the 'pink dollar' has dominated discourses on LGBT tourists as a niche market, the segment is no more homogeneous than the heterosexual market (Hughes, 2005; Pritchard et al., 2002).

Advertisers have been critiqued for their reliance on non-threatening symbols that pass by heterosexual consumers and are only understood by the LGBT community, often termed 'gay window dressing' (Schroeder & Zwick, 2004). Gay tourism marketing might also run the risk of reinstating common stereotypes (Coon, 2012), perhaps especially through the use of symbolism such as the pink triangle or rainbow flag (Stuber, 2002). While tourism scholars are beginning to challenge the reductionist tendency to conceptualise LGBT as gay, white, man (Lucena et al., 2015), historically gay advertising has targeted white gay men (Baxter, 2010). While, 'mainstream' advertisements may often remain unmodified due to economic limitations (Hughes, 2005), the findings of Dotson et al. (2009) suggest that an LGB market may want overt images of people similar to themselves. While symbolism may be an important feature in LGBT advertising, less scholarly attention has been placed on the importance of authenticity of LGBT tourism advertisements.

Authentic advertising is often considered a contradiction in terms, especially when commodification is understood as the antonym of authenticity. Yet, for LGBT tourism, authentic advertising is imperative if destinations are to welcome and care for all their guests with equal respect. Authentic advertising must be based on an authentic anchor, in this case equal rights, in order to avoid pink washing. The politics of LGBT tourism are multitude as highlighted by Binnie and Klesse (2011), and there is some pressure on homophobic destinations to encourage gay law reform.

Gay-Friendly Buenos Aires

There is a history of LGBT activism in Argentina, which has been pivotal in increasing public awareness of the need to advance the LGBT agenda in general. Arguably, the most remarkable proponent of LGBT rights was Carlos Jáuregui, who was the first President of the Comunidad Homosexual Argentina (Argentinean homosexual community) and founder of the Associacion Gays por los Derechos Civiles (Gay association for Civil Rights). This activism has changed the map of Buenos Aires, and in recognition of Carlos Jáuregui a metro station in the capital city bears his name (Meccia, 2015). Memorialising activists in this way is certainly a symbolic gesture of representation, but discourses of acceptance have permeated legislation and Argentinian governments have granted equal rights.

The Egalitarian Marriage Law (Law 26.618), promulgated in 2010, placed Argentina at the forefront of LGBT rights in the region and set an example to be followed by countries such as Brazil, Colombia and Uruguay. The Egalitarian Marriage Law was not the only first for Argentina: in 2002 the city of Buenos Aires was the first city in South America to grant equal rights to same sex couples. Furthermore, in 2012 the Argentinian government passed legislation allowing Argentinean citizens to decide their legal sex based on their personal preferences. Same-sex sexual activity was decriminalised in the country in 1853. Thus the right space, born of activism but supported by government, has been created for LGBT tourism to flourish.

Government initiatives that support LGBT tourism in Buenos Aires include a webpage that promotes and provides information for LGBT tours in Buenos Aires, and also the BA Diversa (Diverse Buenos Aires) festival, a festival to promote and celebrate diversity in the city with a focus on the LGBT community. According to Bowman (2015), Buenos Aires is an example of innovative inclusive tourism. One of the main features that makes Buenos Aires stand out in the region is its entrepreneurial bureaucracy, which in essence means a local government willing to take LGBT tourism seriously and able to provide and innovate within its regulatory framework. Since the late 1990s and early 2000s, tourism planning has been built out of a belief that tourism is culture, and that promotion should focus on local aspects of Buenos Aires like its café culture and independent theatres or libraries to position Buenos Aires as a cultural tourist attraction. This approach has paid off, as numbers of visitors to Buenos Aires have been increasing in general, and in particular in terms of the LGBT segment.

This cultural approach is linked to the idea of authenticity, which in many cities is developed at the expense of local hosts. A key example of this might be Tropicana in Havana, Cuba, which is now a show for tourists rather than a social space for Cubans. In contrast, in Buenos Aires, tours do not exclude local 'Porteños' from cultural attractions like Café Tortoni or any of the theatres of Calle Corrientes. This level of inclusivity within the cultural attractions provides tourists visiting Buenos Aires with a feeling of authenticity difficult to replicate – an environment where tourists do as the locals do and where hosts and guests interact. This authenticity is quite unique to Buenos Aires. Although other cities such as Havana also have an entrepreneurial bureaucracy, they are limited by a shortage of adequate infrastructure; Rio de Janeiro might have many touristic sites, but bureaucracy and the enclavic nature of tourism space limits opportunity for growth of the sector in general and LGBT tourism in particular.

Traditional Argentine culture has also proved dynamic, and advances made by the LGBT movement have challenged these traditions to become more inclusive. A clear example of this is queer tango, which has emerged to challenge traditional gender roles in society. Queer tango disrupts the dance that has for years reinforced gender roles – where the man leads the woman follows – by allowing performers of the same sex. Yet, critical scholars have understood these practices as a form of cultural entrepreneurialism that works to benefit city planners over citizens (Kanai, 2015). Other examples of cultural practices include 'Los Dogos', the first openly gay football team in South America, a continent crazy about football. Football in Latin America is linked to a masculine heterosexual macho identity, but this team and others are challenging these deeply rooted social norms. According to Pablo De Luca, President of CCGLAR and Pablo Singerman, CEO and Camilo Makón, CEO of Singerman & Makón LATAM Tourism Consulting, these activities are often among the most sought out by LGBT tourists in Buenos Aires as among other reasons they include opportunities to socialise with locals (UNWTO, 2017).

The move to challenge gender roles and heteronormativity has been fomented by activists and is now supported by legislation. Yet, these movements are also spatial in that they are shaped by and shape place and space. Unlike other cities such as Toronto or Sydney (Gorman-Murray & Nash, 2017), Buenos Aires has not territorialised the LGBT community; there has never been a gay ghetto. Buenos Aires is home to the largest LGBT parade in Latin America and is one of the most important LGBT destinations in South America, having gained 'international recognition as an LGBT mecca of Latin America' (UNWTO, 2017: 95). The move to make Buenos Aires an LGBT urban tourism destination owes its authenticity and arguably its success to grass roots movements, which were later supported by legislation.

Key dates

- 2003 – Argentina first country in South America to legalise civil partnerships
- 2010 – Law 26.618: Equal rights in matrimony between persons of the same sex
- GMaps360 (gay tourist maps of Buenos Aires) produced between 2010 and 2011 (after this date they went online, but these maps are still available in tourist info)
- 2011 – National and local BA governments aimed to increase number of LGBT tourists – by positioning Argentina as LGBT friendly and segment not based solely on sexuality

---

Figure 13.1 Key dates for LGBT tourism development in Argentina
Source: Authors' own elaboration

Interviewing Stakeholders

In 2016, as part of a wider project on social inequality, five semi-structured interviews with key LGBT tourism stakeholders were carried out in Buenos Aires; the interviews lasted between one and two hours. The interviews were designed to explore the role and space of Argentina as an LGBT tourism destination within Latin America. Participants were identified using snowball sampling and included a representative from INPROTUR (the government organisation responsible for promoting Argentina as a tourism destination abroad), two representatives from the Camara de Comercio Gay y Lesbica Argentina (CCGLAR), one straight-friendly bar owner and one same-sex marriage travel agency owner. These interviews were conducted in English or Spanish depending on the participants' preference; the interviews were carried out by the first and second author. The first author is a British female, who speaks Spanish fluently albeit with a 'funny accent', and the second author is an Argentinian man. The interviews were recorded and then transcribed using the language of the interview.

Two prominent themes that emerged from the interviews were the importance of authenticity which links to a feeling of gratitude towards government support and activism, and (heteronormative) disruption through the use of space categorisation which is used in marketing materials. Utilising the participants' own words in line with the overall importance of authenticity to this chapter, we (re)present these themes in both English and the original Spanish below.

Authentically Gay Buenos Aires

UNWTO (2017) have stated that authenticity is key to creating successful LGBT destinations, but ironically if the primary motive of a destination is to attract the LGBT market then arguably the product will not be authentic nor will it achieve its aim. INPROTOUR highlight this contention:

> You can have the best destinations, but if people think that your enthusiasm is only based on gay and lesbian money it's very probable that gays and lesbians won't go.
>
> *Podés tener el mejor destino, si se percibe que tu interés está sólo basado en el dinero de gays y lesbianas es muy probable que no vayan gays y lesbianas.*

Authenticity should also be strived for within institutions and attempts to market the destination. CCGLAR embed authenticity within their marketing activities:

> Our concept, the idea, is that you have to have a gay photographer or a gay model to complete a publication, I mean who am I speaking to? To gays and lesbians
>
> *En nuestro concepto, la idea ... si es necesario tener un fotógrafo gay o un modelo gay para llevar adelante una producción, yo digo a quién le habló? - a gays y lesbianas*

Working with authentic models takes into account that we look for our own (re)presentation in advertising (Dotson *et al.*, 2009) and avoid 'gay window-dressing' (Schroeder & Zwick, 2004). Similarly, Fort Lauderdale ensure that they work with models who have transitioned when marketing to the trans community (UNWTO, 2017). However, there is also the risk of hyper-homosexualising a destination, as CCGLAR explain after being asked to give feedback on another destination's promotional video:

> Inside, we were saying 'it's gayland!' It's all gay, there isn't even one heterosexual person in the video.
>
> *por adentro dijimos, es gaylandia, es todo gay, no hay un solo heterosexual en el video.*

As previously noted, gay tourism marketing might also run the risk of reinstating common stereotypes (Coon, 2012) through the use of symbolism such as the pink triangle or rainbow flag (Stuber, 2002). CCGLAR explain how they are aware of this and how they tried to move away from stereotypes to create a more authentic image when Buenos Aires became the first Latin American destination in ITB's (Internationale Tourismus-Börse Berlin) 'pink corner':

> We changed the esthetics of the stand, which was pink. We didn't want it to be pink so we made it white with photos of Argentina ... It's a stereotype that might not represent the whole community, we don't rule it out just as we don't rule out the flag, but we believe that it isn't our only resource.
>
> *Nosotros lo que hicimos fue cambiar la estética del stand que era rosa. Y no queríamos que fuera rosa y pusimos blanco con fotos de Argentina*

… es un estereotipo que quizás no representa a toda la comunidad y no lo descartamos, como tampoco descartamos la bandera que nos identifica, pero consideramos que no es el único recurso.

However, the most important element of creating an authentic LGBT tourism destination is inclusivity. Legislation does not automatically equate to equality in society, but without it equality is impossible. Legislation is also key to promoting the destination on a global stage, according to CCGLAR:

> It is what has made Argentina, on the one hand it promotes the destination, but on the other it gives us recognition as equal, I mean I can legally get married, I can adopt, I can buy a house with my partner.
> *[La ley] justamente es lo que hace Argentina, por un lado promociona su destino, pero por otro lado nos reconoce como iguales, o sea a nivel leyes yo puedo casarme, puedo adoptar, puedo comprarme una casa con mi pareja.*

Certainly, without legislative legitimisation, certain businesses could not exist, but as highlighted by a same-sex marriage travel agency owner, it is not only the law but bureaucratic processes that enable an international tourism destination:

> Argentina is the only country, as far as I know, if it changed somewhere a week ago I might not have heard, but it's the only country that doesn't have any restrictions. Actually, if I wanted to get married here, as an Argentinian with my Argentinian girlfriend, the process would take 21 days and it costs, not a lot, but it has a price. For foreigners, it takes 5 days and it's free.
> *Argentina sí es el único país, hasta donde yo sé, digamos si cambió hace una semana a veces no me entero, pero es el único que no tiene ningún tipo de restricción. Es más, si yo me quiero casar a aquí, yo como argentino con mi novia argentina, el trámite entero se va a 21 días y tiene un costo, no muy caro, pero tiene un valor. Para gente extranjera, son cinco días y es gratis.*

In Buenos Aires, the legislation has been an important factor in creating an authentic LGBT tourism product; equality as promulgated by law evidences more than mere pink washing. In addition to the law, the simplification of processes surrounding international weddings has helped to attract LGBT tourists wishing to marry. Interestingly, the law that makes Argentina an authentic LGBT tourist destination is also the primary pull factor. As CCGLAR state:

> This is being authentic. And this is why other countries can't do it.
> *Eso es ser auténticos. Y por eso hay otros países que no pueden decirlo.*

Marketing as Rebellion

As previously highlighted, CCGLAR supported by the Argentinian government have used promotional materials to disrupt stereotypical symbolism such as the use of the colour pink or the rainbow flag. While

CCGLAR are working towards authentic (re)presentations of the LGBT community within their promotional materials, there is also evidence of what might be understood as a political manoeuvre against homonormativity that 'does not contest dominant heteronormative assumptions and institutions, but upholds and sustains them' (Duggan, 2003: 50). This manoeuvre lies in the categorisation of space as found in LGBT tourism marketing materials.

The commonly used adjective 'gay-friendly' highlights how space is normalised as straight: the use of gay-friendly as a category is political as it informs the public that gays are allowed in. In the 21st century, we can argue that there should not be a need to identify certain spaces as gay and others as straight. Yet reports in the media (see, for example, Davies, 2018) highlight that in certain spaces in the West, the notion of gay-friendly can be used as an excuse to exclude LGBT people. Within this politic of inclusive/exclusive space, the use of 'straight-friendly' by the government, CCGLAR and local entrepreneurs in promotional materials targeting LGBT tourists can be understood as activism to highlight the political use of gay-friendly.

A 'straight-friendly' bar owner utilises and understands the categorisation 'straight-friendly' in opposition to the term 'gay-friendly':

> It's like condescending – We can be condescending too! They [heterosexuals] only think to go to a bar and they basically just go in and that's it, whereas gay bars like we have to try and think where it is.

The government's INPROTOUR situates the creation of the category 'straight-friendly' within a wider discourse of inclusion:

> We thought it would be funny to use the term straight friendly in certain nightclubs, bars and hotels that aren't totally gay, there aren't any gay hotels in Buenos Aires. So, one day one of the hotel owners told me my hotel is not a gay hotel, it is straight friendly. It's a gay hotel that also welcomes straight people.
> *A lo que voy es que el término hetero friendly nos pareció divertido utilizarlo en algunas discos o bares u hoteles que no son totalmente gay, que ya no existen hoteles gay en Buenos Aires. Entonces, un día uno de los dueños que es español, que es dueño de los Hoteles en España me dijo mi hotel no es un hotel gay es hetero friendly. Es un hotel gay que también está abierto para gente hetero.*

Conclusion

Authenticity has been described by UNWTO (2017) as key to developing LGBT tourism destinations, but authenticity is often conceptualised by tourism researchers as impossible to attain when there is a price tag attached. The case of Buenos Aires highlights how LGBT tourism has grown out of authentic equal rights gained by the efforts of activists. Equal rights have allowed stakeholders such as CCGLAR and

INPROTOUR to market the destination authentically and in turn these stakeholders attempt to move away from stereotypes such as the colour pink. In addition to this, authenticity informs their choice of models and their marketing materials become an act of entrepreneurial activism. This activism is particularly clear in the categorising of space as 'straight-friendly'; this contrasts with the term 'gay-friendly', which should be redundant by now.

While Argentina, and Buenos Aires specifically, evidences patterns of normalisation and defiance alongside growing popularity as an LGBT destination, there are still caveats to be found within the offering. LGBT tourism follows similar patterns evidenced elsewhere (Pritchard *et al.*, 2002) of a growing homo-patriarchy with few (perhaps even no) lesbians or women involved in decision making. Additionally, while legislation has been passed to allow citizens to decide their legal sex based on their personal preference, the trans community lack representation within the LGBT tourism sector. Argentina still plays a leading role in gay policy making across Latin America, and within this LGBT tourism and its Argentine proponents are the primary influencers. For this the country should be applauded, but more costly rights, such as women's reproductive freedom, are yet to be granted.

Acknowledgments

This chapter was elaborated in the context of the INCASI Network coordinated by Dr Pedro López-Roldán, a European project which has received funding from the European Union's Horizon 2020 research and innovation programme under the Marie Skłodowska-Curie GA No. 691004.

References

Baxter, S. (2010) Evidence on the marketing approaches targeting gay and lesbian consumers. *Global Journal of Business Research* 4, (2), 125–139.

Binnie, J. and Klesse, C. (2011) 'Because it was a bit like going to an adventure park': The politics of hospitality in transnational lesbian, gay, bisexual, transgender and queer activist networks. *Tourist Studies* 11 (2), 157–174.

Bowman, K. (2015) Policy choice, social structure, and international tourism in Buenos Aires, Havana, and Rio De Janeiro. *Latin American Research Review* 50 (3), 135–156.

Cole, S. (2007) Beyond authenticity and commodification. *Annals of Tourism Research* 34 (4), 943–960.

Coon, D.R. (2012) Sun, sand, and citizenship: The marketing of gay tourism. *Journal of Homosexuality* 59 (4), 511–534.

Davies, S. (2018) Gay men told Leeds bar was for 'mixed couples only'. *BBC News*, 11 April. See https://www.bbc.com/news/uk-england-43683033 (accessed 15 October 2018).

Dotson, M.J., Hyatt, E.M. and Petty Thompson, L. (2009) Sexual orientation and gender effects of exposure to gay-and lesbian-themed fashion advertisements. *Journal of Fashion Marketing and Management: An International Journal* 13 (3), 431–447.

Duggan, L. (2003) *The Twilight of Equality? Neoliberalism, Cultural Politics, and the Attack on Democracy.* Boston, MA: Beacon Press.

Foucault, M. (1980) Power/knowledge: Selected interviews and other writings, 1972–1977. New York: Pantheon Books.

Gorman-Murray, A. and Nash, C. (2017) Transformations in LGBT consumer landscapes and leisure spaces in the neoliberal city. *Urban Studies* 54 (3), 786–805.

Hughes, H.L. (2005) A gay tourism market: Reality or illusion, benefit or burden? *Journal of Quality Assurance in Hospitality & Tourism* 5, 2–4, 57–74.

Kanai, J.M. (2015) Buenos Aires beyond (homo)sexualized urban entrepreneurialism: The geographies of queered tango. *Antipode* 47 (3), 652–670.

Lucena, R., Jarvis, N. and Weeden, C. (2015) A review of gay and lesbian parented families' travel motivations and destination choices: Gaps in research and future directions. *Annals of Leisure Research* 18 (2), 272–289.

Markwell, K. (2002) Mardi Gras tourism and the construction of Sydney as an international gay and lesbian city. *GLQ: A Journal of Lesbian and Gay Studies* 8 (1–2), 81–99.

Meccia, E. (2015) Cambio y narración. Las transformaciones de la homosexualidad en Buenos Aires según los relatos de homosexuales mayores. *Sexualidad, Salud y Sociedad – Revista Latinoamericana* 19.

Oswin, N. (2008) Critical geographies and the uses of sexuality: Deconstructing queer space. *Progress in Human Geography* 32 (1), 89–103.

Pritchard, A., Morgan, N. and Sedgley, D. (2002) In search of lesbian space? The experience of Manchester's gay village. *Leisure Studies* 2, 105–123.

Puar, J. (2001) Global circuits: Transnational sexualities and Trinidad. *Signs* 26 (4), 1039–1065.

Schroeder, J.E. and Zwick, D. (2004) Mirrors of masculinity: Representation and identity in advertising images. *Consumption Markets & Culture* 7 (1), 21–52.

Stuber, M. (2002) Tourism marketing aimed at gay men and lesbians: A business perspective. In S. Clift, M. Luongo and C. Callister (eds) *Gay Tourism: Culture, Identity and Sex* (pp. 88–124). London and New York: Continuum.

UNWTO (2017) *Second Global Report on LGBT Tourism.* Affiliate Members Global Reports Vol. 15. Madrid: World Tourism Organization. See https://www.e-unwto.org/doi/pdf/10.18111/9789284418619.

Vorobjovas-Pinta, O. (2018) Gay neo-tribes: Exploration of travel behaviour and space. *Annals of Tourism Research* 72, 1–10.

Waitt, G., Markwell, K. and Gorman-Murray, A. (2008) Challenging heteronormativity in tourism studies: Locating progress. *Progress in Human Geography* 32 (6), 781–800.

14 Out of the Closet and into the Streets: Reflections on the Considerations in Hosting Rural Pride Events

Clifford Lewis and Oscar Vorobjovas-Pinta

Introduction

The academic literature has typically noted that gender, sexuality and romantically diverse individuals (GSRD) travel away from small towns in an effort to realise their identity in a more holistic way (Annes & Redlin, 2012; Provencher, 2007; Vorobjovas-Pinta & Hardy, 2016). Travel, in general, allows closeted individuals who may socially identify as heterosexual/cis-gendered within their home environment to experience GSRD lifestyles without fear of identification (Hughes, 2006; Waitt & Markwell, 2006). Travel to metropolitan locations provides the individual with anonymity, allowing visitors to engage in lifestyles they may be denied within their home environment (Provencher, 2007; Waitt & Markwell, 2006) – either due to a lack of provision or because of a need to be discreet. Metropolitan locations based on their population density also provide greater prospects for the individual to meet others who share a similar lifestyle (Hughes, 2003; Vorobjovas-Pinta, 2018). Such interactions with other GSRD individuals are key to building a healthy self-identity and accepting one's own sexual and gender disposition (Blichfeldt *et al.*, 2013; Hughes, 1997).

In recent times, however, there has been a growth in GSRD individuals moving towards regional destinations and either relocating as new residents (Brown, 2015) or visiting for a holiday (Gorman-Murray *et al.*, 2012). This has in part been spurred on by the increasing acceptance of LGBTIQ+ people, and by more and more rural destinations repositioning themselves as ally places. Pride events have been used as part of these repositioning campaigns, and pride parades which initially were an act of defiance have now been transformed into celebrations of acceptance. Such events are often portrayed as places that facilitate a physical gathering of often marginalised LGBTIQ+ people and as change agents that may lead to 'opposition in the form of contestations in respect to social and legal identities' (Ong & Goh, 2018: 967). Johnston (2005, 2007) positions gay pride festivals as socially contested events embodied with political significance that foster community conversations around the topics of tolerance, acceptance and diversity. However, while pride events are considered to be 'visible expressions of collectivities', they may also homogenise the lived experiences of pride attendees and, indeed, exclude the voices of those who do not conform to norms set by the majority (Johnston, 2007: 33). On the other hand, Gorman-Murray *et al.* (2012) frame LGBTIQ+ rural events as idylls that blur the urban/rural binary. Indeed, over the last couple of years there has been a surge in the number of gay festivals and events organised in rural and remote areas worldwide. Examples of rural pride events can be found around the world, including Broken Heel in Broken Hill (New South Wales, Australia), Pride on the Plains in Auburn (Alabama, United States) and Agrogay Festival in Monterroso (Galicia, Spain), to name but a few (Vorobjovas-Pinta & Hardy, 2021). Following the notion of rural pride events, this chapter focuses on the first Mardi Gras hosted in the township of Hay, located in regional New South Wales (Australia) in 2018.

The value of events to a destination has been well documented in the literature (Hankinson, 2005; Jago *et al.*, 2003). Economically, events help attract visitors and tourist income, stimulate employment, encourage spending and contribute to public infrastructure development (Getz, 1997). In regard to a destination's brand, events can help build awareness, position a destination as fashionable and help destinations manage their brand image over time (Lewis *et al.*, 2013b). Within a regional context, events help build social and cultural bonds (Frost & Laing, 2015) and form part of a package which provides a greater value experience for visitors (Wilson *et al.*, 2001). In light of declining rural visitor numbers, many places in Australia have sought to revitalise their communities and foster economic development by staging events and festivals that cater to particular sub-segments (Gibson & Stewart, 2009).

Given the socioeconomic value of tourism to regional destinations, and the value of events in promoting equality, an understanding of the considerations with respect to developing such events in rural locations is relevant. In this regard, Australia offers a notable case study due to its rural expanse and the recent passage of the same-sex marriage act which has made *pride* a topical area of discussion. With only 0.18% of the land area classified for urban use (Department of Agriculture and Water Resources, 2018), the expanse of rural Australia and the importance of rural tourism is evident. At the same time, in 2017, the Australian government commissioned a public survey to determine if same-sex marriage should be legalised. The results indicated that 61.6% supported same-sex marriage, voting 'yes' (Australian Bureau of Statistics, 2017). The survey achieved a participation rate of approximately 80% of Australians eligible to vote, indicating that it is highly likely that 20% did not have an opinion on the matter. Interestingly, the state of New South Wales (NSW), which hosts the annual Sydney Mardi Gras, had the highest percentage of NO voters (42%). For readers who are not familiar with it, the Sydney Mardi Gras is the biggest gay pride event in Australia and has been hosted each year since 1978, attracting an estimated 500,000 spectators in 2018 (Sydney Gay and Lesbian Mardi Gras, 2018), positioning Sydney as an international gay-friendly city.

Despite this division, it is interesting that rural towns in NSW have been increasingly developing and hosting pride events (Lewis & Markwell, 2020). This chapter explores the considerations in developing rural pride events by reflecting on the town of Hay, which conducted its inaugural Mardi Gras in 2018. The aim of this chapter is to highlight these considerations as aspects that need to be managed and accounted for when developing such events within a rural setting. The findings presented may accordingly be used by regional towns to enhance the process of creating such events. Key literature is briefly reviewed.

Rural gay pride events

The multidimensional nature of rural tourism makes it difficult for scholars to achieve a consensus in relation to its understanding (Frochot, 2005). Nonetheless, Pesonen and Tuohino (2017) explain it as tourism that happens outside densely populated areas and centres. Literature on rural travel identifies escape and relaxation as being key motives for rural travel (Devesa et al., 2010; Park & Yoon, 2009). Hattingh and Spencer (2017) found that homosexual travellers are pushed to escape heteronormative environments, to pursue sex/romance and to construct or validate their gay identity. On the other hand, homosexual travellers are pulled to destinations that are perceived to be gay-friendly, places where same-sex partnerships are legal or places that host gay events and festivals (Hattingh & Spencer, 2017).

Gay events provide a safe space for GSRD individuals (Hughes, 2006) while helping attendees to communicate their identity and seek support in their community (Kates, 2004). Attending gay pride events has been found to function as an essential step in the coming out process by allowing the individual to display their sexuality in a more public manner (Hughes, 2006). This is particularly relevant within rural environments which are typically perceived as being unwelcoming of LGBTIQ+ people and where heterosexuality is believed to be the only orientation (Gorman-Murray et al., 2008). By bringing like-minded people and supporters together, gay events provide attendees with an opportunity to share experiences (Hahm et al., 2018), and help pressure the government on policies and legislation (Ong & Goh, 2018). Gay events in rural areas can promote social change and help the destination benefit from economic and sociocultural development. Gorman-Murray *et al.* (2012) position rural gay events as an idyllic escape from urban gay lives. It is therefore argued that, if managed effectively, rural environments can provide an escape for GSRD individuals hoping to have a break from the strictures of their home environment and help reflect on their sexual identity.

This chapter focuses on the Hay Mardi Gras and, therefore, the uniqueness of a pride parade needs to be acknowledged. Originating in 1969 at Stonewall Inn in New York, pride events have been defined as a celebration of Otherness (Lamond, 2018). Such events have morphed from being Gay Liberation marches into street parties (Laughland, 2012). Pride parades function as cultural festivals emphasising fun and celebration (Markwell, 2002) and have been defined as being carnivalesque in nature (Markwell & Tomsen, 2010). The event represents a form of co-creation where attendees are the entertainment, and the spectators contribute to the atmosphere. This uniqueness imposes specific considerations on their organisation – especially within a rural environment.

The Hay Mardi Gras

Originally known as Lang's Crossing, this regional town in NSW was officially named Hay in October 1859, after local politician Sir John Hay. Since its exploration by Charles Sturt in 1829–1830, the town has functioned as a route for transporting livestock, as a regional farming hub and as a World War II Prisoner of War and internment centre. Hay is part of one of the best merino wool growing regions in Australia and is home to a range of specialist agricultural enterprises growing irrigated and pastured crops. Politically, it is part of the Farrer electorate in NSW where only 55% of voters supported same-sex marriage (Australian Bureau of Statistics, 2017) – stated differently, almost one out of every two residents voted against it.

Touted as a 'bush Mardi Gras' (Lewis, 2018), the Hay Mardi Gras (HMG) started off as an idea between three resident mums who were planning to host a small social event to watch the 2018 Sydney Gay and Lesbian Mardi Gras on a big screen in the local community centre. The 2018 Mardi Gras celebration is of particular significance because it marked the 40th anniversary of the Sydney Mardi Gras, and was the first one after the same-sex marriage legislation was passed. From there, the idea evolved into a town event, gaining support and sponsorship from local businesses and administrators. Running over three days, the event included a civic reception, a parade, an after party and a recovery breakfast. The event was positioned as a celebration of acceptance and love to help and support GSRD rural residents in realising their identity publicly.

Prior to the event, the local Member of Parliament proudly informed the House of Representatives that they were expecting a 'bumper crowd of around 250' (Ley, 2018), while the organisers indicated they would be pleased if they got three or four floats in the parade (Lewis, 2018). However, the event exceeded expectations, attracting more than 20 floats in the parade, 400 people who marched, another 400 estimated spectators and 360 who attended the after party (Hay Shire Council, 2018; King, 2018). The event raised approximately $17,000, of which $11,000 was donated to the Cancer Assistance Network, $1000 was given to the Hay Junior Magpies (a local sports team) and $5000 was retained by the committee as seed funding for 2019 (Hay Shire Council, 2018).

Reflections

This chapter provides a reflection on the considerations required in hosting pride events in rural communities by focusing on the HMG. Reflections help provide an understanding of a phenomenon that can inform practice and further research (Zahra & Sharma, 2004). They allow for an opportunity to explore underlying meanings that can be used to build knowledge (Lew & Schmidt, 2011). As explained above, this chapter aims to present an initial exploratory view of the considerations associated with hosting pride events in rural locations. Only publicly available data, such as news articles, event reports and government acknowledgments, were used to inform this reflection.

Getz's (1997) event management system was adapted to structure the reflection presented in this chapter. The framework recognises that events are hosted within a socioeconomic context and proposes four interdependent and interacting components that need to be managed. These are the event, the internal environment of the organiser, the community context and the general environment. As a management system, it serves to point that each component could pose considerations in terms of event development – particularly when it comes to pride events in rural locations. Accordingly, the model was adapted for this purpose and is presented in Figure 14.1. The considerations identified below represent the factors organisers need to bear in mind while developing such events within a rural community.

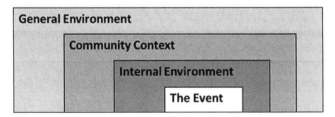

Figure 14.1 The event management system
Source: Adapted from Getz (1997).

General Environment

The general environment encompasses the overall context within which the event is staged. Two considerations are identified in this regard.

Geographical location

The rural nature of the event represents the most significant consideration in the context of rural pride events. The location limits the catchment area for volunteers and spectators and ultimately impacts the scope of the event and its viability. Located almost equidistant from four capital cities in Australia, Hay is 724 km from Sydney (the state capital of NSW), 423 km from Melbourne (the state capital of Victoria), 655 km from Adelaide (the state capital of South Australia) and 509 km from Canberra (the capital of Australia). Its geographic location positions it as an important regional and national transport node in Australia, making it accessible to visitors from different Australian capital cities. The Mardi Gras was attended by spectators who came from more than 700 km away, demonstrating the geographic reach of the event (King, 2018). The rural location of the HMG, coupled with its perceived identity of being a 'bush Mardi Gras', could create a sense of authenticity and contribute to greater acceptance by the GSRD community. This is because, as mainstream city-based pride marches become more commercialised, they depart from the authenticity and purpose they first represented (Lamond, 2018). On the other hand, LGBTQI+ events in rural areas and their carnivalesque nature may be disruptive to the perceived image of a masculine and 'rough' countryscape. Both urban and rural geographies are imbued with their particular 'symbolic codes' which have a shared meaning in our societies. For many, the observation of an urban 'symbolic code' in rural settings is rather conflicting. This is because queer identities have been entrenched and predominantly associated with urban spaces in both cultural and personal domains (Kazyak, 2011).

Generating awareness

Given the scale of the event and the associated limited budgets, opportunities to generate awareness must be considered. Keeping in mind that volunteer participation in the event by building floats and marching is a core event product, and that spectators are necessary to create the environment, awareness is therefore essential. The HMG was able to leverage its position as a 'bush Mardi Gras' as the first regional Mardi Gras in NSW to attract interest and media attention. A total of 47 news media outlets either contacted or were contacted by the committee for media releases – resulting in free promotion of the event (Hay Shire Council, 2018). In addition, residents were a key part of the event promotion – as is evident by the proportion of event visitors who stayed with family and friends (Hay Shire Council, 2018). Greater awareness through traditional and digital advertising channels beyond news releases may be essential to growing the awareness of such events.

Community Context

The community context includes the nuances of the host location that could impact the event. These encompass the people and amenities within the local area that could impact the development of the event and the visitors' experience at the event.

Social attitude

Rural events may be unpopular with locals who do not identify with the theme of the event (Zahra & Sharma, 2004). Two key components of this discourse need to be considered – the members of the community and the business organisations in the community. A positive social discourse is essential to creating the environment and seeking support from publicly elected stakeholders. Such discourse needs to extend not just in the rural town but also the to surrounding region that would most likely contribute a large proportion of visitors and spectators. Locals explain Hay as being a place 'where men work hard, drink hard and have a blinkered view of the world' (Stuart & McDonald, 2018). In her speech to the House of Representatives, the local Parliamentary member acknowledged that Hay was not known for being socially progressive. However, she recounted a conversation she had with a local resident who imagined a float that would say, 'I voted No. But I'm okay with it now' (Ley, 2018) – indicating the role of events in changing social attitudes. Organisers were overwhelmed by the support the event received (Lewis, 2018). On the weekend of the event, some local residents who were not in favour decided to leave town without protest (King, 2018).

The business community represents another social group that needs to be considered. It is through their cooperation that a regional town is able to provide visitors with the services they require during their visit. Kerr and Lewis (2010) note that the tourism outcome for an individual is based on the sum of the different components of the experience, from the moment the individual leaves their home environment to when they return. This includes accommodation, entertainment, catering, retail and other consumption experiences an individual may have at a host destination. Businesses in Hay acknowledged the economic value of the HMG and demonstrated support for the event (Leighton-Dore, 2018). Some businesses decorated their shop windows, while others created special rainbow products or promotions (Coates, 2018). While a cynic may question the motive driving this support, the utilitarian outcome is undoubtedly a more inclusive environment. The experience visitors have while interacting with the business community during their visit could influence their overall satisfaction with the experience – and is particularly critical for a start-up destination event where dissatisfaction could result in negative word-of-mouth.

Social misperceptions

The way the local community understands the event and their perceptions of what to expect can influence social discourse. This understanding may not always be aligned with the true aims or purpose of the event and, therefore, may need to be managed. The purpose of the HMG was to promote inclusion and to raise funds for local causes, as opposed to pushing an agenda (Lewis, 2018). Many locals, however, worried that it was going to be a naked parade down the street (Stuart & McDonald, 2018). Such perceptions can originate from the general discourse on the heightened promiscuity of GSRD individuals and can bias perceptions of LGBTIQ+ events. Effective positioning can help avoid community backlash. For instance, the Pink Dot event – a gay event in Singapore – positioned itself as a family event in order to avoid protest and violence (Ong & Goh, 2018). By doing so, the aim of Pink Dot was not to legalise gay rights in Singapore – which may be confrontational in nature – but rather to ease the gay agenda into the mainstream (Tan, 2015).

Amenities

The amenities represent the tourism infrastructure that needs to be in place in order for the event to be possible. Amenities function as hygiene factors in that their absence could erode the tourists' satisfaction at the destination. The level and type of amenities expected are dependent on the context of the destination (Lewis *et al.*, 2013a); accordingly, visitors may not expect luxurious amenities within a rural context. The definition of tourism as per the World Tourism Organisation (UNWTO, 2008) requires that at the very minimum individuals stay away from home for one night. Accommodation is, therefore, an important component of the tourism experience. Seven out of the nine accommodation venues in Hay had bookings for the HMG, and informal feedback received indicated that visitors stayed with friends and family or in camping facilities (Hay Shire Council, 2018). This is indicative of the importance of social and community support in promoting the event among friends and family and creating a safe environment for visitors to set up campsites.

Internal Environment

The internal environment represents the working structures that are required to create and deliver an event (Getz, 1997). At its core, it comprises those who organise the event – that is, those that came up with the event idea and work on organising it – and the associated stakeholders necessary to transform the event idea into a reality.

Organisation committee

Small organisation committees that typically work on rural event management lack succession plans and the professional knowledge required for the event's long-term success (Pesonen & Tuohino, 2017). This results in the event either dying a natural death when the organisers are no longer able to manage it or being limited in potential to the skills the organisers can bring to it. The HMG was organised by three mums who did not initially plan for it to be an event. In some ways, the inaugural parade provided a litmus test to determine if there was sufficient demand for such an event to be organised annually. Noting its success, the organisers have commenced planning the 2019 Hay Mardi Gras and are seeking funding to secure the skills required to grow the event.

Government support

Wilson *et al.* (2001) note that support and participation from local government are important for a place to be positioned as a rural destination. Such support is essential to building the popularity of the event and ensuring that the relevant resources and infrastructure are available. Frost and Laing (2015), when studying the Elvis festival in the rural town of Parkes (Australia), found that popularity surged once local government supported the event. Government bodies may also provide both financial and in-kind support such as road closures and the security presence required for hosting a pride parade. In regard to the HMG, the local government council provided traffic management and printing support totalling $2700 in value (Hay Shire Council, 2018). As local councils are elected officials, securing such support can be dependent on the value the event can provide and the social discourse of residents.

Sponsorship

Funding is an essential component of organising any event and may come from both governmental and private entities. For a private organisation, event sponsorship provides a means of building a brand and gaining awareness – it is through awareness of the sponsorship that the meaning of the event gets transferred to the brand (Keller, 2013). However, this level of awareness may not be achievable within a rural event context, potentially defeating the purpose of corporate sponsorship from entities that do not operate in the local community. Government bodies, on the other hand, may be more likely to sponsor the event due to its impact on the local economy and social environment. As noted, the Hay City

Council contributed support totalling $2700 in value (Hay Shire Council, 2018). In addition, local businesses also sponsored aspects of the event, and even businesses that were initially not interested in sponsorship eventually came on board (Lewis, 2018), potentially demonstrating the impact of changing social perceptions on securing funding.

The Event

Kerr and Lewis (2010) note that different aspects of the trip can hold different degrees of importance in attracting visitors to a destination. Within the context of this chapter, the event is the core product and pull factor for the regional destination. Due to the distance involved in rural travel, visitors need to be provided with an experience that demonstrates value – in that the experience anticipated should outweigh the distance required to travel or other perceived costs.

Activities and attractions

The activities and attractions that are a part of the event provide the reason to attend. Lewis *et al.* (2013a) found that having a variety of events and attractions is essential to making a destination fashionable and argued that such a variety could help appeal to the interests of different groups. Having a variety of activities within the event could provide visitors with a more holistic experience of the event and the destination. The HMG ran over a three-day period and included a civic reception, a parade, an after party, a recovery picnic and a live stream of the Sydney Mardi Gras. The multiplicity of this event helped create a more holistic experience for visitors to engage with.

Attractions in this context may also include personalities who attend and perform at the event. Attracting high-profile celebrities may be difficult given the location of the events and the limited budget available. There is, however, an expectation to have a headline act at the event or after party because of the entertainment value they provide – with the Sydney Mardi Gras hosting the likes of Cher, The Veronicas, Conchita Wurst, Dannii and Kylie Minogue, Tina Arena, and others over the years. As part of the HMG, Dragolog (a popular regional drag troupe with a strong online presence) was invited to perform at the after party – providing an element of celebrity appeal.

Participation of volunteers

Given the nature of the event, volunteers build and host floats in the parade – making their participation a core component of the event experience. Without volunteers marching in the parade and managing floats, there would be no parade for spectators to experience. Because of the rural location of the event and stereotypical associations with masculinity within these communities, encouraging a sufficient number of volunteers to travel to the rural town and participate can be a challenge. The HMG had more than 20 groups and floats participating in the parade – far exceeding the organisers' expectation of having only four floats (Hay Shire Council, 2018; Lewis, 2018).

Conclusions

This chapter discussed the considerations relevant to hosting rural pride events based on a reflection on Hay's Mardi Gras. Specifically, publicly available reports were reviewed to identify factors organisers need to keep in mind while developing such events. The considerations identified in this work fundamentally stem from the nature of the event, the rural host environment and the social contexts of the environment. Understanding these factors could help rural locations develop such events – ultimately contributing to a greater acceptance of those that are GSRD. This chapter takes the first step towards this aim, and further research is encouraged to understand how such events can be successfully implemented within a rural context. This could include extensive formal research on the supply side to understand challenges that may exist and techniques to manage them, on the demand side to understand what could attract visitors to such events, and in the community context to understand how they may be encouraged to participate.

As a final note, the authors would like to dedicate this chapter to the 78ers who bravely hosted Australia's first Mardi Gras – whose fight we benefit from.

References

Annes, A. and Redlin, M. (2012) Coming out and coming back: Rural gay migration and the city. *Journal of Rural Studies* 28, 56–68.

Australian Bureau of Statistics (2017) *1800.0 Australian Marriage Law Postal Survey, 2017*. See http://www.abs.gov.au/ausstats/abs@.nsf/mf/1800.0.

Blichfeldt, B.S., Chor, J. and Ballegaard Milan, N. (2013) Zoos, sanctuaries and turfs: Enactments and uses of gay spaces during the holidays. *International Journal of Tourism Research* 15 (5), 473–483.

Brown, G. (2015) Rethinking the origins of homonormativity: The diverse economies of rural gay life in England and Wales in the 1970s and 1980s. *Transactions* 40 (4), 549–561.

Coates, J. (2018) Country pride: Hay comes alive for Mardi Gras in the outback. *The Area News*, 5 March. See https://www.areanews.com.au/story/5263830/smash-hit-rainbow-on-the-plains-to-return-for-another-year/.

Department of Agriculture and Water Resources (2018) *National Scale Land Use (Based on Land Use of Australia 2010–11, Version 5, ABARES 2016)*. See http://www.agriculture.gov.au/abares/aclump/land-use.

Devesa, M., Laguna, M. and Palacios, A. (2010) The role of motivation in visitor satisfaction: Empirical evidence in rural tourism. *Tourism Management* 31 (4), 547–552.

Frochot, I. (2005) A benefit segmentation of tourists in rural areas: A Scottish perspective. *Tourism Management* 26 (3), 335–346.

Frost, W. and Laing, J. (2015) Avoiding burnout: The succession planning, governance and resourcing of rural tourism festivals. *Journal of Sustainable Tourism* 23 (8–9), 1298–1317.

Getz, D. (1997) *Event Management & Event Tourism*, Elmsford, NY: Cognizant Communications.

Gibson, C. and Stewart, A. (2009) *Reinventing Rural Places: The Extent and Impact of Festivals in Rural and Regional Australia*. Wollongong: University of Wollongong.

Gorman-Murray, A., Waitt, G. and Gibson, C. (2008) A queer country? A case study of the politics of gay/lesbian belonging in an Australian country town. *Australian Geographer* 39 (2), 171–191.

Gorman-Murray, A., Waitt, G. and Gibson, C. (2012) Chilling out in 'cosmopolitan country': Urban/rural hybridity and the construction of Daylesford as a 'lesbian and gay rural idyll'. *Journal of Rural Studies* 28, 69–79.

Hahm, J., Ro, H. and Olson, E.D. (2018) Sense of belonging to a lesbian, gay, bisexual, and transgender event: The examination of affective bond and collective self-esteem. *Journal of Travel & Tourism Marketing* 35 (2), 244–256.

Hankinson, G. (2005) Destination brand images: A business tourism perspective. *Journal of Services Marketing* 19 (1), 24–32.

Hattingh, C. and Spencer, J. (2017) Salient factors influencing gay travellers' holiday motivations: A push-pull approach. *African Journal of Hospitality, Tourism and Leisure* 6 (4), 1–26.

Hay Shire Council (2018) Business Paper, Ordinary Meeting, Tuesday 1.00pm 27th March 2018.

Hughes, H.L. (1997) Holidays and homosexual identity. *Tourism Management* 18 (1), 3–7.

Hughes, H.L. (2003) Marketing gay tourism in Manchester: New market for urban tourism or destruction of 'gay space'? *Journal of Vacation Marketing* 9 (2), 152–163.

Hughes, H.L. (2006) *Pink Tourism: Holidays of Gay Men and Lesbians*. Wallingford: CABI.

Jago, L., Chalip, L., Brown, G., Mules, T. and Ali, S. (2003) Building events into destination branding: Insights from experts. *Event Management* 8 (1), 3–14.

Johnston, L. (2005) *Queering Tourism: Paradoxical Performances at Gay Pride Parades*. London: Routledge.

Johnston, L. (2007) Mobilizing pride/shame: Lesbians, tourism and parades. *Social & Cultural Geography* 8 (1), 29–45.

Kates, S.M. (2004) The dynamics of brand legitimacy: An interpretive study in the gay men's community. *Journal of Consumer Research* 31 (2), 455–464.

Kazyak, M. (2011) Disrupting cultural selves: Constructing gay and lesbian identities in rural locales. *Qualitative Sociology* 34 (4), 561–581.

Keller, K. (2013) *Strategic Brand Management: Global Edition*: Upper Saddle River, NJ: Pearson Higher Education.

Kerr, G. and Lewis, C. (2010) Planning for the tourism outcome: An industries approach. In P. Jayashree and M. Balakrishnan (eds) *Academy of International Business Middle East and North Africa Conference: Manara – Reigniting Growth, Dubai*.

King, R. (2018) Hay celebrates diversity with inaugural Rainbow on the Plains Festival. *ABC News*, 4 March. See https://www.abc.net.au/news/2018-03-04/hay-runs-its-own-mardi-gras-rainbow-on-the-plains/9507110.

Lamond, I.R. (2018) The challenge of articulating human rights at an LGBT 'mega-event': A personal reflection on Sao Paulo Pride 2017. *Leisure Studies* 37 (1), 36–48.

Laughland, O. (2012) Is Pride today about gay rights or just partying? *The Guardian*, 6 July. See https://www.theguardian.com/commentisfree/2012/jul/06/conversation-pride-gay-rights-party.

Leighton-Dore, S. (2018) Meet the small town throwing its very own Mardi Gras festival. *SBS*, 1 March. See https://www.sbs.com.au/topics/sexuality/mardigras/article/2018/02/23/meet-small-town-throwing-its-very-own-mardi-gras-festival.

Lew, M.D. and Schmidt, H.G. (2011) Self-reflection and academic performance: Is there a relationship? *Advances in Health Sciences Education* 16 (4), 529.

Lewis, A. (2018) Hay hosting its first Mardi Gras celebration. *The Area News*, 27 February. See https://www.areanews.com.au/story/5254691/putting-the-gay-into-hay-with-first-mardi-gras/.

Lewis, C., Kerr, G. and Burgess, L. (2013a) The application of fashion to destinations. Paper presented at the 23rd International Research Conference of the Council for Australian University Tourism and Hospitality Education (CAUTHE), Lincoln, New Zealand.

Lewis, C., Kerr, G. and Burgess, L. (2013b) A critical assessment of the role of fashion in influencing the travel decision and destination choice. *International Journal of Tourism Policy* 5 (1), 4–18.

Lewis, C. and Markwell, K. (2020) Drawing a line in the sand: The social impacts of an LGBTQI+ event in an Australian rural community. *Leisure Studies* (online).

Ley, S. (2018) *Rainbow on the Plains Hay Mardi Gras Festival speech.* Canberra: House of Representatives, Parliament of Australia. See https://parlinfo.aph.gov.au/parlInfo/search/display/display.w3p;query=Id:%22chamber/hansardr/418e385e-5a3e-4ec1-9392-e323a8dfd488/0080%22;src1=sm1.

Markwell, K. (2002) Mardi Gras tourism and the construction of Sydney as an international gay and lesbian city. *GLQ: A Journal of Lesbian and Gay Studies* 8 (1), 81–99.

Markwell, K. and Tomsen, S. (2010) Safety and hostility at special events: Lessons from Australian gay and lesbian festivals. *Event Management* 14 (3), 225–238.

Ong, F. and Goh, S. (2018) Pink is the new gray: Events as agents of social change. *Event Management* 22, 965–979.

Park, D.-B. and Yoon, Y.-S. (2009) Segmentation by motivation in rural tourism: A Korean case study. *Tourism Management* 30 (1), 99–108.

Pesonen, J.A. and Tuohino, A. (2017) Activity-based market segmentation of rural well-being tourists: Comparing online information search. *Journal of Vacation Marketing* 23 (2), 145–158.

Provencher, D.M. (2007) Mapping gay Paris: Language, space and sexuality in the Marais. *Contemporary French and Francophone Studies* 11 (1), 37–46.

Stuart, R. and McDonald, P. (2018) Gay Hay. *ABC News*, 25 February. See https://www.abc.net.au/news/2018-02-25/mardi-gras-comes-to-hay-the-tiny-town-in-nsw/9465076.

Sydney Gay and Lesbian Mardi Gras (2018) *40 Years of Evolution: 2018 Annual Report.* See https://www.mardigras.org.au/images/uploads/images/mg19-annual-report-final-artwork-v3-web.pdf.

Tan, C. (2015) Pink dot: Cultural and sexual citizenship in gay Singapore. *Anthropological Quarterly* 88 (4), 969–996.

UNWTO (2008) *Glossary of Tourism Terms.* See https://www.unwto.org/glossary-tourism-terms.

Vorobjovas-Pinta, O. (2018) Gay neo-tribes: Exploration of travel behaviour and space. *Annals of Tourism Research* 72, 1–10.

Vorobjovas-Pinta, O. and Hardy, A. (2016) The evolution of gay travel research. *International Journal of Tourism Research* 18 (4), 409–416.

Vorobjovas-Pinta, O. and Hardy, A. (2021) Resisting marginalisation and reconstituting space through LGBTQI+ events. *Journal of Sustainable Tourism* 29 (2–3), 448–466. doi:10.1080/09669582.2020.1769638

Waitt, G. and Markwell, K. (2006) *Gay Tourism: Culture and Context.* Binghamton, NY: Haworth Hospitality Press.

Wilson, S., Fesenmaier, D.R., Fesenmaier, J. and Van Es, J.C. (2001) Factors for success in rural tourism development. *Journal of Travel Research* 40 (2), 132–138.

Zahra, S.A. and Sharma, P. (2004) Family business research: A strategic reflection. *Family Business Review* 17 (4), 331–346.

Afterword

Rodrigo Lucena

Gay Tourism: New Perspectives is a much anticipated and needed book. While there have been a number of peer-reviewed publications on the topic over the last few years (Blichfeldt *et al.*, 2013; Monterrubio, 2019; Therkelsen *et al.*, 2013; Vorobjovas-Pinta, 2018, to name but a few), much of the iconic work on gay tourism is from the 1990s and early 2000s. It is not surprising therefore that the works by Hughes (1997, 2003, 2005, 2006), Clift (Clift & Forrest, 1999; Clift *et al.*, 2002) and Pritchard (Pritchard *et al.*, 2000) continue to inform current research and have thus been cited repeatedly in this collection. Yet, if sexuality is a fluid construct (Sell, 1997) that has evolved since the 1990s (and continues to do so), then, as Lewis and Vorobjovas-Pinta suggest in Chapter 14 of this book, so have the gay community and gay tourism. Therefore, there is a critical need for academia to look at gay tourism in a way that not only reflects the diversity of tourism practices and choices but also draws upon and informs wider discourses in society.

Such a need is even more important in times when institutional and social homophobia is (still) an issue in many countries, as highlighted on diverse occasions in this book (see, for example, Hattingh's report in Chapter 5 on the treatment given to LGBTQI+ people in some African countries, or Gao's account in Chapter 6 of how, despite no longer being considered a pathology, homosexuality is still stigmatised and heavily monitored in China). This, of course, does not mean that sexuality-related discrimination does not exist in the so-called 'Western' nations, often viewed by many as the epitome of freedom and individual expression. Indeed, over the last few years in particular, quite a few Western societies have seen the emergence of populist governments that have adopted regressive policies and discourses towards issues of sexuality and gender, with Donald Trump's ban on transgenders in the US army (Pilkington, 2019) being just one example of this.

Gay tourism is implicated in, and influenced by, this politically-charged context, but at the same time has potential to reshape it. In addition to the impact tourism can have on national and regional economies and individuals' well-being (as evidenced in Chapter 14 by Lewis & Vorobjovas-Pinta and Chapter 12 by Andrade, Breda & Dinis), gay tourism can foster societal changes. As exemplified in Dahl and Barreto's Chapter 10, gay tourism, particularly when combined with volunteer tourism, can generate opportunities for support of LGBTQI+ local causes and advance acceptance in the destination. As reminded by Monterrubio in Chapter 3, in helping construct gay identity through socialisation, bonding and learning, gay tourism spaces can also have a significant role in reinforcing gay local communities.

Yet, gay tourism is not without its own issues, contradictions and criticisms. As Ooi discusses in Chapter 2, gay tourism can indeed be an exercise of democratic choice. But such a choice is often limited and moulded by heteronormative standards and businesses. Jeffrey and Sposato remind us in Chapter 13 that the sheer use of the expression 'gay-friendly' by businesses is condescending as it implies that LGBTQI+ people are 'allowed in'. As highlighted in the example provided in Vorobjovas-Pinta's Chapter 8, gay businesses and other spaces are often characterised by an enclavic nature which, it is argued here, rather than disrupting heteronormativity, reinforces heterosexuality as the norm. In frequenting and often being confined to gay businesses, the LGBTQI+ subject, rather than 'coming out of the closet', simply moves to another – larger and arguably more comfortable – closet.

While gay tourism can generate, among both tourists and locals, a sense of togetherness and belonging based on shared values and practices, a key question that has emerged from this book relates to whether gay tourism is really any different from generic tourism (or would it, as Ooi implies, just be business-as-usual?). In this sense, Jeffrey and Sposato appropriately call into question the authenticity of gay tourism. The 'pink washing' phenomenon, addressed quite a few times in this book (see, for example, Vorobjovas-Pinta & Grimmer's Chapter 11), highlights the lack of 'authenticity' of many tourism businesses and destinations, which promote themselves as 'gay-friendly' in order to obtain the 'pink dollar' rather than to make a genuine political statement. Jeffrey and Sposato also note that, in the tourism literature, authenticity is often understood in juxtaposition to its antonym (i.e. commodification). Yet, the dichotomy between authenticity and commodification is not clear cut and the authors insightfully call for the use of marketing in activism, which has significant potential for social change.

However, it is undeniable that, as with most forms of tourism, gay tourism is also a reflection and result of capitalist production and ideology. As explained in Chapter 8, the sheer dichotomy between work and leisure is a product of industrial capitalism. In that sense, gay tourism does risk alienating less affluent LGBTQI+ segments of society. This is fully acknowledged in this book. Most chapters questioned the traditional assumption, reinforced by the tourism industry, that gay people are affluent and educated aesthetes. As highlighted throughout the book, the depiction of gays and lesbians as DINKs (dual income, no kids) with high disposable incomes no longer holds true. In many countries, families parented by LGBTQI+ people have become more common due to legal recognition and increased visibility. Yet they are largely missing in tourism scholarship, as Cai and Southall remind us in Chapter 4. Importantly, future research on gay tourism should adopt an intersectional approach and investigate, for example, whether and how factors such as social class and cultural background, but also age and bodily (dis)abilities, interplay with sexuality as far as holiday choices are concerned.

The book also offers new and unique insights into LGBTQI+ communities from non-Western countries, which have been largely overlooked by both the tourism industry and academia. It is refreshing to see, for example, the perspectives of Asian (Gao's Chapter 6 and Nghiêm-Phú & Suter's Chapter 9), Muslim (Coşkun's Chapter 7), Latin American (Monterrubio's Chapter 3 and Jeffrey & Sposato's Chapter 13) and African (Hattingh's Chapter 5) gay tourism stakeholders and players. It is true that some of these depictions reinforce what Puar (2007) called 'homonationalism' – namely the portrayal of Western societies as accepting towards non-heteronormative sexualities and that of non-Western countries as barbaric and backwards. Not only does this approach reinforce the Western/non-Western schism but it also conceals the reality of homophobia which also exists in the West. On the other hand, it should be noted that these chapters shed unique light on the multiple meanings assigned to sexuality in these countries. Some highlight how homophobia was, in many cases, a construct imported from the West (Chapter 7), and how the concept of 'coming out' is deeply rooted in Western individualism and thus may not 'transfer' well to other cultures (Chapter 6).

As novel as these insights and perspectives are, it is true that some significant gaps still remain. Future research on LGBTQI+ tourism needs to go beyond the 'G' and look further into all the letters of the acronym. Lesbians have notably been neglected in tourism research, and studies on bisexuals and transgenders in tourism are virtually non-existent. As suggested by Jeffrey and Sposato (Chapter 13), LGBTQI+ tourism (public and private) policies and strategies are often designed by men, via the use of a patriarchal lens, with few women (if any) involved in decision making. I argue that future studies need to go beyond, and even challenge, the prevalence of gay men as subjects of LGBTQI+ tourism scholarship.

In several instances, the book disrupts the notion of the LGBTQI+ community as a homogeneous monolith. As Ooi puts it (p. 18), 'if there is a sense of community, it is imagined and maintained by a common challenge to heteronormativity'. At times, the book also reveals the underlying tensions among members of the community. In Chapter 3, for example, Monterrubio brings to the fore the stigmatisation of effeminate men by (presumably) 'butch' gay men. In Chapter 9, Nghiêm-Phú and Suter uncover the discriminatory practices hidden under the pricing strategies of gay saunas in Asia, where older and heavier gay men are sometimes charged more than other patrons. This is not to mention the LGBTQI+

members who, in adopting more 'transgressive' lifestyles (e.g. polyamorous or fetishist sub-groups), further deviate from the norm and are stigmatised within the community. As Jeffrey and Sposato explain, the inclusion of LGBTQI+ tourists in marketing (and, by analogy, LGBTQI+ businesses) often comes 'at the cost of exclusion of those who may not identify with the commercial scene' (p. 202). As gay tourism and the functioning of many gay spaces rely on the encounters among the diverse members of the community, it is imperative that more scholarly attention be given to these frictions.

One of the strengths of this book lies in the fact that it does reinforce gay tourism motivations as complex and multi-layered constructs, which cannot be explained through the prism of sexuality alone. In Chapter 10, Dahl and Barreto underline that these motivations interplay and intersect among themselves, further highlighting the need for research on gay tourism to explore more than the stereotypical 'city/beach combo' which has characterised much of the existing research on gay destinations and spaces. This type of information needs to be better recognised and employed by tourism businesses willing to cater for the LBGTQI+ 'market'. As concluded by Hattingh (Chapter 5), an all-encompassing umbrella approach to gay tourism marketing would not successfully reach and attract all types of LGBTQI+ tourists.

Arguably, the most important contribution of this collection relates to the discussions around the existence of a mainstream gay culture and the mainstreaming of gay culture itself. If, as explained above, gay tourism motivations (and, by analogy, other motivations) are multiple and the LGBTQI+ community is diverse and heterogeneous, then it does not make sense to talk about one singular gay culture. Indeed, several authors in this book refuted the assumption of one uniform gay culture, thereby calling for a more holistic, but also less compartmentalised, understanding of LGBTQI+ tourism (and, I argue, non-heteronormative sexualities).

Importantly, due to the enhanced acceptance of such sexualities in several countries, many of these gay cultures have themselves become mainstream to wider (heterosexual) segments of society. As noted by Monterrubio (Chapter 3) and Cai and Southall (Chapter 4), many gay spaces have gone through a 'de-gaying' process. This phenomenon is further amplified by the increasing use of virtual spaces (i.e. dating websites and apps) by members of the LGBTQI+ community (Vorobjovas-Pinta & Dalla-Fontana, 2019), some of whom may no longer see the need to patronise gay spaces, causing them to become (or be perceived as) obsolete. While the mainstreaming of gay cultures and spaces both reflects and reinforces the increased visibility of LGBTQI+ people, it is also seen by some activists as eroding their shared values and alienating members of the community. For example, gay pride events headlined by international pop stars (examples in the UK include Ariana Grande, Britney Spears and Kylie Minogue) naturally attract a large number of people from both inside and outside the gay community, which forces ticket prices up, discouraging less affluent LGBTQI+ members from attending. This also adds to the previously mentioned argument that the commodification of the gay tourism (and event) industry also undermines its authenticity.

The debates about the mainstreaming of gay culture(s) and its ramifications for LGBTQI+ tourism are of extreme relevance and, therefore, need further scrutiny. Because mainstreaming draws upon, and leads to, the absorption of gay culture by heteronormative societies, it is inextricably linked to the academic discussions about gay assimilation that have long marked the LGBTQI+ literature (Robinson, 2012). Many chapters of this book have picked up on such debates. Indeed, questions about similarity and difference (i.e. are LGBTQI+ people similar or dissimilar to their straight counterparts?) have often found echoes in this book. For example, as mentioned earlier, Ooi questions whether gay tourism is in essence different from heteronormative tourism or just a reframing of heteronormative tourism through clever (yet clichéd) marketing.

It is true that there may be more pressing issues for the LGBT cause than investigating the nature of gay tourism. Nevertheless, understanding its very core might lead to unique knowledge about how gay tourists (and gay people in general) navigate their identities in the public arena, which has much wider implications. Further questions need to be asked as to whether or not LGBTQI+ tourists want to/seek to be seen as different from other tourists and whether they want to 'stand out' in holiday spaces or, in a nutshell, whether they want their differences to be highlighted or downplayed. Duggan (2002) is credited with having coined the word 'homonormativity', namely, the politics of gay assimilation that maintains and reinforces heteronormativity rather than contesting it. Thus, the homonormative LGBTQI+ subject, also termed by some the 'good gay', may prefer to minimise, rather than emphasise, such differences. Whether, as Ooi seems to suggest, these differences are invented and accentuated through social, cultural, political and economic dynamics or not, it is crucial to understand what sense LGBTQI+ people make of them, as this will have profound implications not only for gay tourism but also gay culture(s) and identity(ies).

References

Blichfeldt, B.S., Chor, J. and Milan, N.B. (2013) Zoos, sanctuaries and turfs: Enactments and uses of gay spaces during the holidays. *International Journal of Tourism Research* 15 (5), 473–483.

Clift, S. and Forrest, S. (1999) Gay men and tourism: Destinations and holiday motivations. *Tourism Management* 20 (5), 615–625. doi:10.1016/S0261-5177 (99)00032-1

Clift, S., Luongo, M. and Callister, C. (2002) *Gay Tourism: Culture, Identity and Sex.* New York: Continuum.

Duggan, L. (2002) The new homonormativity: The sexual politics of neoliberalism. In R. Castronovo and D.D. Nelson (eds) *Materializing Democracy: Toward a Revitalized Cultural Politics* (pp. 175–194). Durham, NC: Duke University Press.

Hughes, H.L. (1997) Holidays and homosexual identity. *Tourism Management* 18 (1), 3–7.

Hughes, H.L. (2003) Marketing gay tourism in Manchester: New market for urban tourism or destruction of 'gay space'? *Journal of Vacation Marketing* 9 (2), 152–163.

Hughes, H.L. (2005) A gay tourism market. *Journal of Quality Assurance in Hospitality & Tourism* 5, 57–74.

Hughes, H.L. (2006) *Pink Tourism: Holidays of Gay Men and Lesbians*. Wallingford: CABI.

Monterrubio, C. (2019) Tourism and male homosexual identities: Directions for sociocultural research. *Tourism Review* 74 (5), 1058–1069. doi:10.1108/TR-08-2017-0125

Pilkington, E. (2019) Revealed: The trans military members living in fear under Trump's ban. *The Guardian*, 13 June. See https://www.theguardian.com/society/2019/jun/12/revealed-how-trumps-transgender-ban-has-forced-military-members-back-into-hiding (accessed 14 September 2020).

Pritchard, A., Morgan, N.J., Sedgley, D., Khan, E. and Jenkins, A. (2000) Sexuality and holiday choices: Conversations with gay and lesbian tourists. *Leisure Studies* 19 (4), 267–282.

Puar, J. (2007) *Terrorist Assemblages: Homonationalism in Queer Times*. Durham, NC: Duke University Press.

Robinson, B.A. (2012) Is this what equality looks like? How assimilation marginalizes the Dutch LGBT community. *Sexuality Research & Social Policy* 9 (4), 327–336.

Sell, R.L. (1997) Defining and measuring sexual orientation: A review. *Archives of Sexual Behaviour* 26 (6), 643–658.

Therkelsen, A., Blichfeldt, B.S., Chor, J. and Ballegaard, N. (2013) 'I am very straight in my gay life': Approaching an understanding of lesbian tourists' identity construction. *Journal of Vacation Marketing* 19 (4), 317–327.

Vorobjovas-Pinta, O. (2018) Gay neo-tribes: Exploration of travel behaviour and space. *Annals of Tourism Research* 72, 1–10.

Vorobjovas-Pinta, O. and Dalla-Fontana, I.J. (2019) The strange case of dating apps at a gay resort: Hyper-local and virtual-physical leisure. *Tourism Review* 74 (5), 1070–1080.

Vorobjovas-Pinta, O. and Hardy, A. (2016) The evolution of gay travel research. *International Journal of Tourism Research* 18 (4), 409–416.

Index